Rich Simon
with
Leslie Koorhan
and
Ken Cox

SAMS

Teach Yourself

Object-Oriented

Programming with

Visual Basic .NET

in 21 Days

SECOND EDITION

SAMS

201 West 103rd St., Indianapolis, Indiana, 46290 USA

Sams Teach Yourself Object-Oriented Programming with Visual Basic .NET in 21 Days

Copyright © 2002 by Sams Publishing

International Standard Book Number: 0-672-32149-1

Library of Congress Catalog Card Number: 00-112014

Printed in the United States of America

First Printing: February 2002

05 04 03 02   4 3 2 1

Learning Resources
Centre

12368571

Trademarks

Warning and Disclaimer

ASSOCIATE PUBLISHER
Linda Ratts Engelman

ACQUISITIONS EDITOR
Dayna Isley

DEVELOPMENT EDITOR
Susan Shaw Dunn

MANAGING EDITOR
Charlotte Clapp

PROJECT EDITOR
Sheila Schroeder

COPY EDITOR
Chuck Hutchinson

INDEXER
Tom Dinse

PROOFREADER
Suzanne Thomas

TECHNICAL EDITORS
Ken Cox, Microsoft MVP
Leslie Koorhan, MCT, MCSD,
MCSE, MCDBA

TEAM COORDINATOR
Lynne Williams

MEDIA DEVELOPER
Dan Scherf

INTERIOR DESIGNER
Gary Adair

COVER DESIGNER
Aren Howell

PAGE LAYOUT
Michelle Mitchell

Contents at a Glance

Contents

About the Author

Richard J. Simon is cofounder of MillenniSoft, Inc., a software development and consulting company that specializes in custom application development with the latest technologies for Windows and the Internet. Before starting MillenniSoft, Richard was a CTO for more than eight years in a software development company that specialized in client/server development with *n*-tier technology.

In 1985, Richard started consulting and developing custom PC software applications. By 1989, he was developing Windows applications for some of the largest Fortune 500 companies in the United States. Richard has always been on the cutting edge of technology and spends his time researching and developing new technologies to bring to market. He has authored *Windows 2000 API SuperBible* (Sams Publishing, ISBN: 0-672-31933-0) and tech edited several books on Windows development.

About the Contributing Authors

Ken Cox is a technical writer and Web developer in Toronto. A Microsoft Most Valuable Professional (MVP), Ken is a frequent contributor to computer books and magazines dealing with Microsoft technologies. During six years with Nortel Networks, he was the senior technical designer on the documentation department's multimedia team. Ken's technical writing has won several awards from the Society for Technical Communication. Before turning his interests to computers and things high-tech, Ken had a successful career as a broadcast journalist in Toronto and Quebec City for Canada's top radio stations and news networks.

Leslie Koorhan is a certified trainer and developer in New Jersey. He works with Microsoft SQL Server and Microsoft Visual Studio. Leslie is a Microsoft Certified Trainer, a Microsoft Certified Solution Developer (MCSD), a Microsoft Certified Systems Engineer (MCSE) using Windows NT 4.0, and a Microsoft Certified Database Administrator (MCDBA). He has been a computer professional for many years and has worked in the PC arena for nearly two decades. As such, he has used many development products over the years—most recently Visual Basic—and has been involved in Internet technologies such as ASP, XML, and XSLT. Leslie has done courseware design, written a book on Access, and written articles for several publications. He can be reached at lkoorhan@earthlink.net.

Ken and Leslie served as both contributors and technical editors for this book.

Acknowledgments

From Ken Cox: Thanks to Dayna Isley, Sondra Scott, and Susan Dunn for making my participation in this book an enjoyable and rewarding experience. Thanks to my wife, Vilia, for her constant support in my quest to explore the best technologies.

From Leslie Koorhan: I'd like to thank my wife first and foremost for supporting me throughout the years in my endeavors. Without her, I would never have the opportunities that I get today. She also makes sure that I don't worry too much in the down times because she is an eternal optimist. I'd also like to thank the fine staff at Sams for all their help on this project. They are a wonderful and professional group that made this experience very positive for me. Finally, I have to thank Ken Cox for all his contributions to making my share of this project run a little smoother.

Tell Us What You Think!

As the reader of this book, *you* are our most important critic and commentator. We value your opinion and want to know what we're doing right, what we could do better, what areas you'd like to see us publish in, and any other words of wisdom you're willing to pass our way.

As an Associate Publisher for Sams, I welcome your comments. You can fax, e-mail, or write me directly to let me know what you did or didn't like about this book—as well as what we can do to make our books stronger.

Please note that I cannot help you with technical problems related to the topic of this book, and that due to the high volume of mail I receive, I might not be able to reply to every message.

When you write, please be sure to include this book's title and author as well as your name and phone or fax number. I will carefully review your comments and share them with the author and editors who worked on the book.

Fax: 317-581-4770

E-mail: feedback@samspublishing.com

Mail: Linda Engelman, Associate Publisher
           Sams Publishing
           201 West 103rd Street
           Indianapolis, IN 46290 USA

Introduction

Welcome to the world of object-oriented programming. Over the next 21 days, you will learn the concepts, terminology, best practices, and practical applications of developing object-oriented software in Microsoft Visual Basic .NET. At the outset, you probably have some notion of objects but are vague on what's really involved. Terms such as *methods* and *properties* don't trouble you, but you start to get hazy when it comes to *classes*, *namespaces*, *inheritance*, *derivation*, *polymorphism*, and *overloads*. By the time you finish the lessons in this book, you'll have a good grasp of these topics and much, much more.

Although we don't assume that you know a lot about programming, this book isn't for a raw beginner. If you don't feel comfortable with program variables and structures such as loops, you might find the going difficult. That said, you can learn anything if you try hard enough. After all, everyone started from zero at some point.

In the "old" pre-.NET days, Visual Basic developers could get along quite well without knowing much about object-oriented programming. For one thing, OOP was a relatively recent addition to VB5 and VB6, and for another, it wasn't a complete implementation of object-oriented capabilities. However, the introduction of the .NET Framework and—specifically—Visual Basic .NET changes all that. Everything is now an object, and you can't start a project without seeing evidence of object-oriented concepts. So, to a certain extent, we're all *forced* to learn about OOP just to feel comfortable in this new environment. But you're probably reading this book for more than comfort. You know that to take your applications to another level of modularity, simplicity, and efficiency, you need to build them with the best tools and the best practices.

In this book, you'll find a mix of theory and practice. Reassure yourself that learning OOP concepts is like any other learning in that you use acquired knowledge on your way to grasping new concepts. For many, just getting your head around what an object is can take awhile. You might remember occasions when a theory, concept, or argument that you were struggling to understand suddenly snapped into place. The proverbial light bulb went on when you weren't even concentrating on the issue. That's often the way it is with object-oriented concepts: All of a sudden you just "get it," and your progress accelerates rapidly from that point.

The lessons in this book aren't devoted exclusively to object-oriented programming. Visual Studio .NET is a heavy-duty development environment, and part of the fun of learning a language is to get your hands on the primary tool that supports the language. In short, you want to build something with Visual Basic .NET. When you study the projects in this book, such as trapping events, using remoting techniques, and serializing data, you'll see that you're still employing all the elements that go into OOP. It's just that the tool hides much of it from you.

By the time you complete the 21 lessons we've created for you, the world of OOP will no longer be mysterious or forbidding. When someone shows you a UML diagram of an object, you'll be able to read it like a roadmap. When a colleague asks whether your object can be overloaded, you'll know the answer. Learning OOP over the next 21 days won't always be easy, but it will certainly be rewarding.

How This Book Is Organized

This book is organized into 21 days—three weeks of lessons. The first week plunges you directly into the subject by building a small OOP application. From there, you learn how to talk the language of OOP with explanations and examples of constructors, destructors, objects, members, and more. By the middle of the first week, you'll be creating interfaces and derived objects and learning to use inheritance. The fascinating area of polymorphism is explored on Day 5, and on Day 6 you'll be extending an object's behavior by using composition. To ease up at the end of the week, you delve into the Visual Studio .NET environment, a fascinating and powerful tool for manipulating the objects exposed in the .NET Framework.

At the end of Week 1, we've included a little bonus project. This is a bit of whimsy in which you use your knowledge of classes and inheritance to build a dog nuisance calculator. We're just throwing you the doggy project as a little bone. You can gnaw on it for a while or maybe bury it for later consumption.

Week 2 begins with a study of the data types used in Visual Basic .NET and a discussion of namespaces. You'll see that you can organize your own classes into your own namespaces. As you progress through the second week, more of your learning is done in the IDE. You'll create Windows Forms, Web Forms, and components that are compatible with other .NET languages. In the second half of the week, you'll learn about Web services and how to create and deploy assemblies. The final lesson of Week 2 revisits programming interfaces and how to expose your objects to the world.

Week 3 takes on more advanced topics, starting with events and notifications and moving into the use of exception classes for handling unexpected errors. Objects that were once local to your machine become available to the whole world by mid-week as you learn the techniques and technologies of remoting. For the remainder of the final week, it's down to business: planning, coding, and implementing an object-oriented interface. These final lessons take you from understanding the objects you require for solving a business problem to delivering them in a working application.

Conventions Used in This Book

While you're reading this book, you will probably notice a few conventions that have been used to make it easier for you to learn the topic being discussed.

All the source code in this book is provided in a monospaced font, as shown in Listing 0.1. This includes all the source code from the applications that you will be building and illustrations of how various namespaces, classes, and objects can be used. In some listings, code lines that are being specifically referenced may be shown in boldface to make them easier to find.

LISTING 0.1   Some Sample Code

```
Class SimpleMsg
    Private strMessage As String
    Public Property MsgText() As String
        Get
            MsgText = strMessage
        End Get
        Set(ByVal Value As String)
            strMessage = Value
        End Set
    End Property
End Class
```

If a topic needs special attention, it will be set apart from the rest of the text by one of several special markers:

Note

Notes offer a deeper explanation of a topic or explain interesting or important points.

Tip

Tips are pieces of information that can make your job easier.

Caution

Cautions warn you about traps that you will want to avoid.

ANALYSIS This icon points to detailed explanations or insights about the programming code and often links the code to concepts discussed elsewhere in the text.

At the end of each day, you'll find a short quiz and an exercise to help ensure that you learned the topic you were studying. Not to worry, we don't abandon you if you're stuck on a question; the answers are provided in Appendix A, "Answers to Quizzes," along with a possible solution to each exercise.

Okay, enough about the book. Let's get to the subject at hand. Put your mind in gear, turn the pages, and immerse yourself in the world of OOP....

WEEK 1

At a Glance

Object-oriented programming isn't simple. Most Visual Basic 6 developers have some notions about OOP but need a solid grounding, thanks to the introduction of Visual Basic .NET. You'll get that solid base during this first week. Keep in mind that some concepts take awhile to sink in. You'll probably find as you work through the next seven days and beyond that issues you found confusing on their first encounter will suddenly "snap" into place.

Day 1, "Object-Oriented Programming 101: Making the Task Application," gets you directly into the Visual Basic .NET environment with your first object-oriented project. You'll create an object, add a property to it, and then get into serialization. Before you finish the day, you'll have created a Windows Form and derived an object from an existing object.

On Day 2, "Learning to Speak OOP," you'll be immersed in the terminology and theory of object-oriented programming. You'll build on these concepts throughout the book. Some terms, such as *events* and *methods*, may already be familiar to you. This lesson has a lot to chew on, however, with objects, classes, inheritance, constructors, and destructors and an introduction to interfaces.

Day 3, "Enclosing Features and Data in Objects," explores encapsulation. It goes into the theory and practice of creating an object that becomes a simple "black box" for the consumer. You'll learn how to design classes that hide their implementation details from users. By the end of the day, you'll see that through encapsulation you can create complex applications with very little code.

1

2

3

4

5

6

7

Day 4, "Making New Objects by Extending Existing Objects," focuses on building your understanding of inheritance. You'll explore the relationships between base classes and derived classes. Before you finish Day 4, you'll understand overrides, abstract classes, and shared members. As you'll see, much of the theory can be explained by looking at a bicycle.

Day 5, "Giving Objects Polymorphic Behavior," explains the benefits and use of polymorphism in object-oriented design. You'll get some hands-on time here in a Windows application that uses polymorphic behavior to generate several transaction forms from one base class.

By Day 6, "Building Complex Objects by Combining Objects," you are ready to dig into the concept of composition; you'll learn how to design classes that include references or data of another class type. As in previous lessons, you'll encounter UML diagrams. This time, the diagrams define the relationships within complex objects.

Day 7, "Getting to Know the Visual Basic .NET Programming Environment," offers a change of pace at the end of a heady week. Here, you'll become comfortable in Microsoft's development environment, Visual Studio .NET. The goal is to make sure that you have a good handle on the tool and its resources. You'll see how to build forms, debug applications, and get the most out of the online Help. Of course, you'll do all of this in an application that fully supports object-oriented development.

It's time to get started. Nobody said this subject would be easy. In fact, if it were easy, you would probably know it already!

WEEK 1

DAY 1

Object-Oriented Programming 101: Making the Task Application

Visual Basic .NET is the biggest update to Visual Basic since Microsoft first released it. Integration with the .NET Framework and full object-oriented language features have given birth to a new way of developing Visual Basic applications. Visual Basic .NET (VB.NET) applications are easier to develop and deploy, safer to execute with exception error handling, and better performing with full threading capabilities.

This book's primary focus is to teach you how to develop Visual Basic .NET applications using object-oriented programming (OOP) techniques in 21 days. Although Visual Basic offered classes in the previous version, most developers didn't fully utilize them and true object-oriented progamming wasn't possible.

Today you will build your first Visual Basic .NET application to get a taste of OOP before you get into the details. Although today's lesson may be a little overwhelming, there's no better way to start learning than to just jump in knee deep. By the end of the day, you will have a working application and know how to do the following:

- Create a project in Visual Basic .NET.
- Create an object in Visual Basic .NET.
- Add a property to an object.
- Write or read object data to or from a file (serialization).
- Derive an object from another object.
- Create a Windows Form and use objects within it.

Creating a Project

I won't get into the details of using the Visual Studio environment today or try to teach you all there is to know about object-oriented progamming. I will, however, give you a base to build on for the rest of the book.

NEW TERM   You need to have an idea of what you are going to build before you can build it. Figure 1.1 shows a class diagram for the Task project you are going to build. The class diagram is just one you can have to describe an application by using the *unified modeling language* (*UML*).

The UML diagram shows that the Task application has three classes: SimpleMsg, SmartMsg, and MsgReader. A fourth class, System.Windows.Forms.Form, is part of the .NET Framework and provides the Windows Forms functionality to MsgReader. You will learn more about the vocabulary and how these classes work together in the following days.

After you start Visual Studio, select the option to create a new project from the start page. The New Project dialog appears (see Figure 1.2). Select Windows Application under Visual Basic Projects. Name your project **Task** and click OK to create it.

FIGURE 1.1

UML class diagram of the Task project.

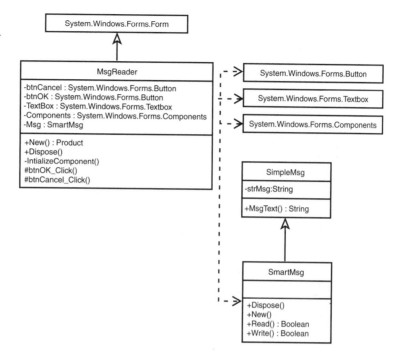

FIGURE 1.2

New Project window in Visual Studio .NET.

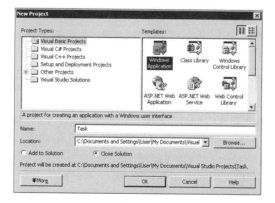

Visual Studio creates a Visual Basic .NET Window Application project with a blank form similar to earlier versions of Visual Basic. However, the appearances are the only similarity. The form is actually a Windows Form, which is an entirely new feature provided by the .NET Framework. You will work with the form after you build the other object classes necessary for the project.

Defining the `SimpleMsg` Object

When you develop an object-oriented application, you typically start by defining the lowest level classes the application will use. You do so to build the foundation on which other application classes are based. For the Task application, you need to define the `SimpleMsg` class, the lowest level class on which other parts of the application rely.

Creating an Object in Visual Basic .NET

NEW TERM An *object* is a collection of data and code that acts on the data. You create an object by using classes. Classes provide a type of template for objects in that they define the objects' characteristics and functionality. For example, an object can be anything—a window, button, text box, and so on. What gives an object its definition is the class. So, a window object would be described by the window class.

Classes are defined in Visual Basic .NET with the `Class...End Class` declarations. If the class builds on another class, it inherits the other class with the `Inherits` keyword.

To begin creating a class, on the Solution Explorer, right-click Task in the tree. (If the Solution Explorer isn't visible, choose Solution Explorer from the View menu.) Select Add and then Add Class to bring up the Add New Item dialog. For this example, name the file **SimpleMsg.visual basic** and click Open. This procedure creates an empty class named `SimpleMsg` in your Task project.

As you saw earlier in the UML class diagram, `SimpleMsg` doesn't inherit from any other class, so it doesn't have the `Inherits` keyword. The only purpose of the `SimpleMsg` class is to store a message and allow that message to be retrieved and changed.

Adding the `Message` Property

Properties are used in classes to make storage and retrieval of simple values easy. For example, name, age, height, and address are all properties of a person. You can define a class with public member data that's accessible without using properties; however, that approach isn't good object-oriented development. It's better for a class to have all its internal data protected or private and provide accessors to set or retrieve values. Properties are very useful in this case.

Properties in Visual Basic .NET aren't the same as properties in previous versions of Visual Basic. They are defined in a class with the `Property` keyword, which then provides `Get`/`Set` functionality. Read-only properties provide only the `Get` functionality, and write-only properties provide only the `Set` functionality. This is illustrated in Listing 1.1, which shows the definition of the `SimpleMsg` class with the `MsgText()` property added. Type this code into the `SimpleMsg` class you created.

LISTING 1.1 SimpleMsg Class

```
 1: Class SimpleMsg
 2:
 3:     'member variable to store the message text
 4:     Private strMessage As String
 5:
 6:     'property to allow get/set functionality on
 7:     'strMessage member variable
 8:     Public Property MsgText() As String
 9:        Get
10:            MsgText = strMessage
11:        End Get
12:        Set (ByVal Value As String)
13:            strMessage = Value
14:        End Set
15:     End Property
16:
17: End Class
```

How a Property Works

ANALYSIS The SimpleMsg class declares a private member, strMessage, on Line 4, which contains the message text. Because other classes can't directly access private class members, you create a property to access strMessage.

The property, MsgText(), declared on Line 8, is called by other classes whenever a value is set into or retrieved from the strMessage member. The following statement shows how to use a property to retrieve the strMessage value from a SimpleMsg object, MyMessage, with the MsgText() property:

strValue = MyMessage.MsgText()

Setting the strMessage member with a property is equally easy:

MyMessage.MsgText = "Hello"

 Note Don't use parentheses on the property when you are *assigning* a value. Instead, use the parentheses when you are retrieving the value.

Accessing a Private Member with Get

When you define a property that allows you to retrieve the value of a private member, you must define the property's Get portion. Within the Get definition, you can do what's necessary to retrieve the value, such as formatting or other special handling of the value.

`Get` ultimately sets the property to the returned value, as shown in the following code segment from the `SimpleMsg` class:

```
Public Property MsgText() As String
    Get
        MsgText = strMessage
    End Get
    ...
End Property
```

A property's `Get` portion is defined with the `Get...End Get` statements within the property definition. If the property is read-only, you define the `Get` only for the property and add the `ReadOnly` specifier to the property declaration.

In the preceding example, the return value of the property is a `String`, the private member is a `String`, and no special handling needs to be done, so the value is simply assigned to the property.

Mutating a Private Member with `Set`

NEW TERM For a property to *mutate* (change) the value of a private member, you must define a `Set` within the property by using the `Set...End Set` statements. Within a property's `Set` statement, you can write the code necessary to set your private member. The most basic version is to simply assign the private member to the `Value` received, as shown in the following code from the `SimpleMsg` class:

```
Public Property MsgText() As String
    ...
    Set (ByVal Value As String)        strMessage = Value
    End Set
End Property
```

The `Value` parameter is the same type as the property containing `Set`. Assigning the private member to the `Value` parameter mutates the private member.

If you are creating a write-only property, define only the `Set` statement of the property and specify `WriteOnly` on the property declaration.

Creating a `SmartMsg` Class

NEW TERM A `SimpleMsg` object is nothing more than a storage place for some message. When the object is gone, the message it stored is lost. The `SmartMsg` class is the same as a `SimpleMsg` class, with the added ability for the state of the object to be saved and read back from a file. The ability for an object to save and read its state is called *persistence*. An object's state is nothing more than the current values of the members within the object.

There's no point in recoding what is already done in the SimpleMsg class, and by using object-oriented techniques in Visual Basic .NET, you won't. Because you are adding capabilities to the already-existing class, SimpleMsg, you will start with that class and build on its features by creating a new class and inheriting all of SimpleMsg's features.

Using Inheritance in Visual Basic .NET

NEW TERM A fundamental concept in object-oriented programming is *inheritance,* which is the ability of one class to inherit all the data, properties, and methods of another class. Very few developers immediately understand the benefits of class inheritance. Most have to work with it and see how it can make writing programs easier before they really understand how to use it to their advantage.

In the Task application, you will use inheritance to build a SmartMsg class from the SimpleMsg class. The SmartMsg class inherits all the features of the SimpleMsg class and adds additional features to allow the message to be saved and read from a file. The relationship between these classes was shown earlier in the UML class diagram in Figure 1.1.

The first step to creating the SmartMsg class is to do the same as you did with SimpleMsg and add a new class to the project, calling it SmartMsg instead of SimpleMsg.

You now have a SmartMsg class that does nothing. To inherit the SimpleMsg class's features, you need to add an Inherits statement to the class declaration:

```
Public Class SmartMsg
    Inherits SimpleMsg
End Class
```

With this one change to the SmartMsg class, SmartMsg now has all the same features and functionality as the SimpleMsg class.

Adding the Write() Method

To save the class data, you need to make a new method, Write(), which saves the class data to a file. For the purposes of this example, you don't care about the filename. Declare the Write() method as follows:

```
Public Function Write() As Boolean
End Function
```

NEW TERM The .NET Framework provides for *serialization* of objects, the process of storing an object's data and other information necessary to reconstruct the object later. To use serialization, add the following statements to the beginning of the SmartMsg.visual basic file, before the class declaration:

```
Imports System.IO
Imports System.Runtime.Serialization
Imports System.Runtime.Serialization.Formatters.Binary
```

These statements import the portion of the .NET Framework that allows your class to use file I/O and serialization. The Write() method is defined as shown in Listing 1.2, which creates a new file and serializes the message text to the file. Type the Write() method code after the Inherits SimpleMsg statement.

LISTING 1.2   Write() Method in the SmartMsg Class

```
Public Function Write() As Boolean
    'declare a file and serialize class
    Dim MsgFile As Stream
    Dim BinSerialize As BinaryFormatter

    'Set the return value to True
    Write = True

    'Use Try/Catch to handle any errors
    Try
        'Allocate and create a new file and serialize object
        MsgFile = File.Open("msg.bin", FileMode.Create)
        BinSerialize = New BinaryFormatter()

        'Serialize the MsgText() property which is a String object
        BinSerialize.Serialize(MsgFile, Me.MsgText())
    Catch
        'Indicate an error occurred
        Write = False
    End Try

        'Indicate an error occurred
    MsgFile.Close()
End Function
```

To make your object automatically save itself whenever it goes away, you need to create a Dispose() method to be called whenever the object needs to be cleaned up before being deleted. The Dispose() method will call the Write() that you previously defined. You can type the following code to define the Dispose() method before the End Class statement:

```
Public Sub Dispose()
    Write()
End Sub
```

It doesn't really matter whether the Write() failed because the object is going away, so the return value isn't needed in this case.

Adding the Read() Method

The other half of making an object persistent is to be able to reload the object state when you're creating a new instance of it. For this to happen, you need to define a Read() method to be able to bring back in the object data that was written out with the Write() method.

The same serialization classes used in Write() are also used in Read(), with the only differences being that you open the file for read instead of creating a new file and use Deserialize() instead of Serialize(). Listing 1.3 shows the definition of the Read() method.

LISTING 1.3   Read() Method in the SmartMsg Class

```
Public Function Read() As Boolean
    'declare a file and serialize class
    Dim MsgFile As Stream
    Dim BinSerialize As BinaryFormatter

    'Set the return value to True
    Read = True

    Try
        'Allocate and create a new file and serialize object
        MsgFile = File.Open("msg.bin", FileMode.Open)
        BinSerialize = New BinaryFormatter()

        'Deserialize the message text from the file into the MsgText property
        Me.MsgText = CType(BinSerialize.Deserialize(MsgFile), String)
    Catch
        Read = False
    End Try

    MsgFile.Close()
End Function
```

Whenever a new instance of the SmartMsg class is allocated, the New() method is called if one is defined. When you define a New() method and call the Read() function from within New(), the object will reload the message if one was saved. The following code segment shows the definition of the New() method:

```
Public Sub New()
    'Always good to call MyBase's New()
    MyBase.New()

    Read()
End Sub
```

NEW TERM Whenever you define a New() method in a class, you should call MyBase.New(), which gives your base class a chance to do any necessary initialization. The *base class* is the class that a class directly inherits.

Building the MsgReader Object

When you first create an application, the default name for the created form is Form1. In the UML class diagram in Figure 1.1, you need a MsgReader class that inherits from System.Windows.Forms.Form. Because Form1 already gives this inheritence to you, simply rename it to **MsgReader** by changing the value of the (Name) property. You also can rename the Form1.visual basic file to **MsgReader.visual basic** with the Solution Explorer. Right-click Form1.visual basic and select the Rename option.

For the purposes of understanding the code behind the scenes, work entirely in the code view instead of the Form designer. Because you are creating a simple form, this process will give you a better understanding than letting the Form designer do everything for you. Listing 1.4 shows the MsgReader class definition with the appropriate name modifications.

LISTING 1.4 MsgReader Class Definition

```
Public Class MsgReader
    Inherits System.Windows.Forms.Form

    Public Sub New()
        MyBase.New()

        MsgReader = Me

        'This call is required by the WinForm Designer.
        InitializeComponent()
    End Sub

    Protected Overloads Overrides Sub Dispose(ByVal disposing As Boolean)
        If Disposing Then
            If Not (components Is Nothing) Then
                components.Dispose()
            End If
```

LISTING 1.4 continued

```
            End If
            MyBase.Dispose(disposing)
        End Sub

#Region " Windows Form Designer generated code "

    'Required by the Windows Form Designer
    Private components As System.ComponentModel.Container

    Dim WithEvents MsgReader As Form

    Private Sub InitializeComponent()
        components = New System.ComponentModel.Container()
        Me.Text = "Task"
    End Sub
#End Region

End Class
```

Making a Windows Form

The MsgReader object is used to view and edit the message contained in a SmartMsg object. The basic form the Application Wizard generates is blank and has no functionality, so the first step is to add some controls.

To view and edit the text, you can easily work with a multiline edit control for this example. To add controls to a Windows Form, you have to allocate a new object and set its properties. All controls within a Windows Form object are declared as member variables and then initialized in the InitializeComponent() method. You add the edit control to the Windows Form with the modifications shown in boldface in Listing 1.5.

LISTING 1.5 Edit Control Added to the Windows Form MsgReader

```
Class MsgReader
    Inherits System.Windows.Forms.Form

    ...

#Region " Windows Form Designer generated code "

    'Required by the Windows Form Designer
    Private components As System.ComponentModel.Container

    'Control variables
    Private WithEvents TextBox As TextBox
```

LISTING 1.5   continued

```
        Dim WithEvents MsgReader As System.Windows.Forms.Form

        Private Sub InitializeComponent()
            components = New System.ComponentModel.Container()

            'Allocate Controls
            Me.TextBox = New System.Windows.Forms.TextBox()

            'Initialize Controls
            Me.TextBox.AcceptsReturn = True
            Me.TextBox.Multiline = True
            Me.TextBox.Name = "TextBox"
            Me.TextBox.ScrollBars = System.Windows.Forms.ScrollBars.Vertical
            Me.TextBox.Size = New System.Drawing.Size(288, 224)
            Me.TextBox.TabIndex = 0
            Me.TextBox.Text = ""

            Me.Controls.AddRange(New System.Windows.Forms.Control() {Me.TextBox})
            Me.Text = "Task"
            Me.ResumeLayout(False)
        End Sub
    #End Region

    End Class
```

After the control is allocated with New, all the properties are set for the control to describe where it should be positioned and its characteristics. For the control to actually appear on the Windows Form, it must be added to the Controls collection with the Add() method. The Controls collection is a list of all the controls on the Windows Form and is defined in the base class, System.Windows.Forms.Form. Because the MsgReader class inherits from System.Windows.Forms.Form, MsgReader has access to the Controls collection.

The process of adding controls is the same for each control, except with different properties depending on the control type. As you can see, the process of building a complex form can generate a lot of code that would be difficult to maintain. Thankfully, a Form designer can generate the code for you. However, it's good to know what the code looks like.

Now you need to add two buttons to the form: OK and Cancel. The OK button will save the message text and close the form, whereas the Cancel button will just close the form.

As with the TextBox control, the buttons are added in the same fashion as shown in Listing 1.6.

LISTING 1.6   OK and Cancel Buttons Added to the Windows Form MsgReader

```
Class MsgReader
    Inherits System.Windows.Forms.Form

    ...

#Region " Windows Form Designer generated code "

    'Required by the Windows Form Designer
    Private components As System.ComponentModel.Container

    'Control variables
    Private WithEvents TextBox As TextBox
    Private WithEvents btnCancel As Button
    Private WithEvents btnOK As Button

    Dim WithEvents MsgReader As System.Windows.Forms.Form

    Private Sub InitializeComponent()
        components = New System.ComponentModel.Container()

        'Allocate Controls
        Me.TextBox = New System.Windows.Forms.TextBox()
        Me.btnOK = New System.Windows.Forms.Button()
        Me.btnCancel = New System.Windows.Forms.Button()

        'Initialize Controls
        Me.TextBox.AcceptsReturn = True
        Me.TextBox.Multiline = True
        Me.TextBox.Name = "TextBox"
        Me.TextBox.ScrollBars = System.Windows.Forms.ScrollBars.Vertical
        Me.TextBox.Size = New System.Drawing.Size(288, 224)
        Me.TextBox.TabIndex = 0
        Me.TextBox.Text = ""

        btnOK.Location = New System.Drawing.Point(128, 232)
        btnOK.Size = New System.Drawing.Size(75, 23)
        btnOK.TabIndex = 1
        btnOK.Text = "OK"

        btnCancel.Location = New System.Drawing.Point(208, 232)
        btnCancel.Size = New System.Drawing.Size(75, 23)
        btnCancel.TabIndex = 2
        btnCancel.Text = "Cancel"

        'Add controls to Windows Form
        Me.Controls.AddRange(New System.Windows.Forms.Control() _
            {Me.TextBox, Me.btnOK, Me.btnCancel})
        Me.Text = "Task"
```

LISTING **1.6**   continued

```
            Me.AutoScaleBaseSize = New System.Drawing.Size(5, 13)
            Me.ClientSize = New System.Drawing.Size(288, 261)
        End Sub
    #End Region

    End Class
```

In addition to adding the push buttons, you add two more statements to set the Windows
Form size to ensure that the form is always the intended size, not a default size.

Referencing a `SmartMsg` Object

The `MsgReader` class is complete from a user interface standpoint; however, it has nothing to display. It needs a reference to a `SmartMsg` object.

Whenever a `MsgReader` object is created, it needs to be given a reference to a `SmartMsg`
object to work with. You do so by adding a parameter to the `New()` method of the
`MsgReader` class. The parameter receives a reference to a `SmartMsg` object, which is then
saved to a member variable of the `MsgReader` class to be used within the object. The following code segment shows the changes needed for the `MsgReader` class:

```
Private Msg As SmartMsg

Public Sub New(ByRef Msg As SmartMsg)
    MyBase.New()

    MsgReader = Me
    Me.Msg = Msg

    'This call is required by the WinForm Designer.
    InitializeComponent()

    'TODO: Add any initialization after the InitializeComponent() call
    TextBox.Text = Msg.MsgText()
End Sub
```

Note

> Within a class, prefacing anything with `Me` forces a reference to the class's
> own variables or methods. If prefaced by `MyBase`, the class that was inherited
> from is referenced. For example, the following code statement assigns the
> `Msg` variable within the class to the reference of the `Msg` variable. Both have
> the same name; however, Visual Basic knows the difference because the `Me`
> qualifier is specified:
>
> ```
> Me.Msg = Msg
> ```

Displaying a `SmartMsg` Object

You can easily display the `SmartMsg` object by using the edit control on the defined Windows Form. If you initialize the edit control's `Text` property to the `MsgText` property of the `SmartMsg` object, the text is displayed. This is done after the `InitializeComponent()` call in the `New()` method, as shown in the following code segment:

```
Public Sub New(ByRef Msg As SmartMsg)
    MyBase.New()

    MsgReader = Me
    Me.Msg = Msg

    'This call is required by the WinForm Designer.
    InitializeComponent()

    'TODO: Add any initialization after the InitializeComponent() call
    TextBox.Text = Msg.MsgText()
End Sub
```

After you make this change, every time a `MsgReader` object is created, the text of the `SmartMsg` object is set into the form's edit control.

Handling OK and Cancel Events

Up to this point, the OK and Cancel buttons added to the form don't have any functionality assigned to them. Because you want the text from the edit control to be saved when the user clicks OK and you want the form to close without saving when the user clicks Cancel, you need to add events to handle the button clicks.

You add event handlers similarly to the way you added them in previous versions of Visual Basic—by declaring a subroutine with the same name as the object and the appended event name. For buttons, you want to know when the user clicks one. Do so by declaring the following subroutines in the `MsgReader` class:

```
Protected Sub btnOK_Click(ByVal sender As Object, _
  ByVal e As System.EventArgs) Handles btnOK.Click
End Sub

Protected Sub btnCancel_Click(ByVal sender As Object, _
  ByVal e As System.EventArgs) Handles btnCancel.Click
End Sub
```

Each subroutine is called when the respective button is clicked.

The common feature for both events is that the form closes when the buttons are clicked. You can easily add this functionality by adding a call to the `Close()` method to each subroutine. The `Close()` method is defined in the `System.Windows.Forms.Form` class and is available through inheritance to the `MsgReader` class. When this method is called, it causes the form to close and all its resources to be closed.

When the user clicks OK, the message is also saved before the form closes. The following code segment shows the assignment that accomplishes this feature:

```
Protected Sub btnOK_Click(ByVal sender As Object, _
    ByVal e As System.EventArgs) Handles btnOK.Click
  ' Save the simple message
  Msg.MsgText = TextBox.Text()

  Close()
End Sub
```

This statement assigns the `Text` property of the `TextBox` object to the `MsgText` property of the `SmartMsg` object referenced by `Msg`.

Because the `SmartMsg` object will save itself when it's disposed, add a call to `Msg.Dispose()` before calling `Close()` in `MsgReader`'s `Dispose()` method. This will cause the message text in the `SmartMsg` object to be serialized to a file so that it can be deserialized when the object is created again.

Putting It All Together

Up to this point, you have been creating class definitions and setting the stage for the application to actually come to life. Now, as in dominos, all that's left is to start the first one.

Adding a `Sub main()`

By default, Visual Basic .NET Windows applications start by running an instance of the default form, `Form1`, which was renamed to `MsgReader`. This works for forms that don't take parameters on the `New()` method of the form and in cases in which the application is based entirely on a main form. This is the case for most applications; however, in an application in which the `New()` method takes parameters as this one does, a `Sub main()` is defined.

In the Solution Explorer, right-click the Task tree item, select Add Module, and use Main for the module name. A new file is created for the module, which is the place where the `main()` subroutine is defined, as shown in the following code segment:

```
Sub main()
   System.Windows.Forms.Application.Run(New MsgReader(New SmartMsg()))
End Sub
```

When you use a `main()` subroutine as the starting point of the application, any pre-initialization can be done, such as looking for previously running instances of an application, initializing options that dynamically change the interface of the application, and so on. In this case, a new `SmartMsg` object is created and passed into a new `MsgReader` object, which is passed to the `System.Windows.Forms.Application.Run()` method. The `System.Windows.Forms.Application.Run()` call won't return until the `MsgReader` form closes. The application then has an opportunity to perform any necessary cleanup before `main()` returns and the application ends.

Setting the Starting Point

All that's left to do is to tell the compiler what to use for a starting point in the application. Select the properties for Task from the Solution Explorer. In the dialog shown in Figure 1.3, the startup object is set to `Sub Main()`. Click OK to accept the changes and compile/run the application.

FIGURE 1.3

Task project property dialog.

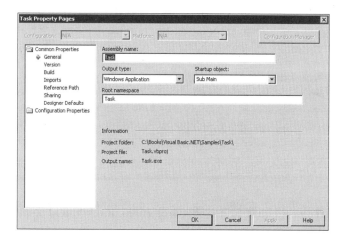

If you see the dialog shown in Figure 1.4, congratulations! You've successfully created your first object-oriented Visual Basic .NET application. If you received any errors compiling or something doesn't look right, try going back through the lesson or looking at the source code for this project at `www.samspublishing.com` (type this book's ISBN in the search field).

Figure 1.4

Finished Task applica-tion.

Summary

Today you learned how to create a simple Windows application by using object-oriented programming techniques in Visual Basic .NET. You learned how to create a simple class and build on it through inheritance. You also learned how to create a Windows Form that has user controls and uses the data class you created.

This exercise laid the groundwork for the upcoming days when you will learn in more detail the techniques used today. You may be a little overwhelmed with the information presented today, and it may take some time to sink in before you fully understand the beauty of object-oriented development. However, you will have a better understanding and appreciation when you complete the book.

Q&A

Q Why do I have to use object-oriented development to develop with Visual Basic .NET?

A To develop a .NET application, you must use the .NET Framework, which is based on an object-oriented design. For example, creating a Windows Form requires you to create a new class and inherit the System.Windows.Forms.Form class. Without inheritance, which is a fundamental part of object-oriented programming, you couldn't create the application you did today.

Q How do I avoid having to supply the fully qualified .NET class name with the namespaces, such as System.Windows.Forms.Form? How can I just use Form?

A You can add an Imports System.Windows.Forms statement before the class decla-ration that uses the Form class. This way, you can eliminate the namespace in front of all classes within the System.Windows.Forms namespace.

Workshop

The Workshop provides quiz questions and an exercise to help solidify your understanding of the material covered and provide you with experience in using what you've learned. Answers are provided in Appendix A, "Answers to Quizzes."

Quiz

1. What does a UML class diagram show?

2. What do you call saving a class's data to a stream such as a file?

3. What feature of object-oriented programming do you use to build a new class from another?

4. What should you provide in a class definition to allow getting and setting values of protected or private member data within a class?

5. What method within a class enables a class to perform cleanup?

Exercise

Add a second SmartMsg object to the MsgReader class and add a second TextBox control to the Windows Form to view and edit the second SmartMsg object. Rather than pass the SmartMsg object in on the New() method as you did in the example today, create it internally to the MsgReader class. You also have to change the SmartMsg class to receive the filename to use on the New() method of the SmartMsg class. This way, each message can be saved to its own file.

DAY **2**

Learning to Speak OOP

NEW TERM For you to start getting serious about object-oriented programming, you first need to learn some basic terms and concepts. Today's lesson covers the common vocabulary used in OOP and how it's implemented in Visual Basic .NET.

Learning the OOP vocabulary and concepts gives you a foundation to build on when you're learning how to do object-oriented development (OOD). A subtle difference between OOP and OOD escapes many junior software developers. However, that difference separates a person who can write an object-oriented application and one who can design an object-oriented application.

Today you will learn what different terms mean and how they apply to building object-oriented applications. By the end of the day, you should have an understanding of the following terms:

- Objects and classes
- Members and properties
- Methods and events
- Constructors and destructors
- Interfaces

Objects

To develop an object-oriented application, you must first understand what an object is and how to put it with other objects to build something complex such as a complete application. In simple terms, an *object* is any item that you can individually select and manipulate. In programming terms, an *object* is a self-contained entity that contains both data and code in the form of subroutines and functions to manipulate and access the data.

Complex software applications are built by using multiple object types, each with its own specialty and identity. An object-oriented view of a company would have employees, buildings, departments, locations, and so on as objects. An object-oriented view of a software package would have buttons, edit controls, windows, data, and so on as objects.

Objects have what's known as *state*. The state of an object is the internal information that describes the object. For example, the state of a check box object indicates whether the check box is checked or unchecked. More complex objects could have a wide range of state information.

State information is internal to an object; however, it generally doesn't change without an outside agent acting on it, such as another object. However, some objects change their own state and are referred to as *actors*, *active objects*, or *objects with life*. A timer object is an example of an object that changes its own state as it keeps track of elapsed time.

Classes

As you learned in the preceding section, an object is an entity with a well-defined boundary, state, behavior, and identity. Classes define an object's functionality, characteristics, and identity. You can think of a *class* as a pattern or template from which to build objects.

When you create an *instance* of a class, you create an object of that class type. The new object has all the functionality, data, and characteristics defined by the class.

A fundamental and powerful feature of classes is the capability to build a new class from another class. This process is known as *deriving* a class from another class. In Visual Basic .NET, a class is derived by *inheriting* a class with the `Inherits` keyword. You learned a little about inheriting yesterday with the `SimpleMsg` and `SmartMsg` classes, shown here again in Listing 2.1.

LISTING 2.1   `SimpleMsg` and `SmartMsg` Classes from the Task Project

```
Class SimpleMsg
   'member variable to store the message text
   Private strMessage As String

   'property to allow get/set functionality on
   'strMessage member variable
   Public Property MsgText() As String ...
End Class

Class SmartMsg
   Inherits SimpleMsg

   Private FileName As String

   Public Sub New(ByVal FileName As String) ...

   Public Sub Dispose() ...

   Public Function Write() As Boolean ...
   Public Function Read() As Boolean ...
End Class
```

With class derivation, you can build progressively more complex classes from a simple base. A good example in Windows applications is building a simple class that represents a basic window. Figure 2.1 illustrates how inheriting the window class builds a progressively more complex user interface window class.

FIGURE 2.1

Class inheritance example.

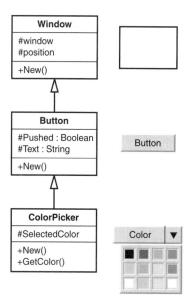

One advantage to building applications from simple classes and inheriting them to build more complex classes is that you can focus your development on a class's unique characteristics. For example, if you inherit a window class to make a button class, the button class doesn't have to deal with anything the window class already does. The button class can focus on what a button does and leave what a window does to the window class.

Members and Scope

Most classes, with few exceptions, have member data defined. The member data stores the state information of an object when a class is *instantiated*, or an instance is created. Some classes provide functionality only and have no state information; however, those classes aren't as common.

In the `SimpleMsg` class from Listing 2.1, the only member is `strMessage`, which stores the message of the object. The `SmartMsg` class in Listing 2.1 doesn't have any state information and therefore no members. It only enhances the `SimpleMsg` class by providing more functionality.

You can think of objects as black boxes in which only the implementer knows how the data is stored and how functionality is implemented. An object's user doesn't care about these details, and in many cases, the object's implementer doesn't want the user to know. A class can define the scope of member data and functionality that determines the type of access users have to an object's member data and functionality. Scope of member data and functionality can either be private, protected, or public.

Private

When you define a class's member data and/or methods that won't be directly accessed by other classes or classes that inherit from this class, you declare them as *private*. Declaring them as private means the data and/or methods are accessible only from within the class.

Classes define member data as private when it's imperative that only that class modifies the data. Even a class that inherits from a class with private members can't modify the data. You might declare it as private when member data requires special processing if it's modified or if it's only for use internally and doesn't have any value to another class.

In general, it's a good practice to declare member data as private and provide accessor functions to retrieve or change its value. For example, the `SimpleMsg` class in Listing 2.1 declares the `strMessage` member as `Private`. An accessor, `MsgText()`, is provided to retrieve and set the value.

Methods within a class can also be declared as private when they should never be called outside the class. If the class has internal functions or subroutines that are used as part of a class's functionality and have no valid use outside the class, they should be declared as private also.

A good time to declare methods as private would be when a subroutine or function is declared in a class and used as part of an overall class-specific process. You don't want another class calling that function directly because it would be out of the context that it was designed to work within. When you declare it with `Private`, no other classes can call the function, which makes the class less vulnerable to bugs caused from misuse.

> **Tip**
>
> When designing a class, you should declare as much as possible of the class's data and methods as private while maintaining the usefulness of the class. Doing so makes your class less vulnerable to misuse by other classes and keeps the class data manipulation under the class's control, where it's less likely to be manipulated incorrectly.
>
> You also can define methods to allow access to all class data so that there is no need for any class data to be declared as anything other than private.

Protected

What if a class needs to have data and/or methods that are visible only within the class but also any classes that inherit it? The *protected* member data and methods provide this level of access. Protected is similar to private in that the user can't directly access the member data or methods, but other classes that inherit a class with protected members and methods can access them as if they were their own.

The most common use of the `Protected` declaration is on methods that are accessible only from derivative classes, as shown in the following:

```
Protected Sub btnCancel_Click(ByVal sender As Object, _
    ByVal e As System.EventArgs) Handles btnCancel.Click
    Close()
End Sub
```

Declaring the `btnCancel_Click()` method as `Protected` keeps other objects from using it but allows a derived class object to use it as necessary. Event handlers are commonly declared this way because they shouldn't be called from outside the object.

Occasionally, member data is marked as protected if a derivative class can safely modify it directly. Again, making member data protected isn't recommended unless it's safe to be modified without any special process.

Public

The last of the three class scope declarations is `Public`. As its name implies, it allows any user or other class to access whatever member data or method is declared public. Generally, classes are designed so that only methods are declared public and member data is private and sometimes declared as protected. Making class member data public is not a good practice because this data can be accessed and modified by any other class. Making data accessible defeats one of the purposes of object-oriented programming: keeping data and functionality contained within objects.

An example of a commonly defined public method within a class is `New()`. All classes in Visual Basic .NET that have initialization work when the class is instantiated declare a `New()` method, which must be declared `Public`. When a class is instantiated with the `New` operator, an object of the class type is allocated, and the `New()` method is called if one is defined.

When you design a class, you need to decide what type of public interface the class should have and declare the appropriate subroutines and functions as `Public`. Users of the class can directly call only those methods that are declared public. Thus, the class designer can control the use of the class and which features are exposed for use by public users.

Static Members

Sometimes all objects of a given class need to share a common value. For example, if you want to track the number of instances of a particular class that are in use, you could add a counter to a class that's incremented every time a new object is created and decremented whenever an object is deleted.

You can declare a global variable to track data; however, the value is then visible to the entire application and is no longer directly tied to your class. Object-oriented programming techniques require declaring such variables as *static* members within the class definition. Visual Basic .NET facilitates declaring static members by declaring them with the `Shared` specification, as follows:

```
Class MyCountClass
    Private Shared InstanceCount As Integer = 0

    Public Sub New()
        InstanceCount += 1

        'Other initialization code
    End Sub
```

```
Public Sub Dispose()
    InstanceCount -= 1

    'Other cleanup code
End Sub
End Class
```

Note   Although the `Static` keyword exists in the Visual Basic language, Microsoft chose to use the `Shared` keyword in Visual Basic .NET to indicate that a class member or method is static.

Unlike typical member variables in which each object of a class type has its own copy of a member variable, static or shared member variables are shared among all instances of a class. So, in the preceding example, the `InstanceCount` variable can keep track of the number of instances of `MyCountClass` currently in use.

Also, any shared member or method within a class can be accessed without an actual instance of the class. You can do this because any shared member is actually allocated when the application starts or when the class is first used because the member is valid for the entire life of the application. For example, if the `InstanceCount` member was declared `Public`, you could access or assign a value to `InstanceCount` at any time within the application with the following:

```
MyCountClass.InstanceCount = 0
```

Final and Abstract

You can create classes that can never exist as an object without being inherited by another class. You also can create a class that can never be inherited by another class. Both concepts are related by the extremes they represent.

As you've learned, you can create a class and then derive another class from the first class by inheriting from it. When you do so, your new class inherits the functionality from the first class and builds on its functionality. Now, suppose that you've created a class that you must derive from and implement additional functionality before it's useful. Such classes are often low-level base classes that don't implement specific functionality but rather contain the building blocks for more complex classes. To enforce a user of such a class to build a new class, Visual Basic .NET provides a `MustInherit` specifier for the class definition.

The code in Listing 2.2 shows a class, `GraphicObject`, that is declared as `MustInherit`, and has a `Draw()` subroutine defined as `MustOverride`. When you declare a method as `MustOverride`, the class becomes *abstract* because functionality is left undefined.

LISTING 2.2   GraphicObject, Circle, and Square Class Definitions

```
MustInherit Class GraphicObject
    Protected Dimensions As System.Drawing.Rectangle

    Public Sub New(ByRef Rect As System.Drawing.Rectangle)
        Dimensions = Rect

        Draw()
    End Sub

    Public MustOverride Sub Draw()
End Class

NotInheritable Class Circle
        Inherits GraphicObject

    Public Sub New(ByRef Rect As System.Drawing.Rectangle)
        MyBase.New(Rect)
    End Sub

    Public Overrides Sub Draw()
        'Draw a Circle
    End Sub
End Class

NotInheritable Class Square
        Inherits GraphicObject

    Public Sub New(ByRef Rect As System.Drawing.Rectangle)
        MyBase.New(Rect)
    End Sub

    Public Overrides Sub Draw()
        'Draw a Square
    End Sub
End Class
```

An application can't instantiate a new GraphicObject class directly because it has the MustInherit declaration; therefore, new classes are created. The first class, Circle, will draw a circle object, whereas the second class, Square, will draw a square.

The only functionality necessary for the Circle and Square classes to implement is the actual drawing code; all other functionality resides in the GraphicObject class. To enforce providing the Draw() functionality, you declare a Draw() subroutine in the GraphicObject class with the MustOverride specifier. Now any classes that inherit from GraphicObject must override the Draw() subroutine to provide the appropriate functionality.

Any time the `GraphicObject` class uses the `Draw()` subroutine, as it does in the `New()` subroutine, the `Draw()` subroutine in the derived class is actually called to draw the appropriate shape.

In this example, the `Circle` and `Square` classes are declared as `NotInheritable`, which means that they are *final* classes and can't ever be inherited to make a new class. This capability can be useful when a class is complete and the class's builder doesn't want any further enhancements made through inheritance.

Say that the design calls for the class to still be inheritable, but a particular method should never be overridden, which would prevent proper function. You can specify `NotOverridable` in the same manner as `MustOverride` was used in Listing 2.2 to protect a function from being overridden. In a class already marked as `NotInheritable`, you don't need to specify `NotOverridable` because no class can inherit from such a class in order to override a method.

Properties

State information of an object is generally not directly available to other classes and users. As you learned earlier, it's good practice to make member data private and provide accessors when you need to give access to other classes and users.

The best approach to creating accessors for member data is to define *properties* for each member variable that you want to allow access. Properties are special in the way they are defined and implemented. The following code segment shows how the `MsgText()` property is defined in the `SimpleMsg` class:

```
Class SimpleMsg

    'member variable to store the message text
    Private strMessage As String

    'property to allow get/set functionality on
    'strMessage member variable
    Public Property MsgText() As String
       Get
          MsgText = strMessage
       End Get
       Set(ByVal Value As String)
          strMessage = Value
       End Set
    End Property

End Class
```

The state information for the SimpleMsg class is the strMessage member variable. The property, MsgText(), provides access to retrieve and set the value of the strMessage member by implementing Get and Set.

Declaring a property is similar to declaring a function, except Property is specified for the type of method. The return type—String, in this case—is defined the same as with a function declaration.

Within the property declaration, Get is defined for all properties that allow access to the state value. You don't need to provide access to the value if you want a WriteOnly property. Set is defined for all properties in which you allow state value changes. If the property is declared as ReadOnly, Set isn't defined.

Properties provide a clean way of implementing the same functionality that's available in object-oriented programming: You declare an *overloaded* subroutine and function. The same functionality is implemented in the following code:

```
Class SimpleMsg

    'member variable to store the message text
    Private strMessage As String

    Public Function MsgText() As String
        MsgText = strMessage
    End Function

    Public Sub MsgText(ByVal Value As String)
        strMessage = Value
    End Sub

End Class
```

The differences in this implementation aren't as obvious until you use the object. With the property declared, you assign the property value as follows:

```
MyMsg.MsgText = "Hello"
```

The second method of implementation doesn't allow for direct assignment of the property because you defined a subroutine for the assignment. The following code shows how you perform the direct assignment:

```
MyMsg.MsgText("Hello")
```

In the second method, what's being done isn't obvious and therefore not self-documenting, which is a goal of good source code design. Therefore, if you declare and use properties instead of subroutines and functions, you can produce better code while effectively providing the same functionality.

Methods and Behavior

The behavior of an object is defined by its methods, which are the functions and subroutines defined within the object class. Without class methods, a class would simply be a structure.

Methods determine what type of functionality a class has, how it modifies its data, and its overall behavior. Methods go beyond what properties do for an object, in that they aren't bound by a rigid implementation guideline and aren't tied to a member data item. They can be subroutines or functions and declared as public, protected, or private.

A class that inherits another class can also override methods of the inherited class to enhance or change its behavior. If the new class changes a method's behavior, it overrides the method and doesn't call the base class's method, as shown in the following:

```
Class DrawName
    Public Overridable Sub Draw()
        System.Console.WriteLine("Nobody")
    End Sub
End Class

Class DrawMyName
        Inherits DrawName

    Public Overrides Sub Draw()
        System.Console.WriteLine("John Doe")
    End Sub
End Class
```

The preceding example shows how overriding the Draw() method can change the results the class produces when the Draw() method is called. The next example shows how overriding the Draw() method can enhance the results the class produces when the Draw() method is called:

```
Class DrawName
    Public Overridable Sub Draw()
        System.Console.WriteLine("What is your name?")
    End Sub
End Class

Class DrawMyName
        Inherits DrawName

    Public Overrides Sub Draw()
        MyBase.Draw()
        System.Console.WriteLine("John Doe")
    End Sub
End Class
```

When you override the `Draw()` method, which then calls the `MyBase.Draw()` method to avoid losing the functionality provided by the base class `DrawName`, the new class enhances or adds to the behavior of the base class.

Events and Delegates

An *event* occurs when an object sends a signal that an action has taken place. The action can be caused by user interaction, such as a button being clicked, or triggered by program logic, such as a timer. The object that raises, or *triggers*, the event is the *event sender*, and the object that receives the event is the *event receiver*. The event receiver does whatever it must do when that event occurs; however, there's no communication back to the object that triggered the event indicating that it was handled or the result if it was handled. Therefore, the event receiver is always a subroutine and not a function because the return value has no meaning.

A class can define events within the class definition; however, no functional code is associated with the event. Functional code is handled by the event receiver when it receives the event notification.

The issue with events is how two objects communicate with each other and know what information is being sent when an event occurs. Delegates come into play here. A *delegate* defines a special function pointer template or blueprint that both the sender and receiver use to communicate at the same level. For example, if an event has a `String` as a parameter, the delegate for that event is declared to have a `String` as the parameter. Whenever an event handler is assigned to handle that event, it must match the delegate's parameter list and define a `String` as a parameter. It can't have anything other than the parameters defined by the delegate.

To define a delegate, you use the `Delegate` keyword. The following shows a delegate that receives `Object` and `System.EventArgs` as parameters:

```
Delegate Sub EventHandler(ByVal sender As Object, ByVal e As System.EventArgs)
```

With a delegate defined, you can declare events that use the delegate as the format of the event notification subroutine. The following `Button` class shows the declaration of some typical events for a push button using the `EventHandler` delegate:

```
Class Button
    Public Event Click As EventHandler
    Public Event DoubleClick As EventHandler
    Public Event RightClick As EventHandler
End Class
```

Although the `Button` class uses the same delegate for all its events, it could have several delegates and use a different one for each event if appropriate.

To handle the events of an object from within another object, you define the object with a `WithEvents` variable and `Handles` clause. For example, the following shows a class with a variable of type `Button`; the class also defines a subroutine to handle the `Click` event:

```
Class Form1
    Private WithEvents Button1 As New Button()

    Protected Sub Button1_Click(sender As Object, _
        e As System.EventArgs) Handles Button1.Click
        ' Place button click code here
    End Sub
End Class
```

Whenever the user clicks the `Button1` object, the `Button` class, defined in the .NET Framework, has code that recognizes that the user clicked the button and uses the `RaiseEvent` statement to raise the `Click` event and signal the `Form1` class that the button has been clicked. The `Form1` class handles the `Button1.Click` event and its subroutine, `Button1_Click()`, which is called when the event is raised. The `RaiseEvent` keyword is used to trigger an event as follows:

```
RaiseEvent Click( Me, New System.EventArgs() )
```

 Note

> The `Button1_Click()` subroutine has the same parameter list as the delegate `EventHandler`. This is enforced by the compiler, so the arguments passed with the `RaiseEvent` statement can be accepted by the event handler.

Constructors

Most classes need to perform some sort of initialization whenever a new instance of the class is allocated. The object-oriented way of performing this initialization is to provide a *constructor* for a class. Whenever a class is instantiated to create a new object, the constructor is called first.

Visual Basic .NET implements constructors by defining a `New()` subroutine within the class. This subroutine can take arguments just as any other subroutine can; however, defining arguments require that they be provided whenever the class is instantiated. The following shows the `New()` subroutine from the `SmartMsg` class:

```
Public Sub New(ByVal FileName As String)
    'Always call MyBase's New()
    MyBase.New()

    Me.strFileName = FileName

    Read()
End Sub
```

A constructor in a class that inherits another class should always call the constructor of the base class by calling the `MyBase.New()` method. Calling this method ensures that any initialization of the base class is performed when necessary.

In the `SmartMsg` class, the constructor assigns the `FileName` argument to the `strFileName` member and calls the `Read()` subroutine for further initialization.

The constructor isn't always a requirement in Visual Basic .NET class definitions, and you might have a class without a `New()` method. However, providing a constructor for a class is generally good practice even if it's not required.

A class can also define multiple constructors. It could have a constructor that takes no parameters and then have constructors that take various parameters to initialize the class at the time it's constructed. For example, the `String` class in the .NET Framework defines three additional constructors besides the default provided by the `Object` class. They are declared as follows:

```
Public Sub New(Char())
Public Sub New(Char, Integer)
Public Sub New(Char(), Integer, Integer)
```

Each of these constructors initializes the new `String` object differently. How the new object is instantiated and what parameters are provided, if any, determine which constructor is used.

Destructors

Whenever an object is destroyed and removed from memory, the object's *destructor* is called. In object-oriented programming, a destructor gives an object a last chance to clean up any memory it allocated or perform any other tasks that must be completed before the object is destroyed.

Like constructors, destructors are defined as subroutines in the class definition. Visual Basic .NET uses two destructor methods, each with distinct differences:

- The `Finalize()` subroutine is called automatically by the .NET Framework if it's defined in the object's class.
- The `Dispose()` subroutine isn't called automatically by the .NET Framework; therefore, the application is responsible for calling it before an object is destroyed.

Finalize()

An object class should define the `Finalize()` method only if the object must execute some code at memory cleanup. But that code must not be time dependent or rely on the existence of other objects. The `Finalize()` method is called automatically by the memory manager within .NET. Because some overhead is involved with the `Finalize()` method being called, don't define this method in a class unless it needs one.

`Finalize()` should also be defined as protected so that another class can't call it directly. If a class inherits another class, it should call `MyBase.Finalize()` from within its `Finalize()` subroutine.

An example of a `Finalize()` destructor follows:

```
Overrides Protected Sub Finalize()
   ' Clean up class

   ' Call my base class's Finalize()
   MyBase.Finalize()
End Sub
```

Because the .NET Framework can destroy an object any time after its last reference is released, you have no way of knowing when the `Finalize()` subroutine will be called. Don't rely on other outside objects being available within `Finalize()` because they may be destroyed already.

Dispose()

Unlike `Finalize()`, `Dispose()` is a destructor subroutine that the .NET Framework doesn't call automatically. If an object must perform cleanup at a specific point, defining a `Dispose()` subroutine is the correct option.

When a `Dispose()` subroutine is defined, it's up to an object's user to call `Dispose()` when the object is no longer needed. As with the `Finalize()` method, `Dispose()` should also call `MyBase.Dispose()` if it inherits another class.

It's not uncommon for a class definition to have both `Finalize()` and `Dispose()` destructors. `Finalize()` calls the `Dispose()` destructor to actually perform the cleanup. Having both destructors gives an object the best of both worlds. The object cleans up itself when it's destroyed and also gives the user a mechanism to force the object to clean up itself with `Dispose()`.

The following sample code segment shows the definition of a `Dispose()` subroutine:

```
Overrides Protected Sub Dispose(ByVal IsDisposing As Boolean)
    ' Clean up class

    ' Call my base class's Dispose()
    MyBase.Dispose(IsDisposing)
End Sub
```

Interfaces

Interfaces are like classes in that they define a set of properties, methods, and events. They vary from classes in that they don't provide an implementation; rather, they are implemented by classes.

An interface is like a contract with a class. If a class implements an interface, it must supply an implementation for every aspect of the interface.

The purpose of creating interfaces and using them in your application is to "future proof" your code. If all your code is based on a set of classes and the methods and data they define, and something changes in a class definition, such as a parameter, the code that uses the class is broken. Interfaces, on the other hand, can't be changed after they are published; however, the implementation of the interface can change.

With interfaces, you can design features into small, related groups. Implementation of the interfaces can be enhanced without changing existing code that uses the interfaces, thus minimizing compatibility problems. You add new features by creating new interfaces and implementations.

To create an interface, you use the `Interface` statement. This process is similar to a class definition without the implementation. The following code sample shows an interface definition, `ICompression`, for a data compression interface:

```
Interface ICompression
    Function Compress(ByVal FileName As String) As Boolean
    Function DeCompress(ByVal FileName As String) As Boolean
End Interface
```

The two functions, `Compress()` and `DeCompress()`, have no implementation. To provide an implementation for the `ICompression` interface, you define a new class using `Implements` to implement the interface as shown in the following class declaration:

```
Class CompressedFile
    Implements ICompression
```

```
Function Compress(ByVal FileName As String) As Boolean
    ' Compress the file and return success
End Function

Function DeCompress(ByVal FileName As String) As Boolean
    ' DeCompress the file and return success
    End Function
End Class
```

Summary

Today you learned what different terms mean in object-oriented programming and how they relate with each other. At this point, you know that an object is an entity with a defined behavior and characteristic defined by the object class. You also know what a constructor and destructor of an object are and what they are used for, along with member data, properties, methods, and events. Finally, you should have a better understanding of what an interface is and how it relates to a class.

The terms you learned today will help you better understand the material in the upcoming days.

Q&A

Q Does an object have to be defined by a class?

A A generic object type is used for dealing with unknown objects. However, when writing applications, you will create a class for each object the application requires; otherwise, the object would have no defined identity or characteristics and wouldn't be of much use.

Q Interfaces seem like extra, unnecessary code. Do I have to use them?

A No, you don't have to use interfaces. It is, however, a good idea to use them in any portion of code that can be shared with other applications or where changes to the underlying code may occur regularly, and you want to make sure existing code isn't broken.

Workshop

The Workshop provides quiz questions and an exercise to help solidify your understanding of the material covered and provide you with experience in using what you've learned. Answers are provided in Appendix A, "Answers to Quizzes."

Quiz

1. What is an object?

2. What is a class?

3. What destructor is called by the .NET Framework when an object is destroyed?

4. What feature is a delegate used with?

Exercise

Create a new class declaration, MyClass1, that implements an interface, IMyInterface1, and is derived from MyClass2.

DAY **3**

Enclosing Features and Data in Objects

NEW TERM One of the most important principles of objects is that they enclose functionality and data while providing an interface with which to interact with other objects. An object's users don't care how the object does what it does; they just want it done well and to have a simple interface. This "black box" characteristic of objects is known as *encapsulation*.

An object encapsulates data and functionality, keeping the implementation details out of users' hands. The object provides a simple interface as a combination of methods, and in some cases member data, for users to control the object's actions at a high level without dealing with the implementation details.

Today you will learn about encapsulation in more detail and how to design classes with encapsulation techniques. You will learn how to design a class with a simple interface that relieves users from dealing with complex implementation details. By the end of the day, you should know how to do the following:

- Create an object with a simple public interface.
- Provide a protected interface for derived objects.
- Keep implementation details private within an object.
- Design an object with good encapsulation techniques.

Designing a Public Class Interface

 When designing an object class, you first decide on the object's function and then determine what type of interface other objects and users will have available for use. The interface you provide in an object class for other users and objects is the *public interface*.

The public interface is fairly self-describing. It's publicly available to all users of an object. The art of object design is to make only what is necessary publicly available and encapsulate as much of the object functionality and attributes as possible. Using encapsulation techniques in object class design will make your objects easier to use and less likely to result in errors caused from misuse.

Most users of an object don't care and don't need to know how a class implements internal functionality. There's no point to provide more interfaces to an object than what's really needed. For example, an object that draws a circle at a given location and draws a supplied string in the middle of the circle would need a public interface consisting of the Draw() method, Pos() property, and Text() property. Listing 3.1 shows the class definition of the CircleButton class.

LISTING 3.1   CircleButton.vb: CircleButton Class Showing Encapsulation

```
Public Class CircleButton
    'Public properties to set/get private member data
    Public Property Pos() As Drawing.Point
        ...
    End Property

    Public Property Text() As String
        ...
    End Property

    'Public subroutine to draw the circle button
    Public Sub Draw(ByRef DrawOn As Windows.Forms.Form)
        ...
    End Sub
End Class
```

Don't worry too much about the implementation with the CircleButton class definition. Recognizing the amount of functionality encapsulated with this simple object class is more important.

The CircleButton class has a public interface with two properties, Pos() and Text(), which get and set the position of the circle and content of the text. It also has the public subroutine, Draw(), which receives a reference to the Form object on which the circle is drawn. There isn't too much to this interface, and it's simple to use, as highlighted in Listing 3.2.

LISTING 3.2   Form1.vb: Form1 Class with CircleButton Object

```
Public Class Form1
    Inherits System.Windows.Forms.Form

    Private MyCircleBtn As CircleButton

#Region " Windows Form Designer generated code "

    Public Sub New()
        MyBase.New()

        'This call is required by the Windows Form Designer.
        InitializeComponent()

        MyCircleBtn = New CircleButton()
        MyCircleBtn.Pos = New Drawing.Point(10, 10)
        MyCircleBtn.Text = "My Circle"
    End Sub

    ...

#End Region

    Public Sub DoPaint(ByVal sender As Object, ByVal e As PaintEventArgs) _
        Handles MyBase.Paint
        MyCircleBtn.Draw(Me)
    End Sub

End Class
```

After you set up the object state in the New() constructor, only a single line of code is required to actually display the circle button in the DoPaint() subroutine. The simplicity of the interface makes it easy and clean to use, and you don't have to deal with complex implementation details.

Protecting Class Members

When a class definition is used to build another class through inheritance, an interface is available to the new class. Like a back door, the new class can call any methods and use any member data declared protected and still remain hidden to any class users.

The protected class interface allows the class definition to provide a specific interface to any new class built to enhance the functionality of an existing class. Member data is commonly defined as protected if the members' usage isn't governed by code. Member data for a class property is a good example. If the property is a simple value and doesn't require special code, it's more efficient for the new class definition to be able to use and set the data value directly.

The following protected members are added to the class definition in Listing 3.1. These members are available through the public properties defined in the class to users and directly available to any class that inherits from it:

```
Public Class CircleButton

    'Protected member data
    Protected ptPos As Drawing.Point
    Protected strText As String

    'Public properties to set/get protected member data
    Public Property Pos() As Drawing.Point
    Get
        Pos = ptPos
    End Get
    Set(ByVal Value As Drawing.Point)
        ptPos = Value
    End Set
    End Property

    Public Property Text() As String
    Get
        Text = strText
    End Get
    Set(ByVal Value As String)
        strText = Value
    End Set
    End Property

    ...
```

You can also define methods as protected to provide a semi-private interface to any class that inherits your class. The methods aren't available to class users, so they are still contained within the "black box." Derived classes can override protected methods to change the functionality of the object or even make a method public, which changes the interface available to users of the new class.

Overall, protected is used whenever the encapsulated functionality and member data are available for enhancement and access by new class definitions. Because the methods and members aren't visible to the class users, the integrity of the object design is maintained.

Defining Private Class Members

All functionality and data truly encapsulated by a class and not available to any outside user or derived class are defined as private. When you're designing "black box" classes, all supporting methods, classes, and data aren't needed by any user except the class itself.

The class definition in Listing 3.3 shows a class that has private member data and methods defined to implement the public interface.

LISTING 3.3 CircleButton.vb: CircleButton Class Modified to Encapsulate Functionality

```
Class CircleButton
    'Public draw functions
    Public Sub DrawRedButton(ByRef DrawOn As Windows.Forms.Form)
        Draw(DrawOn, Drawing.Color.Red)
    End Sub

    Public Sub DrawBlackButton(ByRef DrawOn As Windows.Forms.Form)
        Draw(DrawOn, Drawing.Color.Black)
    End Sub

    'Private subroutine to draw the circle button in the specified color
    Private Sub Draw(ByRef DrawOn As Windows.Forms.Form, _
            ByVal Color As Drawing.Color)
        ...
    End Sub
End Class
```

Listing 3.3 shows a simple instance in which a class has a public interface that calls a private method. In this case, the Color parameter is added to the Draw() method, and two new public methods, DrawRedButton() and DrawBlackButton(), are defined to draw red and black buttons. The object's user doesn't have to know or care what it takes to draw the red or black button—and doesn't need to. The details are hidden from the public interface, providing object users a more intuitive interface. In more complex classes, providing simple public interfaces that encapsulate more complex interfaces is one feature that makes object-oriented programming quicker and self-documenting.

Sometimes it's necessary for a class to define other classes used only within the class implementation. By encapsulating other class definitions, a class defines its own private objects for implementation of the overall functionality. Without encapsulation, these class definitions are available for other classes to use, which sometimes isn't desirable. The following code shows how a class defines its own classes:

```
Public Class MyTestClass

    ' Can be used as MyTestClass.PublicInnerClass by anyone
    Public Class PublicInnerClass
       '...
    End Class

    ' Can only be used by MyTestClass or derivatives
    Protected Class ProtectedInnerClass
       '...
    End Class

    ' Can only be used by MyTestClass
    Private Class PrivateInnerClass
       '...
    End Class

End Class
```

As you can see in the code segment, a class also can provide other class definitions available for use outside MyTestClass. For example, an object may have a closely related object class that it uses for keeping internal information. However, if that information is made available as part of the public interface, the internal class must also be publicly available. The internal public class, PublicInnerClass, is referenced by using the following statement:

```
MyTestClass.PublicInnerClass
```

Attempts to reference nonpublic classes defined within MyTestClass won't compile because they aren't available for public use.

Designing Objects Using Encapsulation

So far, the information provided has been used in simple examples. By now, you should understand encapsulation principles but probably don't have a firm grasp on how it's used in object design and the creation of real-world object classes.

Think about the real-world instance of an application that deals with a database. This example uses a book database that stores a list of books and authors. The application you are creating deals with the list of books in several different areas of the application, and some developers working on the application don't have much knowledge about databases.

The goal is to design a class that encapsulates a list of books and all the functionality required to query the list from the database while providing a simple interface to retrieve the data. With this class, any area of the application and any developer could retrieve the list of books without any knowledge of the underlying database or how it works. Also, the database code could change, and it would require a single class to change instead of several modules in a large application.

The design of class Books is shown in the UML diagram in Figure 3.1. The BookData class is defined within the Books class as Private and isn't accessible for use outside the Books class.

FIGURE 3.1

UML class diagram of Books *class.*

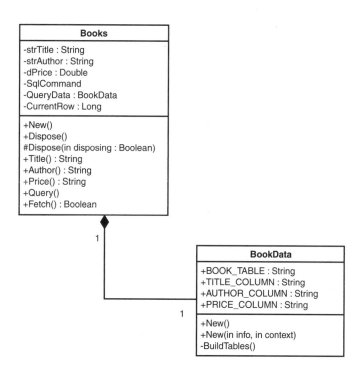

Without getting into how things are implemented in the Books class, concentrate on the public interface of the class. Listing 3.4 has all the public interfaces defined for the Books class.

LISTING 3.4   Book.vb: Books Class Definition of Public Interface

```vb
Public Class Books
      Implements IDisposable

  'Private members for internal usage
  Private SqlCommand As SqlClient.SqlDataAdapter
  Private QueryData As BookData
  Private CurrentRow As Int32

  'Public New() interface for constructing the object
  Public Sub New()
    strTitle = Nothing
    strAuthor = Nothing
    dPrice = 0
    CurrentRow = -1

    SqlCommand = New SqlClient.SqlDataAdapter()
    SqlCommand.SelectCommand = New SqlClient.SqlCommand()
    SqlCommand.TableMappings.Add("Table", BookData.BOOK_TABLE)
  End Sub

  'Public dispose interface
  Public Overridable Sub Dispose() Implements IDisposable.Dispose
    Dispose(True)
    GC.SuppressFinalize(True)
  End Sub

  'Public Query method provides the user of the object a method to
  'start the query of the books in the database
  Public Sub Query()
    If Not QueryData Is Nothing Then
      QueryData.Dispose()
    End If

    CurrentRow = 0
    QueryData = New BookData()

    With SqlCommand
      Try
        With .SelectCommand
            .CommandType = CommandType.Text
            .CommandText = "SELECT title, au_lname, price FROM " & _
                  BookData.BOOK_TABLE
            .Connection = New System.Data.SqlClient.SqlConnection( _
                  "data source=(local)\NetSDK;initial catalog=pubs;" & _
                  "persist security info=False;user id=sa;")
        End With
        .Fill(QueryData)
      Finally
```

LISTING 3.4   continued

```
          If Not .SelectCommand Is Nothing Then
            If Not .SelectCommand.Connection Is Nothing Then
              .SelectCommand.Connection.Dispose()
            End If
            .SelectCommand.Dispose()
          End If
          .Dispose()
      End Try
    End With
  End Sub

  'The public Fetch method provides the object user a method
  'of fetching each record that was returned from the query
  'The results are loaded into members for access via public properties
  Public Function Fetch() As Boolean
    Fetch = False

    If CurrentRow < 0 Then
      Exit Function
    End If

    With QueryData.Tables(BookData.BOOK_TABLE).Rows

      'If there are no more records, exit
      If CurrentRow >= .Count() Then
        CurrentRow = -1
        Exit Function
      End If

      Try
        strTitle = CType(.Item(CurrentRow).Item(BookData.TITLE_COLUMN), _
            String)
        strAuthor = CType(.Item(CurrentRow).Item(BookData.AUTHOR_COLUMN), _
            String)
        dPrice = CType(.Item(CurrentRow).Item(BookData.PRICE_COLUMN), _
            Double)
      Catch
        'Do nothing...
      Finally
        Fetch = True
        CurrentRow += 1
      End Try

    End With
  End Function

  #Region " Property Definitions "
```

3

LISTING 3.4   continued

```
Private strTitle As String
Private strAuthor As String
Private dPrice As Double

'The public properties provide read only access to the
'data returned from the query after each call to Fetch()
Public ReadOnly Property Title() As String
Get
  Title = strTitle
End Get
End Property

Public ReadOnly Property Author() As String
Get
  Author = strAuthor
End Get
End Property

Public ReadOnly Property Price() As String
Get
  Price = dPrice.ToString("c")
End Get
End Property

#End Region

End Class
```

You can compare the class definition to the UML class diagram in Figure 3.1 and get an idea of the interface. Adding the additional protected and private code to the class as shown in Listing 3.5 completes the Books class definition.

LISTING 3.5   Book.vb: Books Class Definition of Private and Protected Interfaces

```
Public Class Books
      Implements IDisposable

  'Private members for internal usage
  Private SqlCommand As SqlClient.SqlDataAdapter
  Private QueryData As BookData
  Private CurrentRow As Int32

  'Public New() interface for constructing the object
  Public Sub New()
      ...
  End Sub
```

LISTING 3.5   continued

```
'Public dispose interface
Public Overridable Sub Dispose() Implements IDisposable.Dispose
    ...
End Sub

'Protected dispose for internal class usage
Protected Overridable Sub Dispose(ByVal disposing As Boolean)
    If Not disposing Then
        Exit Sub ' we're being collected, so let the GC take care of
                 ' this object
    End If

    If Not SqlCommand Is Nothing Then
            If Not SqlCommand.SelectCommand Is Nothing Then
                If Not SqlCommand.SelectCommand.Connection Is Nothing Then
                    SqlCommand.SelectCommand.Connection.Dispose()
                End If
                SqlCommand.SelectCommand.Dispose()
            End If
            SqlCommand.Dispose()
            SqlCommand = Nothing
    End If
End Sub

'Public Query method provides the user of the object a method to
'start the query of the books in the database
Public Sub Query()
    ...
End Sub

'The public Fetch method provides the object user a method
'of fetching each record that was returned from the query
'The results are loaded into members for access via public properties
Public Function Fetch() As Boolean
    ...
End Function

#Region " Property Definitions "

    Private strTitle As String
    Private strAuthor As String
    Private dPrice As Double

    Public ReadOnly Property Title() As String
    Get
        Title = strTitle
    End Get
    End Property
```

3

LISTING 3.5   continued

```
    Public ReadOnly Property Author() As String
    Get
       Author = strAuthor
    End Get
    End Property

    Public ReadOnly Property Price() As String
    Get
       Price = dPrice.ToString("c")
    End Get
    End Property

#End Region

    'The BookData class provides a DataSet that represents the data
    'returned from the query
    <SerializableAttribute()> Private Class BookData
            Inherits DataSet

       Public Const BOOK_TABLE As String = "TitleView"
       Public Const TITLE_COLUMN As String = "title"
       Public Const AUTHOR_COLUMN As String = "au_lname"
       Public Const PRICE_COLUMN As String = "price"

       Public Sub New(ByVal info As SerializationInfo, _
              ByVal context As StreamingContext)
          MyBase.New(info, context)
       End Sub

       Public Sub New()
          MyBase.New()
          BuildDataTables()
       End Sub

       Private Sub BuildDataTables()
          '
          ' Create the Books table
          '
          Dim table As DataTable = New DataTable(BOOK_TABLE)

          With table.Columns
               .Add(TITLE_COLUMN, GetType(String))
               .Add(AUTHOR_COLUMN, GetType(String))
               .Add(PRICE_COLUMN, GetType(Double))
          End With

          Me.Tables.Add(table)
       End Sub
```

LISTING 3.5 continued

```
    End Class
End Class
```

The Books class obviously has a significant amount of code to provide the implementation logic needed by design. The good part is that the Books class user has very little code to write to retrieve a list of books. The use of the Books class is shown in the following code segment:

```
Public Sub MySub()
    Dim BookQuery As Books = New Books()

    BookQuery.Query()
    While BookQuery.Fetch()
        'Do something with data by accessing the properties within
        'the Books object
    End While

End Sub
```

By building classes, such as Books, and encapsulating as much functionality as possible within the class, you can create complex applications with little code.

When a new instance of the Books class is created and assigned to the BookQuery object, all the initialization in the Books.New() constructor is executed. You can see how much code you would have to write repeatedly to duplicate the functionality without the Books class.

When the Books.Query() method is called, a SQL connection is made to a SQLServer, and a query is executed to bring back a list of books with author names and prices. The query results are saved in a DataSet for future processing. Users of the Books object execute only one statement while the class implementation takes care of all the dirty work in dealing with the database.

Finally, the users process the results of the query by repeatedly calling the Books.Fetch() method until it returns false. After each call to Fetch(), the Books object properties are set to the current record, and users can retrieve those values with the property methods.

Summary

Today you learned how encapsulation in class design can hide a complex process in an object and provide a simple interface. By using object-oriented programming, you learned that encapsulation can speed development and limit the number of errors within an application.

As you design object-oriented applications, remember that encapsulating functionality and data in a class is a fundamental goal of object-oriented development. If you use encapsulation effectively and creatively, writing stable, complex applications will become simple.

Q&A

Q Isn't there a standard that dictates how to encapsulate?

A The quick answer is no. Encapsulation is facilitated by object-oriented development. You can write an application with objects and classes that don't really encapsulate much of anything. It's up to the class designer to encapsulate functionality and data into a "black box" that users can easily use without knowing the internal implementation.

Q Can I go too far with encapsulation?

A Yes. If you take encapsulation too far, a class becomes rigid and useful only for its original purpose. Rigid classes don't provide a flexible enough interface to allow new classes to inherit and enhance its functionality. Also, the interface is too rigid for its intended use because it evolves and is constantly being changed to accommodate new requirements. Encapsulation is a good thing, but too much can be a bad thing.

Workshop

The Workshop provides quiz questions and an exercise to help solidify your understanding of encapsulation and provide you with experience in using what you've learned. Answers are provided in Appendix A, "Answers to Quizzes."

Quiz

1. What's the recommended scope for member data in a well-encapsulated class design?

2. What's the purpose of encapsulation in class design?

3. What interfaces are available to users of an encapsulated class?

Exercise

Modify the Books class in Listing 3.5 to add a subroutine, FillList(), that queries the book data and loads the results into a supplied ListView object. By defining this subroutine, you extend the functionality of the Books class, which in turn removes the code from the user application.

3

DAY **4**

Making New Objects by Extending Existing Objects

In the first few lessons, you read a little about inheritance and probably have some idea of what it is by now. However, it's unlikely that you have a firm grasp on inheritance and how to use it effectively in object-oriented programming (OOP).

Without inheritance, which is new to VB in .NET, you can't write a truly object-oriented application. Inheritance provides the mechanism that allows you to build increasingly complex classes from more simple ones. Inheritance is also necessary to change an object's behavior without modifying the original object class.

Today you will gain a better understanding of inheritance, the features and capabilities it provides, and how to use it effectively in your application design. In this lesson, you will do the following:

- Learn about base classes.
- Derive from a class and add data and behavior.
- Build abstract classes.
- Override methods to provide new functionality.
- Use inheritance with .NET objects.
- Designate a class as final.

Understanding Inheritance

Inheritance is the OOP feature that allows new object classes to be created from existing ones. If a class inherits another class, it inherits all the features and characteristics of the class from which it inherits. For example, an object class that represents a bike would have behavior and characteristics. The bike has two wheels and brakes, moves by peddling, and so on. There are many types of bikes in the world with the same characteristics; however, every type of bike has unique characteristics and behavior.

You can design a class to represent all types of bikes, but then the class would be very large and filled with "if this bike type…then this" logic. A better, object-oriented approach is to build a new class for each bike type that inherits the basic bike, as shown in Figure 4.1. Each new class then implements only the behavior and characteristics specific to each bike type and leaves the basic bike behavior and characteristics up to the Bike class.

FIGURE 4.1

Base class and derived class relationship.

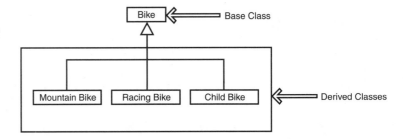

The Base Class

In a pure form, a base class is a class that inherits no other classes and from which other classes are derived. However, in common object-oriented programming terms, the base class is relative to the class being referenced. In other words, the base class is whatever class is inherited by a class and can itself inherit from another class.

> **Inherited Versus Derived**
>
> Today you are learning about inheritance and how it relates to object-oriented program-ming. As you learn, *inheritance* means that a class inherits from another class and extends or enhances its functionality.
>
> When speaking to other developers in the object-oriented community, you are most like-ly going to hear them talk about a class *derivation* and a class being *derived* from anoth-er class. You may never hear *inherit* used to describe the relationships between classes. However, you may hear *class inheritance*, which talks about how a class is derived. The Inherits keyword, new to Visual Basic .NET, brings inheritance into the realm of discus-sion.
>
> When you get down do it, *inherits* and *derived* mean the same thing, and it is the same to say a class is derived from another class and a class inherits from another class. Therefore, when you are trying to figure out the difference between *inherits* and *derived*, realize that there's no difference and the terms are synonymous with each other.

With the bike example in Figure 4.1, the base class for the specific Bike classes is the Bike class. The Bike class could have its own base class as well.

By their nature, base classes are generic and provide functionality common to all classes that derive from them. A well-designed base class shouldn't include behavior or charac-teristics unique to a single object type. Those behaviors and characteristics are imple-mented in a derived class.

Let's go back to the example of the Bike class. When designing this class, you ask your-self, "What features do all bikes have?" The answer dictates the Bike class's design. The class would have a seat, pedals, two wheels, handle bars, chain, and so on. It would also have the behavior of moving forward when the pedals are operated and steering when the handle bars are turned.

Why wouldn't the base class of a bike have brakes? If you think about all the bike types, they have different types of brakes. Some kids' bikes don't even have brakes. So, brakes aren't part of the base Bike class.

Deriving a Class

When you derive a class from another class, you inherit the class's behavior and charac-teristics from which you are deriving. Without the ability to inherit from another class, you couldn't design a truly object-oriented application. This key feature allows you to further define an object class by starting with a base class and adding to and enhancing the base class's characteristics and behaviors.

In the bike example shown in Figure 4.1, three classes are derived from the base Bike class. Each one of the three bikes looks and acts different; however, they have the basic bike characteristics and behavior in common.

For example, you create a Mountain Bike class by deriving from the Bike class. This gives the mountain bike all the basic characteristics and behavior of a bike. Next, the bike is enhanced by further defining its characteristics, such as tires, seat, handle bar, and so on. The bike is then extended by adding features that a basic bike doesn't have, such as brakes, gears, water bottle, and so on.

You can apply the same principles in OOP as the bike example does. Applications typically start from a series of basic classes, and then new classes are derived from the basic classes to further define the functionality they provide. You can't write an object-oriented application that has only base classes and uses no derivation. Such an application may claim to be object-oriented, but in fact it's nothing more than a traditional nonobject-oriented application with structures.

Adding Data

When a class inherits another class's properties and data, it's common for the resulting new class to add additional data. Back to the bike example, the Mountain Bike class has more characteristics than the standard Bike class. It has hand brakes, gear shifter, water bottle, and so on.

Any time the new class has more characteristics than the base class, the new class requires more data members to keep track of them. Adding new data members adds to the overall size of the class; therefore, the new class should add only what it needs.

Adding Behavior

Adding behavior is almost a given when deriving a new class. The new behavior adds to the already-existing behavior the base class provided. Adding new behavior shouldn't be confused with enhancing already-existing behavior—that's covered a little later.

Adding a new behavior to the class gives the new class a behavior that the base class never had. A mountain bike has gears and can switch the gears to make it go faster or slower for speed and climbing. This behavior isn't present on a basic bike and is unique to the mountain bike.

> **The MyBase Keyword**
>
> In Visual Basic .NET, a class can always reference its base class with the MyBase keyword. For example, in the New() subroutine, it's common to call MyBase.New() to call the base class's New() subroutine.
>
> MyBase is a keyword, not a real object; therefore, it can't be assigned as a pointer and can't be used to qualify itself. For example, you can't have this statement: MyBase.MyBase.MyFunction().

Fine-tuning the Class

Up to this point, everything is basic object-oriented programming with base classes and derived classes. You can use more advanced techniques when designing classes that allow the base class to control how it's used by its derivatives.

Object-oriented programming techniques allow the designer to be creative; however, it's up to you to make use of these techniques when building your objects.

You can create an object-oriented application with simple classes and derivation. However, if you have a complex application with thousands of objects and multiple developers, or are creating a class library for use by some other organization, fine-tuning the classes becomes a necessity.

Overrides: Giving an Existing Method New Behavior

You read a little about overriding methods in previous lessons and until now probably didn't fully understand what this procedure was or the point of it. When a class is derived from another class, it can add new behavior by adding new methods, and it can modify or enhance existing behavior of the base class.

Often a base class implements basic functionality in a method appropriate for most, if not all, derived classes. When you create a special derived class that requires more complex implementation of the same method, the new class can override the base class's implementation and replace it completely or add to it by calling the base class's implementation with the MyBase keyword. Listing 4.1 shows a base class and derived class that overrides the base class method CalculatePrice().

LISTING 4.1 Example of Overriding a Method

```
Class Product
    Protected Price As Double
    Protected Shipping As Double
```

LISTING 4.1 continued

```
    Public Overridable Function CalculatePrice() As Double
        CalculatePrice = Price + Shipping
    End Function
End Class

Class LargeProduct
    Inherits Product

    Protected ShippingSurcharge As Double

    Public Overrides Function CalculatePrice() As Double
        CalculatePrice = MyBase.CalculatePrice() + ShippingSurcharge
    End Function
End Class
```

ANALYSIS In Listing 4.1, the `LargeProduct` class overrides the `CalculatePrice()` function of the `Product` class to add the `ShippingSurcharge` onto the total price. Notice the keywords `Overridable` and `Overrides`; these keywords tell Visual Basic .NET when a method is overridable and when it's being overridden. This code is somewhat different from traditional C++, in which any method can be overridden within a base class unless it's marked `Private`. Visual Basic .NET gives class designers control over what's overridable and when they intend to actually override a method.

When a derived class overrides a method, the new implementation is used whenever that method is called, even from within the base class. The one exception to this rule is that the base class can call its own implementation of a method by prefacing the call with the `MyClass` keyword. Doing so ensures that whenever the base class calls a method, it gets its version of the implementation. It also defeats some of the features that overriding methods provides.

Working with Abstract Classes

NEW TERM You can build classes that by themselves can't be used directly. Maybe the class requires something unknown at the base class level or requires additional implementation before it's useful. These classes are known as *abstract classes*.

An abstract class has one or more methods with no implementation details. The implementation is too specific, and only a derived class can provide the implementation. The base class provides the method declaration because it has its own need for the implementation.

For example, the Bike class was designed to know it has to be able to stop but doesn't know how. So, it defines a Stop() method without an implementation and leaves it up to the derived classes to provide the implementation. The Mountain Bike class then provides the stop implementation of pulling the hand brakes. Listing 4.2 shows the pseudo code for the Bike and Mountain Bike classes with a Stop() method.

LISTING 4.2   Abstract Bike and Mountain Bike Classes

```
MustInherit Class Bike
    Protected MustOverride Sub Stop()
End Class

Class Mountain Bike
    Inherits Bike

    Protected Overrides Sub Stop()
        Use Hands to Apply Brakes with Brake Levers
        While Wheels Moving
            Apply more pressure to brakes
        End While
    End Sub
End Class
```

4

When a class has one or more methods that have no implementation, a new object of that class type can't be instantiated. Therefore, you could never have just a Bike object; only one of its derivatives can exist as an object.

In Visual Basic .NET, a class is abstract when it has the MustInherit keyword on the class definition. It should also contain one or more methods with the MustOverride keyword, as shown with the Bike class in Listing 4.2.

Working with Protected Members

Protected member data and methods in a base class can be accessed by the base class or any class that inherits the base class. Any user of the base class object or derived class object cannot use the protected members as they are usable only within the base class or derived classes.

When you're designing a class that you intend other classes to inherit, it's very important to decide where the line is drawn between private and protected. If the base class is allowed to use only certain members, which is often the case with member data represented by properties, make sure that they are marked private. Members marked as private aren't accessible by any derived class and are accessible only from within the class that declares the private members. All other members marked protected and public are freely accessible to derived classes.

A derived class can even change a method's scope to public or private if it's allowed to override the method. If this change isn't acceptable, the only thing the base class can do is not make the method overridable. Table 4.1 shows a matrix of what each scope provides to other classes.

TABLE 4.1   Class Member Access and the Resulting Access to Derived Classes and Object Users

Access	Derived Class	Object User
Public	Available	Available
Protected	Available	Not Available
Private	Not Available	Not Available

If any method is marked to allow overriding, the access can be changed by a derived class. However, a private member can't be marked to allow overriding, and therefore it cannot be changed.

Working with Shared Members

Shared members within a class definition are somewhat unique in that each object of a class type that has shared members doesn't have its own copy of the member. In other words, if a member data item is declared as Shared, all instances of a class share the same member data item.

You also would use shared members when you have methods within a class that are conceptually part of a class but that need to be called directly without the user having to declare and instantiate an object of that class type. The only rule is that a shared method can't use an internal nonshared method. You call a shared method by prefacing the method name with the class name, as follows:

```
MyClass.MySharedFunction()
```

When a class has shared member data, those members may need to be initialized before they can be used. Normally, the class constructor initializes member data when necessary. However, if an instance of the class is never created, how is shared member data initialized?

To initialize shared member data, you can declare a shared constructor for the class. This constructor is the same as the normal constructor of a class, except that it can access only shared class members and runs only once after the program begins executing. The shared constructor stands alone and doesn't override the normal class constructor. The following code segment shows how a class would declare and use a shared constructor:

```
Class Job
   Private Shared ds As DataSet

   Private Name As String
   Private Salary As Double

   Shared Sub New()
      ds = New DataSet()
   End Sub

   Public Sub New()
      Name = Nothing
      Salary = 0
   End Sub
End Class
```

In the Job class, the shared New() is called when the application executes, initializing the ds shared member variable. When an instance of the Job class is created, the regular New() constructor is called, initializing the Name and Salary member variables.

Making the Class Final

When designing a class that you don't want to allow anyone to inherit into a new class, you make the class final. Making a class final means that it implements all the functionality necessary to perform its desired goal and that it's no longer appropriate to extend or enhance the class with another class.

A typical place to make a class final is in class libraries. The class library's publisher can protect classes from alteration through inheritance by making them final.

Visual Basic .NET uses the NotInheritable keyword to declare a class as final. When you're defining the class definition, add NotInheritable to the class declaration, as shown in the following code segment, and no other classes are allowed to inherit from it:

```
NotInheritable Class MyClass

   <Class Body>

End Class
```

Using Inheritance in Visual Basic .NET

Up to now, everything you've learned today has dealt with hypothetical classes and examples. The best way to relate what you've learned so far is to actually put it to use in Visual Basic .NET.

The process of implementing base classes and inheriting from them in Visual Basic .NET is straightforward. The `Inherits` specifier indicates the base class from which a class is derived. In most object-oriented languages, a class can also inherit from multiple base classes, which is known as *multiple inheritance*. However, in Visual Basic .NET, classes can inherit only from a single base class. Interfaces can, however, inherit multiple interfaces if you specify multiple `Inherits` specifiers. You will learn more about interfaces on Day 14.

The examples covered today use single inheritance and aren't too complex for ease of understanding.

Simple Class Inheritance: Making a `MailMsg` Class

By using the `SimpleMsg` class created on Day 1, you can create a new class, `MailMsg`, using simple inheritance in Visual Basic .NET. As you recall, the `SimpleMsg` class contains a member to store the message text and a property to access and set the message member. The UML class diagram in Figure 4.2 shows the `MailMsg` class and the derivation from `SimpleMsg`.

FIGURE 4.2

UML class diagram of `MailMsg` *class.*

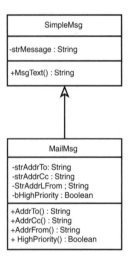

The `MailMsg` class adds additional members and corresponding properties to what is provided by `SimpleMsg`. The corresponding Visual Basic .NET code to implement the `MailMsg` class is shown in Listing 4.3.

LISTING 4.3 SimpleMsg.vb and MailMsg.vb: SimpleMsg and MailMsg Classes

```
Class SimpleMsg
    'member variable to store the message text
    Private strMessage As String

    'property to allow get/set functionality on
    'strMessage member variable
    Public Property MsgText() As String
        Get
            MsgText = strMessage
        End Get
        Set(ByVal Value As String)
            strMessage = Value
        End Set
    End Property
End Class

Class MailMsg
    Inherits SimpleMsg

    'Private member data
    Private strAddrTo As String
    Private strAddrCc As String
    Private strAddrFrom As String
    Private bHighPriority As Boolean

    'Public properties
    Public Property AddrTo() As String
    Get
        AddrTo = strAddrTo
    End Get
    Set(ByVal Value As String)
        strAddrTo = Value
    End Set
    End Property

    Public Property AddrCc() As String
    Get
        AddrCc = strAddrCc
    End Get
    Set(ByVal Value As String)
        strAddrCc = Value
    End Set
    End Property

    Public Property HighPriority() As Boolean
    Get
        HighPriority = bHighPriority
    End Get
```

4

LISTING 4.3 continued

```
        Set(ByVal Value As Boolean)
            bHighPriority = Value
        End Set
        End Property

        Public Property AddrFrom() As String
        Get
            AddrFrom = strAddrFrom
        End Get
        Set(ByVal Value As String)
            strAddrFrom = Value
        End Set
        End Property
End Class
```

The MailMsg class has the features of the SimpleMsg class—the message text—and the member data and properties it defined directly—the address and priority information normal for a mail message.

Form Inheritance: Making the Transaction Forms

To build applications in Visual Basic .NET, you use the Windows Forms class in the .NET Framework to provide the user interface. All Windows forms in the .NET Framework ultimately inherit the System.Windows.Forms.Form class to provide Windows form functionality. You can create a new Windows form either by creating a new class that inherits the System.Windows.Forms.Form class directly or by inheriting from an existing form class.

Looking at a form that represents a transaction in a checkbook as the generic form from which others are built, you could build the classes shown in the UML class diagram in Figure 4.3.

The transaction form has all the base controls common to the other two forms. It's derived from the System.Windows.Forms.Form class and sets up most of the information for the other two forms. Listing 4.4 shows the TransactionForm class definition.

FIGURE 4.3

UML class diagram of
TransactionForm,
DepositForm, *and*
WithdrawForm *classes.*

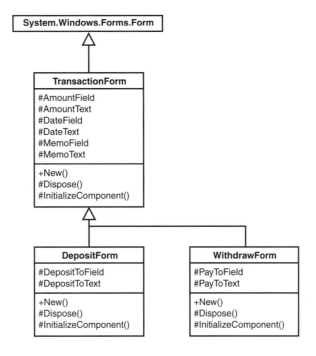

LISTING 4.4   TransactionForm.vb: TransactionForm Class Definition

```
Public Class TransactionForm
    Inherits System.Windows.Forms.Form

    Public Sub New()
        MyBase.New()

        'This call is required by the Windows Form Designer.
        InitializeComponent()
    End Sub

    'Form overrides dispose to clean up the component list.
    Protected Overloads Overrides Sub Dispose(ByVal disposing As Boolean)
        If disposing Then
            If Not (components Is Nothing) Then
                components.Dispose()
            End If
        End If
        MyBase.Dispose(disposing)
    End Sub
```

LISTING 4.4   continued

```
Protected WithEvents AmountField As System.Windows.Forms.TextBox
Protected WithEvents AmountText As System.Windows.Forms.Label
Protected WithEvents MemoField As System.Windows.Forms.TextBox
Protected WithEvents MemoText As System.Windows.Forms.Label
Protected WithEvents DateField As System.Windows.Forms.TextBox
Protected WithEvents DateText As System.Windows.Forms.Label

'Required by the Windows Form Designer
Protected components As System.ComponentModel.Container

Protected Overridable Sub InitializeComponent()
    Me.AmountField = New System.Windows.Forms.TextBox()
    Me.AmountText = New System.Windows.Forms.Label()
    Me.MemoField = New System.Windows.Forms.TextBox()
    Me.MemoText = New System.Windows.Forms.Label()
    Me.DateField = New System.Windows.Forms.TextBox()
    Me.DateText = New System.Windows.Forms.Label()
    Me.SuspendLayout()

    '
    'DateField
    '
    Me.DateField.Location = New System.Drawing.Point(320, 16)
    Me.DateField.Name = "DateField"
    Me.DateField.TabIndex = 0
    Me.DateField.Text = ""
    '
    'DateText
    '
    Me.DateText.Location = New System.Drawing.Point(256, 16)
    Me.DateText.Name = "DateText"
    Me.DateText.Size = New System.Drawing.Size(56, 16)
    Me.DateText.TabIndex = 1
    Me.DateText.Text = "Date:"
    '
    'AmountField
    '
    Me.AmountField.Location = New System.Drawing.Point(320, 40)
    Me.AmountField.Name = "AmountField"
    Me.AmountField.TabIndex = 2
    Me.AmountField.Text = ""
    '
    'AmountText
    '
    Me.AmountText.Location = New System.Drawing.Point(256, 42)
    Me.AmountText.Name = "AmountText"
    Me.AmountText.Size = New System.Drawing.Size(56, 16)
    Me.AmountText.TabIndex = 3
```

LISTING 4.4 continued

```
            Me.AmountText.Text = "Amount:"
            '
            'MemoField
            '
            Me.MemoField.Location = New System.Drawing.Point(80, 88)
            Me.MemoField.Name = "MemoField"
            Me.MemoField.Size = New System.Drawing.Size(176, 20)
            Me.MemoField.TabIndex = 4
            Me.MemoField.Text = ""
            '
            'MemoText
            '
            Me.MemoText.Location = New System.Drawing.Point(10, 90)
            Me.MemoText.Name = "MemoText"
            Me.MemoText.Size = New System.Drawing.Size(70, 16)
            Me.MemoText.TabIndex = 5
            Me.MemoText.Text = "Memo:"
            '
            'TransactionForm
            '
            Me.AutoScaleBaseSize = New System.Drawing.Size(5, 13)
            Me.ClientSize = New System.Drawing.Size(456, 133)
            Me.Controls.AddRange(New System.Windows.Forms.Control() _
                {Me.DateText, Me.DateField, Me.MemoText, Me.MemoField, _
                Me.AmountText, Me.AmountField})
            Me.Name = "TransactionForm"
            Me.Text = "Transaction Form"
            Me.ResumeLayout(False)
        End Sub
    End Class
```

As you can see, the `TransactionForm` class adds the date, amount, and memo fields to the form when the `InitializeComponent()` subroutine is called from the `New()` constructor. The transaction form looks like the window shown in Figure 4.4.

FIGURE 4.4

Displayed Windows Form defined by the `TransactionForm` *class.*

The `DepositForm` class has all the same features that the `TransactionForm` class provides with the addition of a combo box field that specifies where to deposit the funds.

The `DepositForm` class is created by inheriting the `TransactionForm`. The `InitializeComponent()` method is then overridden to create the new controls needed, as shown in Listing 4.5.

LISTING 4.5   DepositForm.vb: `DepositForm` Class Definition

```
Public Class DepositForm
    Inherits TransactionForm

    Public Sub New()
        MyBase.New()

        'This call is required by the Windows Form Designer.
        InitializeComponent()

        'Add any initialization after the InitializeComponent() call

    End Sub

    'Form overrides dispose to clean up the component list.
    Protected Overloads Overrides Sub Dispose(ByVal disposing As Boolean)
        If disposing Then
            If Not (components Is Nothing) Then
                components.Dispose()
            End If
        End If
        MyBase.Dispose(disposing)
    End Sub

    '
    'Additional Controls
    '
    Protected WithEvents DepositToField As System.Windows.Forms.ComboBox
    Protected WithEvents DepositToText As System.Windows.Forms.Label

    Protected Overrides Sub InitializeComponent()
        MyBase.InitializeComponent()

        Me.DepositToField = New System.Windows.Forms.ComboBox()
        Me.DepositToText = New System.Windows.Forms.Label()

        '
        'DepositToField
        '
        Me.DepositToField.Location = New System.Drawing.Point(80, 62)
        Me.DepositToField.Size = New System.Drawing.Size(176, 20)
        Me.DepositToField.TabIndex = 4
```

LISTING 4.5 continued

```
            Me.DepositToField.Items.Add("Checking")
            Me.DepositToField.Items.Add("Savings")
            '
            'DepositToText
            '
            Me.DepositToText.Location = New System.Drawing.Point(10, 64)
            Me.DepositToText.Name = "DepositText"
            Me.DepositToText.Size = New System.Drawing.Size(70, 16)
            Me.DepositToText.TabIndex = 5
            Me.DepositToText.Text = "Deposit To:"


            '
            'Re-order the memo field and text
            '
            Me.MemoField.TabIndex = 6
            Me.MemoText.TabIndex = 7

            MyBase.InitializeComponent()
            Me.Text = "Deposit Form"


            '
            'Re-add controls to form
            '
            Me.Controls.Clear()
            Me.Controls.AddRange(New System.Windows.Forms.Control() _
                {Me.DateText, Me.DateField, Me.DepositToText, Me.DepositToField, _
                Me.MemoText, Me.MemoField, Me.AmountText, Me.AmountField})
        End Sub
End Class
```

When the New() constructor of the DepositForm is called, the overridden version of the InitializeComponent() subroutine is executed, which in turn executes the TransactionForm class's InitializeComponent() subroutine. All the same controls for the TransactionForm are created first. The DepositForm class then creates its controls and makes sure the order is correct for the form. Figure 4.5 shows the DepositForm class when it's displayed.

FIGURE 4.5

Displayed Windows Form defined by the DepositForm *class.*

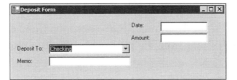

Summary

Today you learned how to create new classes from existing ones and give them new characteristics and modified behavior through inheritance. Inheritance is a fundamental principle of object-oriented development, and understanding it will help you build robust applications with maximum code reuse.

You also learned how to apply inheritance to a couple of Visual Basic .NET examples, with the MailMsg and DepositForm classes. They are just two examples of the many ways that inheritance is used within Visual Basic .NET applications. You will gain more experience with it as you continue through the following lessons.

Q&A

Q Is there a limit to the number of levels class derivation can go?

A Not any practical limit. As far as you should be concerned, there's no limit to the number of times you can derive from a class and make a new class. However, if you find yourself going several layers deep, you might be designing your classes too light. Most applications will never go more than 10 levels of derivation.

Q If MyBase keyword references the class that my class is derived from, how do I reference MyBase's base class?

A Generally, referencing the base class of a class's base class isn't a good practice, and Visual Basic .NET is enforcing that by not allowing MyBase to be chained. A derived class should know only what class it's derived from and not any other classes beyond that point. Therefore, if you need access beyond your base class, provide the appropriate methods in your base class to supply the information. This method keeps every class dealing with a single level back and cuts down on errors caused when a class changes.

Q In the DepositForm class, fields were added to the form. Is it possible to remove fields defined by the base class?

A First, the quick answer is yes. However, you have to ask yourself, "Why am I removing fields from the base class's form?" If you are removing something defined in the base class, you most likely need to modify the base class and remove the field from that form. If all other forms need that field except for a single form, you still remove the field from the base class. You then create a new form that adds the field and use the new class as the base class for all forms that require the field.

Now back to how the field is removed. If you still want it removed, simply don't add the field to the Controls member.

Q Why would I want to inherit from multiple base classes?

A Using multiple inheritance isn't a common practice in most object-oriented programming. However, sometimes it can be useful. For example, if all classes in an application derive from a common base class named `Error` to provide application-level error handling functionality to all classes in the application and you need to create a new class that also must derive from a .NET Framework class, that wouldn't be possible in Visual Basic .NET. Instead, you need to design around the problem or create an `IError` interface that all the classes in the application implement.

Workshop

The Workshop provides quiz questions and an exercise to help solidify your understanding of inheritance and provide you with experience in using what you've learned. Answers are provided in Appendix A, "Answers to Quizzes."

Quiz

1. What's the keyword to derive a class from another class in Visual Basic .NET?

2. What scopes can a derived class access from its base class methods and members?

3. What keyword is necessary to make a class abstract?

4. What two keywords are used together to override a method from a base class?

Exercise

In case you are wondering what happened to the `WithdrawForm` class shown in Figure 4.3, now is the time to create it. For today's exercise, create the third class, `WithdrawForm`, as it's shown in Figure 4.3. Add two fields: PayToField as a TextBox control and PayToText as a Label. This class is similar to the `DepositForm` class and can be used as a guide to help you figure out what to do.

DAY 5

Giving Objects Polymorphic Behavior

Polymorphism is the capability to have multiple classes with the same interface implemented in different ways. For example, a car class and a sailboat class both have a `TurnRight()` method. The car class implements this functionality by turning the steering wheel to the right, which then turns the front wheels to the right. A sailboat class implements the `TurnRight()` functionality by adjusting the sails and turning the rudder, which causes the boat to turn right. Here you have the same method in two classes with two different implementations.

Today you will learn how to use polymorphism in Visual Basic .NET to build classes with the same interface and different implementations. By understanding polymorphism, you will gain a better understanding as to why methods are overridden in derived classes. By the end of the day, you will learn the following:

- How polymorphism benefits object design
- How to create classes in Visual Basic .NET that use polymorphism
- How to use different techniques to create polymorphic classes

Understanding the Benefits of Polymorphism

NEW TERM *Polymorphism* is the capability of a group of objects, typically related, to have the same interface with different underlying implementations. Users of objects that have polymorphic characteristics use the same interface on all object types to perform a task while the underlying object performs the task in whatever way is applicable to that class type.

The benefit comes from being able to interchange the object types without any change in the user code. Each object implements the polymorphic interfaces appropriately, and the user code stays the same. For example, a group of shape objects all implement a Draw() method. The Draw() method for a circle shape object draws a circle, but for a rectangle object it draws a rectangle. Each shape object is interchangeable, and the user of the objects simply uses the Draw() method, letting each object deal with what is actually drawn.

A graphic design application could have a list of shape objects that are all derived from a common base shape class. The list is made up of the base shape class and doesn't know what combination of shapes it has. When it's time to display the shapes, the application iterates through the list of shape objects, calling the Draw() method. Each shape object then has a chance to display its own unique shape. This works because all the different shape classes are derived from the same common base class, which has a Draw() method defined but not necessarily implemented. Each derived class provides the implementation of the Draw() method.

Using Polymorphism in Visual Basic .NET

No special syntax signifies whether a method is polymorphic. Polymorphism is a byproduct of using object-oriented programming techniques to provide different implementations for the same method. In object-oriented languages, you can create polymorphic objects through inheritance and interfaces.

Remember, polymorphic objects have the same interface with different behavior. You created some polymorphic classes yesterday—possibly without even realizing it—when you created the DepositForm and WithdrawForm classes from the TransactionForm base class. They all implemented the InitializeComponent() method, each with a different implementation.

Inheritance Polymorphism

Inheritance in Visual Basic .NET is an effective method of building new classes and providing polymorphic behavior in classes. When a class has methods that are overridable, you can create a new derived class that overrides the methods marked as overridable and provide new or enhanced behavior. Hence, both the base and derived classes have the same method with different behavior.

The `TransactionForm`, `DepositForm`, and `WithdrawForm` classes you created yesterday present a good opportunity to highlight polymorphic behavior. They already have a common `InitializeComponent()` method with polymorphic behavior; however, this method is protected and not visible to the objects' user.

For this example, you define a polymorphic `Save()` method that is `Public`. First, the `Save()` method needs to be defined in the base class, `TransactionForm`. In the base class, the `Save()` method saves the part of the transaction information for which it's responsible using serialization similar to the `SmartMsg` class from the first day. Listing 5.1 shows the changes to the `TransactionForm` class.

LISTING 5.1   TransactionForm.vb: `TransactionForm` Class with `Save()` Method Added

```
Public Class TransactionForm
    Inherits System.Windows.Forms.Form

    Public Sub New()
        MyBase.New()

        'This call is required by the Windows Form Designer.
        InitializeComponent()
    End Sub

    Public Overridable Function Save(ByVal FileName As String) As Boolean
        'declare a file and serialize class
        Dim TranFile As Stream
        Dim BinSerialize As BinaryFormatter

        'Set the return value to True
        Save = True

        'Use Try/Catch to handle any errors
        Try
            'Allocate and create a new file and serialize objects
            TranFile = File.Open(FileName, FileMode.Create)
            BinSerialize = New BinaryFormatter()

            'Serialize the form data
            BinSerialize.Serialize(TranFile, AmountField.ToString())
            BinSerialize.Serialize(TranFile, MemoField.ToString())
            BinSerialize.Serialize(TranFile, DateField.ToString())
        Catch
```

5

LISTING 5.1   continued

```
            'Indicate an error occurred
            Save = False
        End Try

        TranFile.Close()
    End Function

    ...

End Class
```

TransactionForm's Save() function saves the amount, memo, and date fields. Both DepositForm and WithdrawForm have an additional field that isn't being saved when Save() is called. Listing 5.2 shows how to declare and implement a polymorphic Save() within the DepositForm and WithdrawForm classes.

LISTING 5.2   DepositForm.vb and WithdrawForm.vb: DepositForm and WithdrawForm with Polymorphic Save() Methods Added

```
Public Class DepositForm
    Inherits TransactionForm

    Public Sub New()
        MyBase.New()

        'This call is required by the Windows Form Designer.
        InitializeComponent()

        'Add any initialization after the InitializeComponent() call
    End Sub

    Public Overrides Function Save(ByVal FileName As String) As Boolean
        'declare a file and serialize class
        Dim TranFile As Stream
        Dim BinSerialize As BinaryFormatter

        'Call MyBase's Save first and return if an error occurs
        If Not MyBase.Save(FileName) Then
            Return False
        End If

        'Set the return value to True
        Save = True
```

LISTING 5.2   continued

```
              'Use Try/Catch to handle any errors
              Try
                  'Allocate and open the same file as MyBase.Save() used and
                  'serialize object
                  TranFile = File.Open(FileName, FileMode.Append)
                  BinSerialize = New BinaryFormatter()

                  'Serialize the MsgText() property which is a String object
                  BinSerialize.Serialize(TranFile, DepositToField.ToString())
              Catch
                  'Do nothing
                  Save = False
              End Try

              TranFile.Close()
          End Function

      ...
  End Class

  Public Class WithdrawForm
      Inherits TransactionForm

      Public Sub New()
          MyBase.New()

          'This call is required by the Windows Form Designer.
          InitializeComponent()

          'Add any initialization after the InitializeComponent() call
      End Sub

      Public Overrides Function Save(ByVal FileName As String) As Boolean
          'declare a file and serialize class
          Dim TranFile As Stream
          Dim BinSerialize As BinaryFormatter

          'Call MyBase's Save first and return if an error occurs
          If Not MyBase.Save(FileName) Then
              Return False
          End If

          'Set the return value to True
          Save = True

          'Use Try/Catch to handle any errors
          Try
              'Allocate and open the same file as MyBase.Save() used
```

LISTING 5.2   continued

```
                'and serialize object
                TranFile = File.Open(FileName, FileMode.Append)
                BinSerialize = New BinaryFormatter()

                'Serialize the MsgText() property which is a String object
                BinSerialize.Serialize(TranFile, PayToField.ToString())
            Catch
                'Do nothing
                Save = False
            End Try

            TranFile.Close()
        End Function

        ...
End Class
```

Now each class has its own polymorphic Save() method. The DepositForm and WithdrawForm classes call their base class's Save() method from within their own Save() method to get the base class's data saved. When the base class's method is called first, all files created by TransactionForm or any of its derivatives have the base class data with the derived class data following. Standardizing where possible is a good practice, especially when data is involved. Doing so allows you to always know the data is in a specific format.

Abstract Classes and Polymorphism

Adding the Save() function to each class is a bit clunky in its current implementation. The derived classes have to reopen a file that the base class already had open so that they can save their information. This means that any time a Save() occurs in a derived class, a file is opened and closed twice. It also means that all the code to open and close the file is duplicated, which also provides a code maintenance issue.

Another way of creating polymorphic classes is to declare abstract methods in the base class and force the implementation in the derived classes. Rethinking the implementation of the Save() method, you could create an abstract method that derived classes implement to save their specific information. Because the TransactionForm class shouldn't be used directly anyway and is useful only as DepositForm and WithdrawForm, making it abstract doesn't hurt the design of the class. Listing 5.3 shows the new implementation of Save() and the declaration of the abstract SaveData() method in the TransactionForm class.

LISTING 5.3 TransactionForm.vb: Changes to the `TransactionForm` Class to Make It Abstract and to Declare a `SaveData()` Method

```vb
Public MustInherit Class TransactionForm
    Inherits System.Windows.Forms.Form

    Public Sub New()
        MyBase.New()

        'This call is required by the Windows Form Designer.
        InitializeComponent()
    End Sub

    Public Function Save(ByVal FileName As String) As Boolean
        'declare a file and serialize class
        Dim TranFile As Stream
        Dim BinSerialize As BinaryFormatter

        'Set the return value to True
        Save = True

        'Use Try/Catch to handle any errors
        Try
            'Allocate and create a new file and serialize objects
            TranFile = File.Open(FileName, FileMode.Create)
            BinSerialize = New BinaryFormatter()

            'Serialize the form data
            BinSerialize.Serialize(TranFile, AmountField.ToString())
            BinSerialize.Serialize(TranFile, MemoField.ToString())
            BinSerialize.Serialize(TranFile, DateField.ToString())

            'Call SaveData() to save derived class's data
            SaveData(BinSerialize, TranFile)
        Catch
            'Indicate an error occurred
            Save = False
        End Try

        TranFile.Close()
    End Function

    'Declare Abstract method to save derived class's data
    Protected MustOverride Sub SaveData(ByRef BinSerialize _
            As BinaryFormatter, ByRef TranFile As Stream)

    ...
End Class
```

5

The changes to the `TransactionForm` class are relatively minor. What makes this approach work better is the base class deals with all the logic in the `Save()` function, which then calls the `SaveData()` subroutine when it's time for the derived classes to save their information. This approach gives the base class all the control over how the serialization occurs, which is a better design.

The changes to the `DepositForm` and `TransactionForm` classes are more dramatic for the better. They no longer have an override of the `Save()` function, so it is removed from each class. Each class now overrides the `SaveData()` subroutine and provides an implementation for it to save the class's specific data. Listing 5.4 shows the new class definitions.

LISTING 5.4   DepositForm.vb and WithdrawForm.vb: Changes to the `DepositForm` and `WithdrawForm` Classes

```
Public Class DepositForm
    Inherits TransactionForm

    Public Sub New()
        MyBase.New()

        'This call is required by the Windows Form Designer.
        InitializeComponent()

        'Add any initialization after the InitializeComponent() call
    End Sub

    Protected Overrides Sub SaveData(ByRef BinSerialize As BinaryFormatter, _
                                     ByRef TranFile As Stream)
        BinSerialize.Serialize(TranFile, DepositToField.ToString())
    End Sub

    ...

End Class

Public Class WithdrawForm
    Inherits TransactionForm

    Public Sub New()
        MyBase.New()

        'This call is required by the Windows Form Designer.
        InitializeComponent()
```

LISTING 5.4   continued

```
        'Add any initialization after the InitializeComponent() call
    End Sub

    Protected Overrides Sub SaveData(ByRef BinSerialize As BinaryFormatter, _
                                    ByRef TranFile As Stream)
        BinSerialize.Serialize(TranFile, PayToField.ToString())
    End Sub

    ...

End Class
```

It should be clear that the new implementation of the `DepositForm` and `WithdrawForm` classes is much easier to maintain and is overall a better design. Again, it relies on OOP polymorphic features, only with a different subroutine, `SaveData()`. The purpose of building an abstract class is to implement as much logic as possible at the base class level, which most likely relies on abstract methods the derived classes implement. As you can see, it's virtually impossible to have an abstract class that doesn't use and rely on polymorphism.

Interface Polymorphism

Another way to create polymorphic behavior is to define and implement interfaces in Visual Basic .NET. Every class that implements an interface can do so differently and have different behavior. The other benefit of interfaces is that they aren't tied to a class until the class implements an interface. Therefore, several unrelated classes can implement the same interface to provide class-specific implementation.

For example, defining and implementing an `IPrint` interface for the `DepositForm` and `WithdrawForm` classes could create totally different implementations. All other classes that implement the `IPrint` interface would have their own implementations. Any user of the classes can use the `IPrint` interface, which is polymorphic by its nature, because each class that implements the interface has to provide its own implementation. The following shows a simple declaration of an `IPrint` interface, which `DepositForm` and `WithdrawForm` will implement:

```
Public Interface IPrint
    Sub Print()
End Interface
```

Whenever a class implements an interface, it must supply an implementation for each method defined in the interface. In this case, only `Print()` is defined. Listing 5.5 shows how `DepositForm` implements the `IPrint` interface.

5

LISTING 5.5   DepositForm.vb: Implementation of the IPrint Interface in DepositForm

```
Public Class DepositForm
    Inherits TransactionForm
    Implements IPrint

    Protected PrintFont As Font

    Protected Sub Print() Implements IPrint.Print
        Dim pd As System.Drawing.Printing.PrintDocument = _
                    New System.Drawing.Printing.PrintDocument()
        PrintFont = New Font("Arial", 10)

        AddHandler pd.PrintPage, AddressOf PrintDeposit

        pd.Print()
    End Sub

    Protected Sub PrintDeposit(ByVal sender As Object, _
                ByVal ev As System.Drawing.Printing.PrintPageEventArgs)

        'Print the deposit form
        ev.Graphics.DrawString("Deposit Form", PrintFont, Brushes.Black, _
                    ev.MarginBounds.Left(),_
                    ev.MarginBounds.Top() + PrintFont.GetHeight())
        ev.Graphics.DrawString("Date: " & DateField.ToString(), PrintFont, _
                    Brushes.Black, ev.MarginBounds.Left(), _
                    ev.MarginBounds.Top() + (PrintFont.GetHeight() * 2))
        ev.Graphics.DrawString("Deposit To: " & DepositToField.ToString(), _
                    PrintFont, Brushes.Black, ev.MarginBounds.Left(), _
                    ev.MarginBounds.Top() + (PrintFont.GetHeight() * 4))
        ev.Graphics.DrawString("Amount: " & AmountField.ToString(), _
                    PrintFont, Brushes.Black, ev.MarginBounds.Left(), _
                    ev.MarginBounds.Top() + (PrintFont.GetHeight() * 5))
        ev.Graphics.DrawString("Memo: " & MemoField.ToString(), _
                    PrintFont, Brushes.Black, ev.MarginBounds.Left(),_
                    ev.MarginBounds.Top() + (PrintFont.GetHeight() * 6))

        ev.HasMorePages = False
    End Sub

    ...

End Class
```

The DepositForm class implements the Print() subroutine in a way that shares a member variable, PrintFont, with the print handler. The Print() subroutine initializes the font, and PrintDeposit() uses it.

The `WithdrawForm` class implements `Print()` in a different way that doesn't have a member variable, and `PrintFont` is declared, initialized, and used in the `PrintWithdraw()` subroutine (see Listing 5.6). It could go even further and not even print to a printer but to a file instead. The point is that the interface's implementation is polymorphic because it's different for each class that implements it. It also provides the same external interface to users of each class that implements an interface.

LISTING 5.6 WithdrawForm.vb: Implementation of the `IPrint` Interface in the `WithdrawForm` Class

```
Public Class WithdrawForm
    Inherits TransactionForm
    Implements IPrint

    Protected Sub Print() Implements IPrint.Print
        Dim pd As System.Drawing.Printing.PrintDocument = _
                    New System.Drawing.Printing.PrintDocument()

        AddHandler pd.PrintPage, AddressOf PrintWithdraw

        pd.Print()
    End Sub

    Protected Sub PrintWithdraw(ByVal sender As Object, _
            ByVal ev As System.Drawing.Printing.PrintPageEventArgs)
        Dim PrintFont As Font = New Font("Arial", 10)

        'Print the deposit form
        ev.Graphics.DrawString("Withdraw Form", PrintFont, Brushes.Black, _
                    ev.MarginBounds.Left(), _
                    ev.MarginBounds.Top() + PrintFont.GetHeight())
        ev.Graphics.DrawString("Date: " & DateField.ToString(), _
                    PrintFont, Brushes.Black, _
                    ev.MarginBounds.Left(), _
                    ev.MarginBounds.Top() + (PrintFont.GetHeight() * 2))
        ev.Graphics.DrawString("Pay To: " & PayToField.ToString(), _
                    PrintFont, Brushes.Black, _
                    ev.MarginBounds.Left(), _
                    ev.MarginBounds.Top() + (PrintFont.GetHeight() * 4))
        ev.Graphics.DrawString("Amount: " & AmountField.ToString(), _
                    PrintFont, Brushes.Black, _
                    ev.MarginBounds.Left(), _
                    ev.MarginBounds.Top() + (PrintFont.GetHeight() * 5))
        ev.Graphics.DrawString("Memo: " & MemoField.ToString(), _
                    PrintFont, Brushes.Black, _
                    ev.MarginBounds.Left(), _
                    ev.MarginBounds.Top() + (PrintFont.GetHeight() * 6))
```

5

LISTING 5.6   continued

```
        ev.HasMorePages = False
    End Sub

    ...

End Class
```

Summary

Today you learned how to use polymorphism to create classes with the same interface and different behavior. Polymorphism is a natural feature of OOD, and if you are creating your classes and using inheritance, you are most likely using polymorphism.

Today's lesson introduced polymorphism by giving you some examples illustrating when it's used and how to use it. Over time, you will further understand and use this feature when building interfaces to your classes.

Q&A

Q Does creating polymorphic classes with inheritance have advantages?

A Whenever you have classes directly related to each other, using inheritance and overriding methods to provide polymorphic behavior is the best method. As today's lesson shows, it's even better in some cases to create an abstract base class and let the derivative classes provide the necessary implementation.

Q What's the advantage of creating polymorphic classes with interfaces?

A Interfaces allow you to create polymorphic behavior between unrelated classes. Because any class can implement an interface, you aren't bound by inheritance. What you lose is the ability to build on a base class's implementation as you can with building an abstract class.

Q Why can't I instantiate an abstract class and use it directly?

A An abstract class doesn't provide an implementation for each of its declared methods. Therefore, if you tried to use it directly, there wouldn't be code for each method to execute. This is why any class that inherits an abstract class must provide an implementation for any methods that don't have an implementation or the class must also be marked as an abstract class. The only classes you can use are the ones with a complete implementation without any unknowns.

Workshop

The Workshop provides quiz questions and an exercise to help solidify your understanding of polymorphism and provide you with experience in using what you've learned. Answers are provided in Appendix A, "Answers to Quizzes."

Quiz

1. Why is an interface considered polymorphic?

2. Can you have a nonpolymorphic abstract subroutine?

3. Can you have a nonpolymorphic normal subroutine that you know will never have another implementation?

4. Are all overridden subroutines polymorphic?

Exercise

Today the Save() method was added to the TransactionForm class, and SaveData() was declared as abstract and implemented in the DepositForm and WithdrawForm classes. Write the corresponding Read() and ReadData() methods for the same classes to read the information and load it into the form. If you need some help with deserializing, look at the SmartMsg class for a sample.

5

Building Complex Objects by Combining Objects

Today you will learn about another way to extend an object's behavior and characteristics. This method is known as *composition*. Composition is a way to extend a class by delegating functionality to other associated classes. It's important to know the differences between composition and inheritance.

The unified modeling language (UML) defines three forms of composition that are covered in today's lesson. One form is actually called *composition*, so the description may get a little confusing. However, with advanced knowledge of this issue, you can be prepared for it. Today you will do the following:

- Learn the difference between composition and inheritance.
- Learn the three forms of composition.
- Use composition within a class in Visual Basic .NET.

Understanding Composition Versus Inheritance

NEW TERM *Composition* and *inheritance* are both techniques for reusing functionality and extending an object class in OOP. The two have some differences, so it's important to understand when one method is used rather than the other.

As you've learned up to this point, class inheritance gives the derived class all the characteristics and behavior of its base class. All public interfaces of the base class become part of the public interface for the derived class, protected members and methods are accessible to the derived class, and so on.

With inheritance, each successive derived class is the same as the base class with enhanced or extended behavior and characteristics. For example, an `8086` CPU class could be a base class for an `80286` CPU class, which in turn could be the base class for an `80386` CPU class. Each class represents CPUs with increasingly more functionality and characteristics.

Object composition, on the other hand, allows objects to achieve more complex functionality by combining several objects into a single object. This method requires that the object classes have well-defined interfaces because none of the internals of classes are available as they are with inheritance. For example, a `computer` class is a composition of a CPU, motherboard, memory, hard drive, floppy drive, computer case, and so on. Each object in a composition is also a standalone object.

Both methods have advantages and disadvantages; however, they aren't necessarily interchangeable, although a creative developer can use composition in place of inheritance. The advantages of class inheritance are that it's done statically at compile time, it's easy to use, and the new class is the same type as the base class. The disadvantage of inheritance is that the derived class depends on the base class implementation, which can cause problems if part of the inherited implementation is no longer desired. Another problem of class inheritance is that it can't be changed at runtime if you have dynamic relationships. Dynamic relationships allow a class to contain different objects and characteristics at runtime instead of design time.

In composition, functionality is dynamically acquired at runtime by collecting references to other objects. The advantages are that the implementation can be changed at runtime, and objects are easily changed out when functionality changes. Also, complex objects are created by bringing together several other object types. The disadvantages of composition are that the source code may be more difficult to read and that the composition object doesn't know the identity of the objects it contains until runtime.

When deciding which is the correct option for designing a class, you can use this simple question for deciding whether inheritance is the correct option: "Is my new object the same basic type as my base object?" If the answer is yes, inheritance is the way to go. The corresponding composition question you can ask is, "Is my new object a collection of other objects and not a simple extension to a single object?" If you're not sure when to use one rather than the other after asking yourself these questions, composition should be favored.

Understanding Association

NEW TERM Three types of composition are defined in UML. The first and loosest type of composition is *association,* which is diagrammed in UML as shown in Figure 6.1 and is typically implemented as a pointer or reference to an object within an object. For example, the Family object in Figure 6.1 doesn't own or create the Person object; it simply has a reference to one or more persons, and a Person object has a reference to one Family object.

FIGURE 6.1

UML class diagram showing association composition between classes.

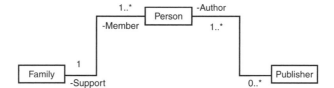

An object that uses association composition typically receives the reference to an object as a parameter of a method. The key is that the object doesn't actually create or control the life span on the associated object, and the use of the associated object isn't required for the object to exist.

Understanding Aggregation

NEW TERM *Aggregation,* the second form of composition, more closely ties the objects together in that the composition object actually stores a reference to the objects contained in the composition, and they must exist for the object to exist.

The life span of composition objects in an aggregation isn't controlled by the object; however, the object that contains the objects needs to have the aggregation objects to exist. In aggregation, the object that contains the other objects needs them to exist in order to exist, but the composition objects don't need the container object to exist. In fact, an instance of an object can be included in more than one aggregation. To ensure that the objects contained in an aggregation exist while the container object exists, a container object class often defines a parameterized constructor to receive the appropriate object references.

6

Figure 6.2 shows the relationship between a `Point`, `Rectangle`, and `Line` class. The `Point` class can exist without the `Rectangle` and `Line` classes, and it's possible that a `Line` object contains the same point as a `Rectangle` object.

FIGURE 6.2

UML class diagram showing aggregation composition between classes.

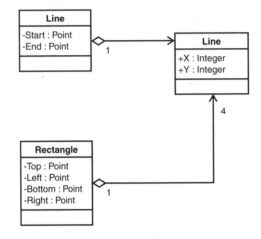

Understanding Composition

NEW TERM *Composition* is the final form of UML composition. This is the strongest form of association in that objects have a whole-part relationship with coexistent life spans. This means that the object class specifically creates the associated objects and controls the life span internally. The associated composition objects are created when the container object is created and destroyed when the container object is destroyed.

This form of association is very common and, in fact, you've already used it in some of the sample code that you've worked through up to this point. For example, if a class has a member data item of type `String`, the class has associated with the `String` class using composition. This happens because, when the container class is instantiated, the `String` member is instantiated also. When the container object is destroyed, the `String` member is also destroyed. Figure 6.3 shows in UML how a `Computer` class would associate with different component classes using composition association.

FIGURE 6.3

UML class diagram showing composition association between classes.

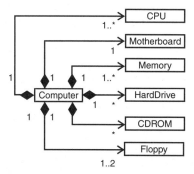

Designing Objects Using Composition

As I just told you, you've already been using composition without realizing it. Any class that includes references or member data of another class type uses composition. In the `TransactionForm` class shown in Listing 6.1, the member data for the form controls uses composition association with the `TextBox` and `Label` classes for the controls. The controls are created when the form object is created and destroyed when the form is destroyed.

LISTING 6.1   TransactionForm.vb: Using Composition Association with the `TransactionForm` Class

```
Public MustInherit Class TransactionForm
    Inherits System.Windows.Forms.Form

    Public Sub New()
        MyBase.New()

        'This call is required by the Windows Form Designer.
        InitializeComponent()
    End Sub

    'Declare Abstract method to read derived class's data
    Protected MustOverride Sub ReadData( _
            ByRef BinSerialize As BinaryFormatter, ByRef TranFile As Stream)

    'Form overrides dispose to clean up the component list.
    Protected Overloads Overrides Sub Dispose(ByVal disposing As Boolean)
        If disposing Then
            If Not (components Is Nothing) Then
                components.Dispose()
            End If
        End If
        MyBase.Dispose(disposing)
    End Sub
```

6

LISTING 6.1   continued

```
Protected WithEvents AmountField As System.Windows.Forms.TextBox
Protected WithEvents AmountText As System.Windows.Forms.Label
Protected WithEvents MemoField As System.Windows.Forms.TextBox
Protected WithEvents MemoText As System.Windows.Forms.Label
Protected WithEvents DateField As System.Windows.Forms.TextBox
Protected WithEvents DateText As System.Windows.Forms.Label

'Required by the Windows Form Designer
Protected components As System.ComponentModel.Container

Protected Overridable Sub InitializeComponent()
     Me.AmountField = New System.Windows.Forms.TextBox()
     Me.AmountText = New System.Windows.Forms.Label()
     Me.MemoField = New System.Windows.Forms.TextBox()
     Me.MemoText = New System.Windows.Forms.Label()
     Me.DateField = New System.Windows.Forms.TextBox()
     Me.DateText = New System.Windows.Forms.Label()
     Me.SuspendLayout()
     '
     'DateField
     '
     Me.DateField.Location = New System.Drawing.Point(320, 16)
     Me.DateField.Name = "DateField"
     Me.DateField.TabIndex = 0
     Me.DateField.Text = ""
     '
     'DateText
     '
     Me.DateText.Location = New System.Drawing.Point(256, 16)
     Me.DateText.Name = "DateText"
     Me.DateText.Size = New System.Drawing.Size(56, 16)
     Me.DateText.TabIndex = 1
     Me.DateText.Text = "Date:"
     '
     'AmountField
     '
     Me.AmountField.Location = New System.Drawing.Point(320, 40)
     Me.AmountField.Name = "AmountField"
     Me.AmountField.TabIndex = 2
     Me.AmountField.Text = ""
     '
     'AmountText
     '
     Me.AmountText.Location = New System.Drawing.Point(256, 42)
     Me.AmountText.Name = "AmountText"
     Me.AmountText.Size = New System.Drawing.Size(56, 16)
     Me.AmountText.TabIndex = 3
     Me.AmountText.Text = "Amount:"
```

LISTING 6.1 continued

```
'
'MemoField
'
Me.MemoField.Location = New System.Drawing.Point(80, 88)
Me.MemoField.Name = "MemoField"
Me.MemoField.Size = New System.Drawing.Size(176, 20)
Me.MemoField.TabIndex = 4
Me.MemoField.Text = ""
'
'MemoText
'
Me.MemoText.Location = New System.Drawing.Point(10, 90)
Me.MemoText.Name = "MemoText"
Me.MemoText.Size = New System.Drawing.Size(70, 16)
Me.MemoText.TabIndex = 5
Me.MemoText.Text = "Memo:"
'
'TransactionForm
'
Me.AutoScaleBaseSize = New System.Drawing.Size(5, 13)
Me.ClientSize = New System.Drawing.Size(456, 133)
Me.Controls.AddRange(New System.Windows.Forms.Control() _
        {Me.DateText, _
         Me.DateField, _
         Me.MemoText, _
         Me.MemoField, _
         Me.AmountText, _
         Me.AmountField})
Me.Name = "TransactionForm"
Me.Text = "Transaction Form"
Me.ResumeLayout(False)
End Sub

...

End Class
```

6

Using the classes created in yesterday's lesson, DepositForm and WithdrawForm, you could create a new class name, CheckBook. The CheckBook class would use the different transaction forms to provide entry screens for the transaction types. Because the DepositForm and WithdrawForm classes aren't required for the entire life span of the CheckBook object and needed only for transaction entry, what form of composition would you use?

Association is the right type of composition to use for this circumstance. Figure 6.4 shows the appropriate relationship in UML.

FIGURE 6.4

UML class diagram of CheckBook *and relationship to* DepositForm *and* WithdrawForm.

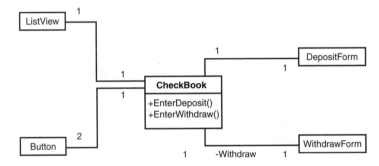

The CheckBook is a form class with the checkbook register displayed. Notice that the CheckBook class also uses the composition association with the ListView and Button classes. When the user enters a deposit, a new DepositForm object is created and displayed. When the user enters a withdrawal, a new WithdrawForm object is created and displayed.

Listing 6.2 shows the code for the CheckBook class with the EnterDeposit() and EnterWithdraw() methods defined.

LISTING 6.2   Checkbook.vb: Using Composition with the ListView, Button, DepositForm, and WithdrawForm Classes

```
Public Class CheckBook
    Inherits System.Windows.Forms.Form

    Public Sub New()
        MyBase.New()

        'This call is required by the Windows Form Designer.
        InitializeComponent()
    End Sub

    'Form overrides dispose to clean up the component list.
    Protected Overloads Overrides Sub Dispose(ByVal disposing As Boolean)
        If disposing Then
            If Not (components Is Nothing) Then
                components.Dispose()
            End If
        End If
        MyBase.Dispose(disposing)
    End Sub

    Private WithEvents ListView1 As System.Windows.Forms.ListView
    Private WithEvents btnDeposit As System.Windows.Forms.Button
    Private WithEvents btnWithdraw As System.Windows.Forms.Button
```

LISTING 6.2   continued

```
Private components As System.ComponentModel.Container

Private Sub InitializeComponent()
        Me.btnWithdraw = New System.Windows.Forms.Button()
        Me.ListView1 = New System.Windows.Forms.ListView()
        Me.btnDeposit = New System.Windows.Forms.Button()
        Me.SuspendLayout()
        '
        'btnWithdraw
        '
        Me.btnWithdraw.Location = New System.Drawing.Point(328, 280)
        Me.btnWithdraw.Name = "btnWithdraw"
        Me.btnWithdraw.TabIndex = 2
        Me.btnWithdraw.Text = "Withdraw"
        '
        'ListView1
        '
        Me.ListView1.Location = New System.Drawing.Point(8, 8)
        Me.ListView1.Name = "ListView1"
        Me.ListView1.Size = New System.Drawing.Size(400, 248)
        Me.ListView1.TabIndex = 0
        '
        'btnDeposit
        '
        Me.btnDeposit.Location = New System.Drawing.Point(240, 280)
        Me.btnDeposit.Name = "btnDeposit"
        Me.btnDeposit.TabIndex = 1
        Me.btnDeposit.Text = "Deposit"
        '
        'CheckBookReg
        '
        Me.AutoScaleBaseSize = New System.Drawing.Size(5, 13)
        Me.ClientSize = New System.Drawing.Size(416, 309)
        Me.Controls.AddRange(New System.Windows.Forms.Control() _
                {Me.btnWithdraw, Me.btnDeposit, Me.ListView1})
        Me.Name = "CheckBookReg"
        Me.Text = "Check Book"
        Me.ResumeLayout(False)
    End Sub
#End Region

    Private Sub btnDeposit_Click(ByVal sender As System.Object, _
                            ByVal e As System.EventArgs) _
                            Handles btnDeposit.Click
      Dim DepositForm As DepositForm = New DepositForm()
      If DepositForm.ShowDialog(Me) = DialogResult.OK Then
          ' Add Deposit Transaction
      End If
    End Sub
```

6

LISTING 6.2   continued

```
Private Sub btnWithdraw_Click(ByVal sender As System.Object, _
                             ByVal e As System.EventArgs) _
                            Handles btnWithdraw.Click
    Dim WithdrawForm As WithdrawForm = New WithdrawForm()
    If WithdrawForm.ShowDialog(Me) = DialogResult.OK Then
        ' Add Withdraw Transaction
    End If
End Sub
End Class
```

Summary

Today you learned the different types of composition. You learned each type's properties and how they are diagrammed in UML. Composition is a feature of OOP that should be used *with* inheritance, not as a replacement—just as inheritance shouldn't replace composition. They both have their uses and should be used for their best purpose.

You should be able to recognize composition within a class definition after creating the CheckBook class and seeing how composition is used. With composition, you can create very complex objects as computer objects from smaller objects that are specialized in their operation and characteristics.

Q&A

Q Is using only composition without inheritance, as some people say, a good practice?

A Eliminating a feature of object-oriented development can't be a good practice. Every feature has its purpose and its best use. As a designer and developer, you must choose the best method for the task. As described earlier today, inheritance has a place and should be used when the new object type is essentially the same as the base object type, just with added features and functionality.

Q With three types of composition, how do I decide which one to use?

A You shouldn't set out to design an object thinking you are going to use a specific type of composition. You should let the design of the object dictate the type of composition. In other words, when you have in mind an object you want to design, as you add characteristics and behavior to the object, the type of composition to use with other objects will present itself. For example, the CheckBook class uses two methods of composition, each one making perfect sense as to why it's used. Don't force a method into working; that is a sign of a bad design.

Workshop

The Workshop provides quiz questions and an exercise to help solidify your understanding of composition and association and provide you with experience in using what you've learned. Answers are provided in Appendix A, "Answers to Quizzes."

Quiz

1. What are the three types of composition as defined in UML?

2. Which form of composition is the loosest?

3. Which form of composition is used with member data of an object type within a class?

Exercise

Add an aggregate relationship between the `DepositForm` and `WithdrawForm` classes and the `CheckBook` class. The purpose of this exercise is to allow `DepositForm` and `WithdrawForm` to have a reference to the `CheckBook` object that created it.

6

DAY 7

Getting to Know the Visual Basic .NET Programming Environment

Microsoft has created a whole new programming environment for its .NET languages. Visual Studio .NET has support for Visual C++, C#, and Visual Basic .NET all within the same environment, which is unlike past versions of Visual Basic that had a separate environment from Visual C++.

The Visual Basic .NET programming environment within Visual Studio .NET is entirely dedicated to creating .NET applications with VB. This means all Visual Basic applications are .NET, and legacy code must be converted to .NET syntax if it will use the same compiler.

Today, you will learn about the Visual Basic .NET programming environment and how to work with VB applications within Visual Studio .NET using the .NET Framework. Covering all features of the environment is beyond the scope of this lesson, but you should have a working knowledge of the environment when you're finished. You will learn more about the following areas in the Visual Basic .NET programming environment:

- The .NET Framework
- The common language runtime (CLR)
- How to build Visual Basic .NET projects and manage them in Visual Studio .NET
- How to build forms in the Form designer
- How to run and debug your applications
- Online help in the programming environment

Working in the Microsoft .NET Framework

The .NET Framework is Microsoft's new application platform designed to simplify application development. The .NET Framework provides support for the Internet as well as traditional client-side applications and is made up of two main components: the common language runtime, known as the CLR, and the .NET class library.

The interesting feature of the .NET Framework is that it allows you to create objects in any .NET language; these objects then can work together in a single application. The language in which you choose to write .NET applications isn't as important as it was with traditional applications and is more of a personal preference.

All .NET applications are object-oriented by their nature and use the .NET class library as the application programming interface (API). Because you need to override methods and derive from classes in the .NET class library to write .NET applications, Visual Basic .NET was given full object-oriented features.

In addition to its language independence, the .NET Framework provides several runtime hosts. Microsoft even provides methods to create your own third-party runtime host. For example, ASP.NET hosts the runtime to provide server-side managed code.

The Common Language Runtime (CLR)

The common language runtime (CLR) provides the code-execution environment for .NET Framework applications. It handles memory management, thread management, security management, code verification, and other system services.

The CLR enforces security in a way that allows applications to perform their operations on a machine without being malicious. For example, an executable attached to e-mail can play an animation but can't access personal information on the computer or access the file system.

The runtime also enforces code correctness by implementing a strict type verification infrastructure called the *common type system* (*CTS*). The CTS makes sure that all code is self-describing, which allows code from multiple languages to be used together. The CLR, with the CTS, enhances developer productivity by allowing each developer to choose his or her favorite language.

The managed environment of the runtime eliminates many common software issues by automatically handling object layout and references to objects, and releasing them when they are no longer being used. Memory leaks and invalid memory references are eliminated.

The .NET Class Library

The .NET class library is a collection of reusable classes and types that tightly integrate with the CLR. The .NET class library is object-oriented and organized into namespaces that enable you to easily find the classes you need in your application.

NEW TERM   A *namespace* is a logical grouping of related classes into a library. By gathering objects into namespaces, there's less chance of a clash between two classes with identical names ending up in your application. Namespaces in .NET are similar to packages in Java. The two main namespaces in the .NET class library are `Microsoft` and `System`.

All namespaces and classes under the Microsoft namespace are specific to the Microsoft platform and provide direct access to Win32 APIs and COM objects when necessary. For most of your application needs, you will use the `System` namespace, which contains the majority of the .NET class library.

Several classes in the .NET class library are designed to be derived from, such as the `Form` class. You therefore can build applications by reusing functionality and extending what's provided by the .NET class library. You can accomplish a wide range of programming tasks with the .NET class library, including string management, database access, file I/O, user interface creation, and so on.

The .NET Framework supports creating the following application types and services:

- Console applications
- Scripted and hosted applications
- Windows GUI applications
- ASP.NET applications
- Web Services
- Windows 2000, XP, and NT services

7

For more information on the actual classes provided by the .NET class library, refer to the online help provided with Visual Studio .NET.

Working with the Visual Basic .NET IDE

The environment in which you spend all your time writing Visual Basic .NET applications is Visual Studio .NET. With this version of the integrated development environment (IDE), all the languages are combined into the same environment. Figure 7.1 shows the IDE after starting in its default state.

FIGURE 7.1

Visual Studio .NET in default startup state.

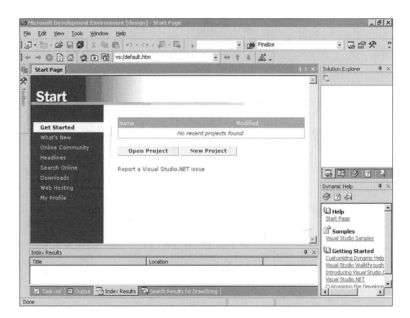

You can easily create a new Visual Basic .NET project from the Start page by clicking the New Project button. If you aren't at the Start page, from the File menu choose New and then Project. Now try creating a new project by clicking the New Project button on the Start page or by using the menu. When the New Project dialog in Figure 7.2 appears, select the type of project to create.

You can view the Visual Basic .NET templates available in the New Project dialog. These starter projects include Windows Application, ASP.NET Web Application, Windows Service, Console Application, Class Library, and so on. The Project Types tree lists other languages and options, but for Visual Basic .NET, use the Visual Basic Projects item.

FIGURE 7.2

The New Project dialog in Visual Studio .NET.

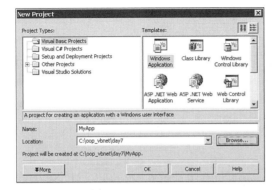

Create a Visual Basic .NET Windows application and name it **MyApp** in the New Project dialog. After the new application is created, your IDE will look something like the one in Figure 7.3, with a blank form displayed.

FIGURE 7.3

MyApp Windows application project in Visual Basic .NET.

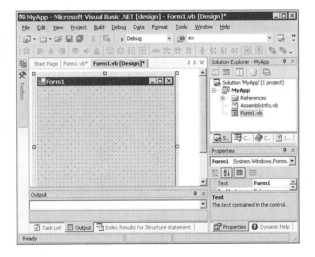

Now that you have a current project, the windows within the IDE will start to come alive with information.

Using Solutions

If you don't already see the Solution Explorer window in your IDE, choose Solution Explorer from the View menu. You should see a window similar to the one in Figure 7.4. It might be docked, as in Figure 7.3, or floating as shown here.

7

FIGURE 7.4

Solution Explorer for the MyApp Windows application project in Visual Basic .NET.

NEW TERM — A *solution* is a container for one or more individual projects. Solutions allow you to group projects of all different languages and types and then build them all with a single build command.

You can set the build configuration for the solution to Debug or Release by changing the selection in the Solutions Configurations combo box on the toolbar. You also can customize the configuration by selecting the Configuration Manager option. By default, all projects will build with the selected configuration. For example, if Debug is selected, all projects in the solution are built for Debug. You'll learn more about debugging later today in the "Running and Debugging Applications" section.

A solution has properties that control the startup project or projects, project dependencies, debug source and symbol files, and configurations. You can access the properties dialog by right-clicking the solution name (for example, Solution 'MyApp') in Solution Explorer and selecting Properties.

Projects

Projects represent a single target within a solution. A project can be one of the types available in the New Project dialog. Figure 7.2 shows some of the project types.

Projects have different properties available depending on the project type with which you're working. Right-click the project you created in the Solution Explorer and select the Properties option. Because you created a Visual Basic .NET Windows application, you should see a properties dialog, as shown in Figure 7.5.

The project properties allow you to control the startup object, assembly name, project output type, root namespace, build options, imported namespaces, and other settings. Web applications in Visual Basic .NET have similar properties to a Windows application, with some additional Web-specific options.

In today's simple exploratory project, you can use the default values in the project properties pages. However, when you are creating a production application, pay attention to options such as the appropriate icon and the imported namespaces.

FIGURE 7.5

Visual Basic .NET project Property Pages dialog for a Windows application.

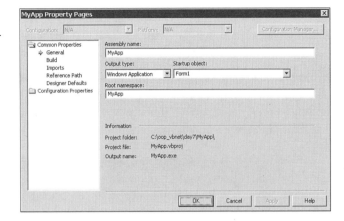

References

References allow projects to link to other files to use external code within a project. Visual Basic .NET relies on references to the .NET Framework to use the classes provided. You can also add references to a project to other files, such as class libraries, that you or someone else has made. After a reference is made, you can use the classes and interfaces exported from the referenced files.

A reference can be made to three types of components: .NET assemblies, .NET projects, and COM automation servers and controls. If you expand the References tree item in the MyApp project, you will see the references, as shown in Figure 7.6, that are added by default to a Visual Basic .NET Windows application.

FIGURE 7.6

Visual Basic .NET Windows application default references.

Web References

A Web reference references code that's published on the Web. The interface is expressed in XML.

7

Web references are generated proxy classes that locally represent the exposed functionality of a Web Service. The proxy class mirrors the actual methods exposed by the Web Service. When an instance of the proxy class is created within a client application, it can call the Web Service as if it was available locally.

Web references are added to the References item under your project in the Solution Explorer. When you right-click the References tree item and select Add Web Reference, the dialog shown in Figure 7.7 appears.

FIGURE 7.7

The Add Web Reference dialog.

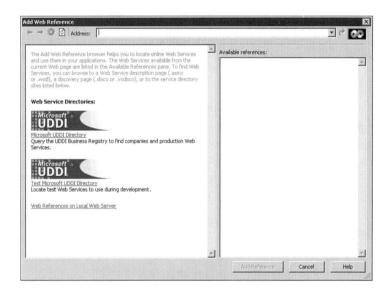

From this dialog, you can search for Web Services that have been registered by companies and other production Web Services. You can also find Web Services that are available during development for testing purposes. Each of these two options is a remote Web Service. The other option is to load a Web Service from your local Web server.

Day 12, "Building Web Applications," provides full details on creating and using Web Services.

The Toolbox

Visual Studio .NET provides a wide array of prebuilt objects that you can drop directly into your forms or Web pages. These objects are contained in the Toolbox. You might not have paid any attention to the Toolbox yet because it's designed by default to stay out of your way. Pass the mouse pointer over the Toolbox label on the left side of the IDE to slide the Toolbox into view. Click the pushpin on the Toolbox's title bar to pin the

Toolbox into place. Keep in mind that the available tools and categories change according to the project type.

As you can see in Figure 7.8, the Windows Forms category in the Toolbox offers a wide range of objects that normally are found in the Windows environment. There are buttons, input controls, and specialized objects that display data in a list or tree-structured view. As you scroll further down the Toolbox, you see a large number of entries for adding special-purpose dialog boxes to your forms, such as OpenFileDialog and PrintPreviewControl.

FIGURE 7.8

The Windows Forms Category of the Toolbox.

To add a tool to a form, you can either double-click the tool or drag it from the Toolbox and drop it on the form.

You can explore other categories in the Toolbox, such as the Data section, which includes objects to create connections to databases and generate datasets. Likewise, the Components category lets you add advanced functionality, such as reporting documents and code to watch for changes to files.

Form Designer

You build the user interface in Visual Basic .NET by using either the Windows Form designer or Web Form designer, depending on the type of application you're creating. The MyApp project is a Windows application, and by default a blank form, Form1, is created.

The Form designer is similar to the one found in previous versions of Visual Basic. You can drag several control types onto the form. Some controls are visible—such as buttons, text boxes, and so on—whereas others are functional only—such as data access controls, clipboard, timer, and so on. Figure 7.9 shows a simple Windows Form in design mode, the control toolbox, and the Properties window for the highlighted button control.

FIGURE 7.9

The Windows Form designer.

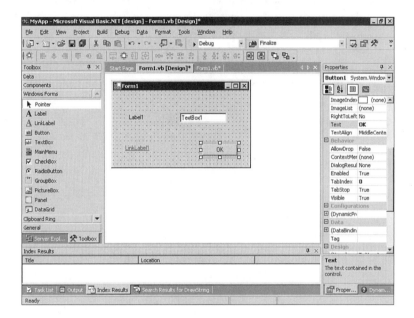

NEW TERM Although we'll stick with a Windows application as our test project today, you should know that in a Web application, the form designer (see Figure 7.10) is somewhat different. It has some of the same controls available for use and some different ones. The layout window is more like what you would find in typical HTML designer with a grid. By default, controls placed on the Web Form are given attributes that fix their precise location on the page. This is called *absolute positioning* and is created when the HTML document's pageLayout property is set to GridLayout. The other positioning option is FlowLayout, where the objects are rendered in the browser according to their place in the HTML code.

Back to the MyApp Windows application. Drag a Button object from the Toolbox and drop it on the form. Do the same with a Label object. Notice that the Properties page shows various settings that you can change for the object. You can drag the items around on the design surface to get the feel of the interface. Before continuing, save your work.

FIGURE **7.10**

The Web form designer.

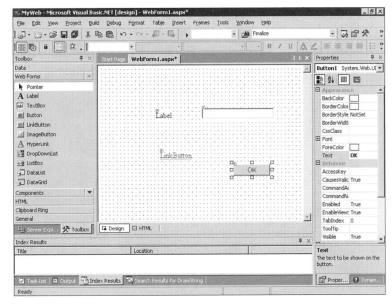

Running and Debugging Applications

You can build (that is, compile) your solution or application by selecting the appropriate item from the Build menu, such as Build Solution.

To run your Visual Basic .NET application after it's built, select Start Without Debugging from the Debug menu or press Ctrl+F5. Click the Close button in the upper-right corner of Form1 to stop the program.

Debugging a Visual Basic .NET application is a little more involved because you can set breakpoints and step through the code as it executes. Before deciding you want to debug your application, you need to select a configuration that builds your application with debugging enabled. By default, a Debug configuration is created so that you can use it for debugging.

For this next step, you need to be in the source code view; double-click the button (Button1) that you added to your form to switch the IDE immediately to the event handler for the Button1 click. Add the following code line just before the End Sub of the Button1_Click subroutine:

```
Label1.Text = "Button1 was clicked"
```

Now add a breakpoint. Click in the gray bar immediately to the left of the line of code you added. As shown in Figure 7.11, a red dot appears and the code is highlighted.

7

FIGURE 7.11

Setting a breakpoint in Visual Basic .NET source code.

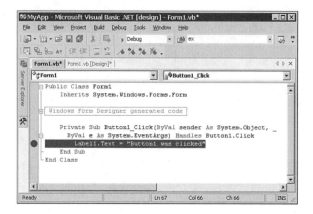

Press F5 to run your program in Debug mode. When the program starts, click Button1 and notice that the program's execution breaks and the Code window appears with a pointer to the line where you set the breakpoint.

To stop the debugger, choose Stop Debugging from the Debug menu. Clear the breakpoint by going to the Debug menu again and selecting Clear All Breakpoints. Finally, run your program without the breakpoint. When you click Button1, notice that the text on the label changes to Button1 was clicked.

Because this is only a tour of the Visual Studio .NET IDE, we won't dwell on the debugging capabilities. However, as you progress, you might want to explore the ability to step into or over functions and set a watch on a variable. Instructions on those tasks is readily available in the online Help, as described in the next section.

As you've seen, debugging is the process of analyzing and correcting problems while you develop an application. Day 16, "Gracefully Capturing Errors," looks at handling errors after the program is in the hands of end users.

Before leaving the source code editor, scroll to the top of Form1.vb. Notice that in the first two lines of code, the IDE generated the statements to create a class and inherit the methods, events and properties of a Windows Form:

```
Public Class Form1
    Inherits System.Windows.Forms.Form
```

Technically, you could write the contents of Form1.vb in Notepad and compile it with the command-line tool. However, you've seen how the IDE generates most of the infrastructure for you and makes short work of thousands of error-prone tasks.

Using Online Help

Visual Studio .NET ships with a complete set of online help files and several ways to retrieve information. For example, if you need help on a topic, locate the Help Index window and type in a keyword. As you see in Figure 7.12, the IDE displays related keywords, matching topics, and the help information. You also can use the Search function to locate topics or phrases. Online help has a nice feature that enables you to filter the topics to a specified language or area of help. Selecting Visual Basic and Related Help will eliminate all the help for C#, C++, and other unrelated help topics.

FIGURE 7.12

Using online help in the Visual Studio .NET IDE.

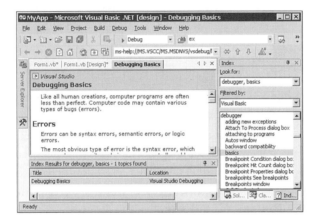

Dynamic Help is an innovative addition to this version of Visual Studio. As you move your cursor's focus to various controls and windows, the Dynamic Help window displays links that relate to the task at hand. Figure 7.13 shows the links that appear as you select a button control.

FIGURE 7.13

Dynamic Help presents different links according to user actions.

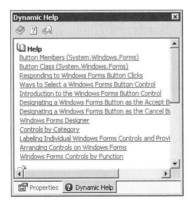

7

Don't forget that whenever you need context-sensitive online help, you can select the object or keyword and press F1. You should use the online help when you need the latest information on the .NET Framework class library and Visual Studio .NET.

Summary

Today's lesson provided an overview of the .NET Framework, common language runtime, and Visual Studio .NET IDE and how it's used with Visual Basic .NET. This overview wasn't meant to teach you how to use Visual Studio .NET, but rather to give you a basic working knowledge of and familiarization with the IDE and the .NET Framework.

Q&A

Q Can I mix a Windows application and Web application within the same solution?

A Yes. You can mix any type of project, including projects of other languages within the same solution. For example, in Day 11 we'll create a component project that can be added to an existing solution.

Q Do all the same object-oriented features and .NET library work for both Web applications and Windows applications?

A Yes. With some obvious exceptions, the .NET Framework works the same with both types of applications, and they are both fully object-oriented. The major exception is that Windows Forms are for Windows applications and Web Forms are for Web applications.

Q Does the Visual Studio .NET IDE support shortcuts and macros?

A Yes. You can save a lot of time by automating repetitive processes. For example, one keystroke can carry out a series of functions such as saving all files, building the project in debug mode, and running the application. You'll find these capabilities under the Tools menu (choose Options, Environment, and then Keyboard).

Q I've been moving and redocking windows in the IDE and now everything is a confusing jumble. How do I organize all the windows?

A From the Tools menu, choose Options. In the Environment area of the properties page, select the General entry. Click the Reset Window Layout button to return your windows to the factory default positions.

Workshop

The Workshop provides quiz questions and an exercise to help solidify your understanding of the Visual Basic .NET environment and provide you with experience in using what you've learned. Answers are provided in Appendix A, "Answers to Quizzes."

Quiz

1. What is a solution?

2. Does the .NET Framework use object-oriented development?

3. Does the program, the .NET Framework, or the CLR deal with memory management?

4. If you have a class in another project and want to use the class in your current project, how do you link that file using the IDE?

5. If your project contains more files than you actually see in Solution Explorer, how do you find out how to make those files visible?

Exercise

Today's exercise is to see whether you are proficient in creating Visual Basic .NET projects and building a simple Windows application. Build a new VB Windows application and name it `MyHello`. Use the form designer and Toolbox to add text box, label, and push button controls. Using the properties page for the text box, set the default text to Hello. Set the text of Label1 to display the contents of the text box whenever the button is clicked. Then, build and run the application. Also, try debugging the application and setting breakpoints.

7

BONUS PROJECT

Putting on the Dog...
With Class

As a reward for your perseverance this week, we've put together a simple, relaxing bonus project. Although you can skip this project without missing much, we think you'll learn something while having a little fun.

This bonus project lets you test some of your new knowledge in a Visual Studio .NET application. It isn't the most challenging application that you'll encounter in your career, but it should give you some experience that you can apply in the real world.

Your project—all in good fun—is to build a type of nuisance calculator for dogs. Let's face it, a big, active dog or a small yappy one can be a great joy as well as a great nuisance. If the dog is still a puppy, the trouble factor will escalate rapidly.

Here's what the calculator should do:

- Create a Dog class that other dog types inherit.
- The Dog class includes properties and a function.

- For each dog type, establish a nuisance factor.
- Make the amount of nuisance in proportion to the dog's weight.
- If the dog is a puppy, dramatically escalate the trouble factor.
- Gather the factors and display the result in a Windows Form.

Peeking Ahead at the Result

Just so you know what you're building, look at Figure BP.1. It shows the graphical interface for the dog trouble calculator. We won't dwell on the cosmetics. You'll find a copy of the files with this book's source code. Suffice it to say that each dog type has its own trouble factor. For example, a golden retriever is very little trouble, but a malamute is another issue. Also, the bigger the dog, the more potential for trouble. If you check the Puppy check box, be prepared for a major increase in chaos.

FIGURE BP.1

The graphical user interface for the dog trouble calculator.

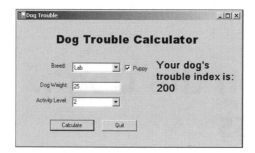

Creating the Base Class

Chihuahuas, Labs, and malamutes all inherit from the same class, Dog. The Dog class has common properties, but the values for a species will vary. For this part of the solution, you work in a class library project called Dogbase. Listing BP.1 shows the Dog class.

LISTING BP.1   Dog.vb: Dog Class with Private Members, Public Properties, and a Public Function

```
Namespace Dogex
  Public MustInherit Class Dog
    'Property holders
    Private mDogWeight As Integer
    Private mActiveLevel As Integer
    Private mPuppyFactor As Integer
    Public Property ActiveLevel() As Integer
      Set(ByVal Value As Integer)
```

LISTING BP.1   continued

```
          End Set
          Get
            ActiveLevel = mActiveLevel
          End Get
        End Property
        Public Property DogWeight() As Integer
          Set(ByVal Value As Integer)
            mDogWeight = Value
          End Set
          Get
            DogWeight = mDogWeight
          End Get
        End Property
        Public Property PuppyFactor() As Integer
          Set(ByVal Value As Integer)
            mPuppyFactor = Value
          End Set
          Get
            PuppyFactor = mPuppyFactor
          End Get
        End Property

        Public Overridable Function DoCalculation() As Integer
          DoCalculation = mDogWeight * mActiveLevel * mPuppyFactor
        End Function

      End Class
    End Namespace
```

ANALYSIS   Notice that you start with a `Namespace` declaration just in case someone else comes along with a `Dog` class within the same project and causes a collision. This `Dog` class is a base implementation of common properties and functions. The `MustInherit` keyword in the class declaration prevents users of this class from creating it directly.

The class has three public properties and three corresponding private variables. `ActiveLevel()` holds the activity level of the pet, indicating whether it's unusually active, average, or sedentary. `DogWeight()` is another integer value, this time representing the dog's weight in pounds. Finally, `PuppyFactor()` comes into play when the Puppy check box is checked. As you'll see later in the code, this quadruples the nuisance factor no matter what the dog type.

The class has one function, `DoCalculation()`. The function is set as `Overridable` so that classes that inherit the `Dog` class can override your implementation. The function performs a calculation based on all nuisance factors and returns an `Integer` as the result.

Using the Base Class

Now that you have a base class with the `MustInherit` keyword, you can take advantage of inheritance in OOP. As you go along, you'll create three separate class files: Lab.vb, Chihuahua.vb, and Malamute.vb.

Lab is the first class to explore here. As you can see in Listing BP.2, there's not much to it.

LISTING BP.2   Lab.vb: The `Lab` Class Doesn't Extend `Dog` But Uses It as Is

```
Namespace Dogex
  Public Class Lab
    Inherits Dog
  End Class
End Namespace
```

A Labrador is the closest thing you can get to the average dog. Therefore, you don't need to extend it in any way. It simply inherits the `Dog` class.

On the other hand, Chihuahuas have a higher nuisance factor. As you can see in Listing BP.3, you need to override the `DoCalculation()` function to take this factor into account.

LISTING BP.3   Chihuahua.vb: The `Chihuahua` Class Overrides the `DoCalculation()` Function

```
Namespace Dogex
  Public Class Chihuahua
    'Inherit the Dog Class
    Inherits Dog
    Overrides Function DoCalculation() As Integer
      DoCalculation = MyBase.DoCalculation * 2
    End Function
  End Class
End Namespace
```

ANALYSIS   Notice that the `DoCalculation` result is doubled in the case of a Chihuahua. The malamute code is the same except that, as a breed, it's three times the trouble. Therefore, create a class file called Malamute.vb with a copy of the `Chihuahua` class code, rename the class to `Malamute`, and change the integer from 2 to 3.

Developing the Doggone Logic

You now have your simple classes in place and can work on the logic that employs the classes and the interface that lets human beings determine the trouble their dogs will get into. In the same solution, add a Windows application project called `Dogclient`. Make sure that you add a reference to the `Dogbase` component in Visual Studio .NET, as shown in Figure BP.2.

FIGURE BP.2

Be sure to add a reference to the Dogbase *class library.*

Listing BP.4 is an abridged version of the Windows Form code from frmDog.vb. We've left out the GUI implementation code for brevity. Be sure to set DogClient as the startup project and DogForm as the startup object.

LISTING BP.4   frmDog.vb: The `DogForm` Class Handles the User Interface

```
Imports System.ComponentModel
Imports System.Drawing
Imports System.Windows.Forms
Imports Dogbase.Dogex

Public Class Dogform
  Inherits System.Windows.Forms.Form
  Public Sub New()
    MyBase.New()
    'This call is required by the Win Form Designer.
    InitializeComponent()
    'Add any initialization after the InitializeComponent() call
    Me.ComboDogType.SelectedIndex = 0
    Me.ComboBoxActive.SelectedIndex = 1
  End Sub

' Windows Form Designer generated code omitted
```

LISTING BP.4   continued

```
Protected Sub btnCalculate_Click _
(ByVal sender As System.Object, ByVal e As System.EventArgs) _
Handles BtnCalculate.Click
  Dim Dog As Object
  Dim Trouble As Integer
  Dim PuppyFactor As Integer

  Select Case Me.ComboDogType.Text()
    Case "Malamute"
      Dog = New Malamute()
    Case "Lab"
      Dog = New Lab()
    Case "Chihuahua"
      Dog = New Chihuahua()
  End Select

  Dog.ActiveLevel = CInt(Me.ComboBoxActive.Text)
  Dog.DogWeight = CInt(Me.txtWeightinPounds.Text)
  If CheckboxPuppy.Checked = True Then
    Dog.PuppyFactor = 4
  Else
    Dog.PuppyFactor = 1
  End If

  Trouble = Dog.DoCalculation()
  Me.LabelResult.Text = "Your dog's trouble index is: " _
  & Trouble.ToString()

End Sub

Private Sub btnExit_Click _
(ByVal sender As System.Object, ByVal e As System.EventArgs) _
Handles btnExit.Click
  End
End Sub
End Class
```

ANALYSIS   On startup, the code goes through its initialization sequence, setting the two combo boxes to their default values. The interesting parts happen in the event handler when the user clicks the Calculate button. The following line isn't intended as a commentary on the intelligence of dogs: instead, it creates a Dog object:

```
Dim Dog As Object
```

You specify the class based on the user's choice of dog. Then, based on the dog's class, you factor in the weight, activity level, and whether this is a puppy. The Trouble value is calculated by calling the Dog.DoCalculation() function.

Summary

Our little bonus project may not get us too far with dog lovers who don't see *any* nuisance factor in their pets, but it has shown how classes and inheritance can shorten the software development cycle. Whenever you want to add more types of dogs to your project, the base class is already in place and is free to use and extend.

WEEK 1

In Review

You made it through the first week. Let's face it, the terminology and concepts in object-oriented programming can be rather daunting.

On the first day, you jumped right into a discussion of properties in OOP and the use of `Get` and `Set`. By the end of the Day 1, you had assembled a Windows Form to demonstrate inheritance using the `SmartMsg` object.

Just getting a handle on the vocabulary can be a challenge. At this point, you can "talk a good game" of OOP thanks to Day 2.

By the middle of the week you became conversant with objects, classes, members, methods, events, constructors, destructors, interfaces, and encapsulation.

Inheritance is a topic that merits a lot of attention in this book—partly because it can be hard to grasp but also because it's so powerful that you'll use it often. Day 4 showed you how to harness that power by creating Windows Forms. Polymorphism, covered on Day 5, is another OOP feature that requires mental exertion, but your understanding of the concept will increase your coding efficiency dramatically. By the end of this week, you learned how to combine complex objects using composition.

Although you're learning OOP in the context of Visual Basic .NET, the concepts apply to many other languages. You'll find that your newly acquired knowledge is quite portable to languages such as C#, JavaScript, and Java.

1
2
3
4
5
6
7

WEEK 2

At a Glance

Having made it through the first week, you now have a solid grounding in object-oriented programming concepts. You're ready to further develop your OOP skills and delve more deeply into Visual Basic .NET.

Day 8, "Working with Visual Basic .NET Data Types," explores the `Object` type, the root of all .NET Framework classes. You'll learn how derivation gives the various data types special characteristics. Day 8's lesson shows the powerful `CType()` function. You'll see how Visual Basic .NET types map to the common language runtime (CLR) types and how there are changes in integral types that you've used in Visual Basic 6. The lesson also covers arrays and enumerations and shows their use in code samples.

Day 9, "Organizing Classes into Groups," explains a lot of terminology that may be new to you in the .NET context. With the vast number of objects in the .NET Framework, you'll see how they needed to be organized into namespaces. In this lesson, you'll use your own namespaces for object classes to avoid naming conflicts. Another key area is the value of assemblies and how they work for you.

Taking a bit of a breather from the theory, Day 10, "Creating a User Interface," starts with in-depth coverage of Windows Forms whose related classes, structures, and enumerations come from the `System.Windows.Forms` namespace. The other major topic is Web Forms, where you leverage your object-oriented skills to design and code Web applications in a brand new way.

OOP is all about re-use. On Day 11, "Creating and Using Components," you'll take re-use to a new level. In this lesson,

8

9

10

11

12

13

14

components written in any of the .NET languages can be incorporated into applications or components in any of the other languages. You'll learn about reflection and how it relates to components and explore working with unknown object types.

On Day 12, "Building Web Applications," you'll continue to expand your abilities in creating Internet applications. This lesson is full of code that uses the rich data objects available in the .NET Framework. Here, you'll see object-oriented development at a very practical level: The design of a Web page is separated from its logic and glued back together with class references.

Day 13, "Deploying Visual Basic .NET Projects," deals with a harsh reality of software development—getting the product into the hands of consumers and getting it working in their environment. This lesson shows how to work with configuration files, deploy assemblies, and create installation projects. You'll also learn about the importance of the Global Assembly Cache (GAC) in the .NET world.

At the end of this week, Day 14, "Working with Object Interfaces," revisits polymorphism and inheritance to build further on the preceding lessons. The topics include using interfaces with class definitions and determining when you should use interfaces in your development projects.

DAY 8

Working with Visual Basic .NET Data Types

Visual Basic .NET has a wide range of types defined, by default, to use in your applications. It offers the traditional types for handling numbers and strings, and other types are provided by .NET to represent objects and collections.

Understanding the types in Visual Basic .NET and how they are used is important in designing objects that best use what .NET provides. It's also important to understand that all data types used in .NET languages are common between the different .NET programming languages so that objects can be shared among them.

Today's lesson will provide an overview of the common data types as they are defined in VB .NET and how they are used. By the end of the day, you will learn the following:

- What the Object type is and how it's used
- What the numerical data types are
- How to work with strings

- How to use the Date data type
- How to work with structures and why
- How to create enumerations
- How to use arrays

Exploring Visual Basic .NET's Array of Data Types

In Visual Basic .NET, all standard data types are provided and controlled by .NET. This way, all types are standardized across all .NET languages. This means that all .NET types conform to the Common Language Specification (CLS).

Each value type in .NET is derived from `ValueType`, which in turn is derived from `Object`. Derivation gives each value type special methods for dealing with it effectively. For example, an `Integer` value type, which is actually the `Int32` .NET class, provides the `ToString()` method to convert the numeric value to a display string.

Understanding the `Object` Type

In previous versions of Visual Basic, a `Variant` variable type was a placeholder for an unknown or dynamic data type. With Visual Basic .NET, the `Variant` data type is no longer supported. Instead, the .NET Framework provides a generic data type from which all other data types are ultimately derived—`Object`.

The `Object` type is used in all situations in which the data type isn't fixed or known at the time of design. Because `Object` is the root of all classes in the .NET Framework, you can reference any .NET data type with an `Object`. The following code segment shows how data types are referenced by `Object`:

```
'Declare variables
Dim UnknownValue As Object
Dim Number As Integer = 10
Dim Name As String = "Hello"

'Assign Number to UnknownValue and display it in a MessageBox
UnknownValue = Number
MessageBox.Show(CType(UnknownValue, Integer).ToString())

'Assign Name to UnknownValue and display it in a MessageBox
UnknownValue = Name
MessageBox.Show(CType(UnknownValue, String))
```

Figure 8.1 shows the two message boxes containing different output by assigning a number and a string to the `UnknownValue` object.

FIGURE 8.1

Display of Integer *and* String *data types referenced by object.*

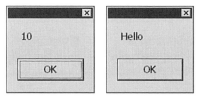

NEW TERM The CType() function is the key to using a value when it's referenced by an Object. CType() converts, or *typecasts*, the Object to the given class type. When it's done, all the members and data of the object are accessible.

This feature is extremely powerful when you're designing objects that dynamically reference other objects or designing interfaces that can take many different data types as parameters. The danger is, of course, that you must check to be sure that the object you reference is actually the type you plan to use it as. The following code segment shows how to check the type before you use it:

```
Public Sub DisplayValue(ByRef value As Object)
    If value.GetType() Is GetType(Integer) Then
        MessageBox.Show(CType(value, Integer).ToString())
    End If

    If value.GetType() Is GetType(String) Then
        MessageBox.Show(CType(value, String))
    End If
End Sub

Public Sub MySub()
    Dim Number As Integer = 10
    Dim Name As String = "Hello"

    DisplayValue(Number)
    DisplayValue(Name)
End Sub
```

By checking the types with GetType(), you can write code that can dynamically adjust based on the type of object referenced, as shown with the DisplayValue() subroutine.

Note

Avoid overusing the Object type, and always declare value types as they are known, if possible. Doing so helps eliminate errors from your code caused by the misuse of object references. When values of the appropriate type are declared, the .NET Framework can employ its strong type checking on all objects before they are used.

Aliasing Common Numeric Data Types

The .NET Framework implements several numeric data types, both integral and noninte-gral. Visual Basic .NET aliases the .NET data types with its own keywords, which are similar to previous versions of Visual Basic. For example, the Int32 .NET class is aliased as Integer in Visual Basic .NET.

The aliases provide developers from earlier versions of Visual Basic some familiarity. They also provide a means for Microsoft to change the underlying class that represents the numeric data type classes. Table 8.1 lists the numeric types available and the related .NET classes.

TABLE 8.1   Numeric Data Types for Visual Basic .NET

Visual Basic .NET Type	CLR Type Structure	Storage Size
Byte	System.Byte	1 byte
Decimal	System.Decimal	16 bytes
Double	System.Double	8 bytes
Integer	System.Int32	4 bytes
Long	System.Int64	8 bytes
Short	System.Int16	2 bytes
Single	System.Single	4 bytes

If you've used previous versions of Visual Basic, you should notice some significant changes in the numeric data types. These changes are for compatibility with other .NET languages and are based on the standard implemented in the common language runtime (CLR).

For starters, the Decimal type is now 16 bytes, whereas it used to be 14 bytes. The good news is that Double and Single are the same as they were before.

The integral types have all changed. Integer, which used to be a Long, is now 4 bytes. Long is now 8 bytes to support the 64-bit integers. New to Visual Basic, Short takes the place of the old Integer and is 2 bytes. The good news: a Byte is still a byte.

Using Strings

The String value type is actually implemented as a class, not as a structure like the numeric data types. It also has a variable size depending on the implementing platform. For example, some platforms implement a String with 2 bytes per character, whereas others implement it as a single byte per character.

The major difference between using `String` in previous versions of Visual Basic and in Visual Basic .NET is that the `String` can't be declared with a fixed length. When a value is assigned to the `String`, the value's length determines the `String`'s length.

Because strings are implemented by the .NET Framework, they also have different internal characteristics than before. An instance of a `String` can't be modified after it's created; even though it appears you are modifying the value, in actuality, a new instance of a `String` is created containing the modification. For example, consider the following code segment:

```
Dim SL As String = "Books"

SL = SL.Remove(4,1)
SL = SL + "s"
```

The first statement declares a `String` variable and assigns a value of `"Books"`. This statement, in turn, allocates the appropriate memory in the `String` to store the value. The second statement uses the `Remove()` method to remove the s from the end of the value. It does so by creating a new instance of a `String` with the modified value and returning a reference to which the `SL` variable is set. The third statement appends the s back to the end of the value stored in `SL`. This statement has the same effect as calling a method within `String` because it also returns a reference to a new instance of a `String` that contains the modified value.

If you want to actually modify the value within a `String`, you can use the `StringBuilder` class. This class allows you to modify a string by inserting and removing characters.

Working with Dates

The `Date` data type within Visual Basic .NET uses the .NET `DateTime` structure. It can represent dates and time values ranging from 12:00:00 AM, 1/1/0001, to 11:59:59 PM, 12/31/9999. The time values have a precision of 100 nanoseconds, which make up one tick.

A particular date and time is made up of several ticks since 12:00:00 AM January 1, 0001. As you can imagine, the number to store a date and time can get very large. The `DateTime` structure can easily handle this large number because it's stored as a 64-bit value.

Calculations with `Date` variables are straightforward considering that they are represented by an integer value. Therefore, subtracting two `Date` variables yields the difference in ticks between the two dates. Because ticks aren't too useful without a conversion, the `DateTime` structure implements different methods for adding and subtracting dates. The results are returned as a `TimeSpan` structure, which provides methods to interpret the result of a `Date` calculation.

You assign `Date` variables to a literal value by enclosing the date literal string within pound (#) characters. For example, a literal value of `#12/12/2001 10:52:30 PM#` is valid to assign to a `Date` variable. The date literal should be in a standard date format, such as the one in the previous example. If the date portion is eliminated, January 1, 0001, is used as the date. If the time is eliminated, midnight is the default.

Creating a date string with the `ToString()` method provides you the flexibility to specify the formatting for the date and time. You can create custom-formatted dates by specifying a formatting string made up of a combination of the values. You also can use one of the predefined date formats. Refer to the .NET online reference for information on the formatting patterns. The following code segment shows how to use the `ToString()` method, and Figure 8.2 shows the onscreen result:

```
Dim Dt As Date = "#12/12/2001 10:52:30 PM#"
MessageBox.Show(Dt.ToString("D"))
```

FIGURE 8.2

Results of the
`ToString()` *method.*

Using Boolean Values

If you've used previous versions of Visual Basic, you are already familiar with the `Boolean` data type. Nothing has changed with the type in Visual Basic .NET except that now it's provided by the `System.Boolean` .NET data type.

The `Boolean` data type is reserved for situations in which a true/false, yes/no, or on/off value is required. `Boolean` types are stored as a 2-byte number and can have a value of `True` or `False` only.

When `Boolean` values are converted to other data types, `False` equates to `0` and `True` to `1`. The opposite is true when other data types are converted to `Boolean`—`0` becomes `False` and any other value becomes `True`.

Creating Structures

In Visual Basic .NET, structures are similar to classes in that they associate one or more members with each other. A structure is also similar to a class in that it can contain

8

member data, properties, methods, and events. Structures do, however, have distinct differences from classes:

- Structures aren't inheritable.
- Structures are implicitly derived from `System.ValueType`.
- A variable of a structure type directly contains its own copy of data.
- Structures are never terminated. The CLR doesn't call the `Finalize` method on a structure.
- Structures require parameters when they have nonshared constructors. However, all structures implicitly have a public `New()` constructor without parameters that initializes the members to their default value.
- Declarations of a structure's data members can't include initializers.
- The default access for members declared with the `Dim` statement is public.
- Members can't be declared `Protected` in a structure.
- Equality testing must be performed with a member-by-member comparison.
- Structures can't have abstract methods.

You declare structures with the `Structure` statement. In previous versions of Visual Basic, you used the `Type` statement to declare a structure. When a structure is declared, it is implicitly derived from `System.ValueType`, which gives the structure the same properties as other value types. The following shows a simple structure declaration:

```
Structure MyStruct
    Public strName As String
    Public strAddr As String
    Public blnReg As Boolean
End Structure
```

Why Use a Structure?

Structures are useful in defining new value types that encapsulate a group of variables. For example, an employee can be represented as a structure that includes all the employee's information. The advantages to using a structure rather than a class as a value type are that a structure isn't allocated on the heap and each instance of the structure has its own copy of the data. For example, if structure A is assigned to structure B, each has its own copy of the data, and any modifications to one don't affect the other. The same example with a class would assign only a reference to B, and any modifications to either one would be reflected in the other because they share the same memory.

If you are designing a new data type that represents a new data element and doesn't need to be extended through inheritance, a structure is a better choice.

Working with Enumerations

Enumerations are types that implicitly inherit from System.Enum and represent a set of values. The underlying type of an enumeration is an integral value and can be specified as either a Byte, Short, Integer, or Long. By default, enumerations are defined as Integer.

You declare an enumeration by using the Enum keyword, followed by the enumeration name and type. If no type is specified, Integer is the default. The following shows the declaration of the enumeration Color:

```
Enum Color
    Red
    Green
    Blue
End Enum
```

Each value defined in the Color enumeration receives an integer value starting with zero—for example, Red (0), Green (1), Blue (2). If you need to define an enumeration in which the values have specific associated integer values, assign the values as follows:

```
Enum Color
    Red = &HFF0000
    Green = &HFF00
    Blue = &HFF
End Enum
```

Now each enumeration value has a specific value. Assigning values is useful in enumerations in which each value is fixed, as it is with colors. Values are fixed and can't be changed at runtime.

Using enumerations is similar to using other variables. All enumeration values must be prefaced by the containing enumeration. For example, the following statement gives MyColor the value of Red:

```
MyColor = Color.Red
```

You can avoid prefacing enumerations by importing them with the Imports statement. In this case, the following code imports the Color enumeration and then makes the same assignment as before:

```
Imports MyApp.Color
```

```
MyColor = Red
```

You can define enumerations as part of a module, class, or structure. If an enumeration is part of a class or structure, you must preface it with the class or structure as follows:

```
Structure tst
    Private blnIsokay As Boolean
    Enum Color
        Red = &HFF0000
        Green = &HFF00
        Blue = &HFF
    End Enum
End Structure
```

You can display the value of an enumeration by either its name or its integral value. The following sample code segment shows how to display both the name and value of Color.Red in a message box:

```
MessageBox.Show(tst.Color.Red.ToString() + " = " _
    + CType(tst.Color.Red, Integer).ToString())
```

Using Arrays

You declare an array as you do any other variable—except that you include a pair of parentheses after the variable name to indicate that it's an array. You can declare an array variable without a predetermined size; however, it must be dimensioned before it's used. For example, the following code segment declares two arrays:

```
Dim MyArray() As Integer
Dim MyOtherArray(10) As Integer
```

Before MyArray can be used, it must be dimensioned; otherwise, the application will have a runtime error.

When you declare an array in Visual Basic .NET, you are specifying the upper bounds of the array and not the size. For example,

```
Dim MyOtherArray(10) As Integer
```

produces an 11-element array, 0 through 10 inclusive. The following code segment shows how to assign values in both arrays:

```
MyOtherArray(0) = 5
MyOtherArray(1) = 8
'Dimension MyArray for use
ReDim MyArray(MyOtherArray(0) + MyOtherArray(1))

MyArray(0) = 10
```

Caution

You access array elements by specifying a zero-based index in parentheses. The zero base in Visual Basic .NET is a significant change from previous versions of Visual Basic where the lowest index was one. This change brings Visual Basic .NET in line with other .NET Framework languages.

Two values are set in the `MyOtherArray` variable and then used as the size to dimension `MyArray`. Dynamic dimensioning at runtime allows an application to decide how much space it requires in an array. If the array size is fixed and known ahead of time, dimension statically. You also can resize arrays dynamically while maintaining the content already loaded into the array by using the `Preserve` keyword as follows:

```
ReDim Preserve MyArray(30)
```

You declare and use multidimensioned arrays by separating multiple indexes with commas within the parentheses. For example, you declare a two-dimensioned array with the following statement:

```
Dim MyArray(10, 20) As Integer
```

Using an array with multiple dimensions is similar to before, except that you specify both indexes to identify an array element. The following statement assigns a value to the first value in the second column of the array:

```
MyArray(2, 1) = 10
```

In .NET, arrays are implicitly derived from `System.Array`, which provides several useful methods for searching, sorting, manipulating, and getting information on the array. For example, you sort an array by using the following statement:

```
Array.Sort(MyArray)
```

Summary

Today you learned about the different common data types in Visual Basic .NET and some of the differences with previous versions of Visual Basic. The data types in Visual Basic .NET are implicitly derived from a .NET Framework class that provides the value types with useful functionality not found in previous Visual Basic types.

As you design your Visual Basic .NET applications and create new data types, remember that all data items in Visual Basic .NET are objects. Even simple data types such as `Integer` are objects.

Q&A

Q In Visual Basic .NET, can I create a data type that's not an object?

A No. All data types and structures are implicitly derived from .NET Framework base classes. Depending on the value type you are creating, the base class can be different. Because all data types are represented by a class, they are all created as objects.

Q Are there alternatives to using arrays in Visual Basic .NET?

A The .NET Framework provides classes that implement the logic to manage collections of objects. Known as *collections*, these classes can be very strict and allow only a single object type, or more relaxed and manage a list of different object types. Collections provide several methods for navigating the list and searching for items. Refer to the .NET Framework reference for more information on collections and how to use them in place of arrays.

Workshop

The Workshop provides quiz questions and an exercise to help solidify your understanding of Visual Basic .NET data types and provide you with experience in using what you've learned. Answers are provided in Appendix A, "Answers to Quizzes."

Quiz

1. What's the class from which all value types are implicitly derived?

2. What's the default integral value of the first value listed in an enumeration?

3. What's the default scope of a member in a structure declared with the `Dim` keyword?

Exercise

Today you need to declare a new structure named `MyNewStruct`. Within the structure, create new members of type `Integer` and `String`. Also, create a member variable that's an array of `Integer` and initialize it with five values you pass as an array argument to a method provided within the structure.

WEEK 2

DAY 9

Organizing Classes into Groups

If you've looked through the .NET Framework reference, notice that there are groups of classes. For example, `System.Windows.Forms` has several classes, some of which are `Form`, `Button`, and `TreeView`. The .NET Framework SDK relies on a language feature known as *namespaces* to define class groupings.

If you had to know all the different classes available in the .NET Framework without knowing what each class was for, you'd have to spend a lot of time studying them. Namespaces are the .NET Framework technique for organizing the classes so that you can concentrate on the groups of classes that fill your particular needs. Furthermore, creating your own namespaces allows you to create class names without having to worry about name conflicts.

An *assembly* is a collection of files used within the .NET Framework. An assembly groups files such as Visual Basic .NET source files, images, and ASP.NET pages so that the common language runtime (CLR) can act on the files as a single, executable unit. In many ways, an assembly is like a dynamic linked library (DLL) except that with assemblies, the .NET Framework has greater control over the component's versioning and security. An assembly has an additional advantage in that it contains metadata about itself, known as the *manifest*. The manifest describes the assembly's name, version, and resources such as the classes that it requires. As a self-describing unit, an assembly in Visual Basic .NET reveals sufficient information about itself that assemblies built in other languages, such as C#, can interact with it. You'll learn more about assemblies on Day 13, "Deploying Visual Basic .NET Projects."

Today's lesson covers the use of namespaces and ways to create namespaces to organize your own object classes. By the end of the lesson, you will learn how to

- Use namespaces in other assemblies.
- Create namespaces for your own object classes.
- Use the .NET Framework namespaces.

Understanding Namespaces

A Visual Basic .NET application is made up of named entities that represent the application as a whole. At the top level, namespaces organize other entities, such as other namespaces or classes. All Visual Basic .NET applications have a default namespace equivalent to your project name. For example, if you have a project named MyApp, all classes defined within the project are part of the MyApp namespace.

Namespaces help prevent naming collisions between different assemblies or class libraries. In traditional coding methods, if a class defined in a library conflicted with a class name in your application, the compiler gave an error because the name was ambiguous, and the compiler didn't know which class to use.

In the .NET Framework, naming collisions aren't an issue because the classes in the application are, at a minimum, part of the default application namespace and therefore won't conflict with any classes found in a class library.

Namespaces can contain other namespaces as they do in the .NET Framework. When a namespace is contained within another namespace, it creates a hierarchical organization that is very useful for organizing related objects to a finer detail than at the assembly level.

For example, you use namespaces within a namespace when any assembly, which has a default namespace, defines a new namespace. For example, MyApp can contain the namespace MyForms. MyForms can contain other namespaces also, as shown in Figure 9.1.

FIGURE 9.1

Namespace hierarchy for MyApp.

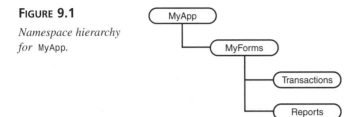

Working with .NET Namespaces

Microsoft uses two top-level namespaces in the .NET Framework: Microsoft and System. The System namespace encompasses the .NET Framework SDK, whereas the Microsoft namespace encompasses all Microsoft-specific classes.

Most classes that Visual Basic .NET applications use are found under the System namespace. It has several levels of namespaces that organize the large number of classes within the .NET Framework. For example, Figure 9.2 shows the namespace hierarchy for the portion of the .NET Framework dealing with the Web.

FIGURE 9.2

The namespace hierarchy for Web-related portions of .NET.

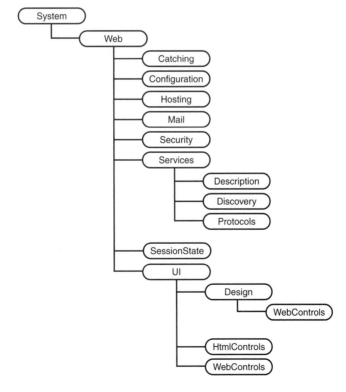

Microsoft created a Web namespace in the System namespace to organize all classes dealing with the Web and related technologies. Within the Web namespace are other namespaces, classes, and structures. If you can imagine the difficulty in creating unique names for all classes and structures within the .NET Framework, you can see why creating the namespaces is more than an organizational method but almost a necessity. Doing so adds clarity and organization to the .NET Framework and the code written to use it.

As I mentioned earlier, the Microsoft namespace includes all Microsoft-specific classes and structures. The classes provide .NET compiler and code generation access for C#, Visual Basic, and JavaScript. This namespace also has classes that handle events raised by the operating system and that manipulate the Registry. Most Visual Basic .NET applications will never use the classes within the Microsoft namespace.

Using Namespaces

When using a class from a namespace, you preface the class name with the namespace hierarchy within which it's defined. For example, when using the .NET Form class, which is defined in the Forms namespace within the Windows namespace within the System namespace, you reference it as follows:

```
System.Windows.Forms.Form
```

Referencing with the entire namespace guarantees that there's no ambiguity with other classes with the same class name. It's also self-documenting in your source code which class you are using. The downside with referencing a class's entire namespace is that the names can get rather long and actually make the source code harder to read.

If several classes from an external namespace are being used within an assembly, you can use the Imports keyword to import the entire namespace and all the classes within the namespace. This approach eliminates the need to preface all classes with the full namespace; however, it also can cause issues with conflicting names. To import the System.Windows.Forms namespace, you place the following statement at the top of the source file:

```
Imports System.Windows.Forms
```

This statement has the effect of zooming into the Forms namespace to where any classes within the Forms namespace don't have to be prefaced. The Form class is now used as Form instead of System.Windows.Forms.Form.

If class names are an issue and collisions occur with the application's class names, you can resort to another alternative. You can create an alias for a class that you want to use within a namespace by using the Imports keyword. If the class has an alias, the class is now referenced with the alias, thus eliminating the collision issues and the need to tediously use the full reference name. The following code segment shows how to declare and use a class alias for the `System.Windows.Forms.Form` class:

```
Imports MyForm = System.Windows.Forms.Form

Class Form1
    Inherits MyForm
End Class
```

Another way to use an alias would be to import the namespace, and then use the alias to qualify the classes within that namespace:

```
Imports MyForms = System.Windows.Forms
Class Form2
    Inherits MyForms.Form
End Class
```

When you use classes from other assemblies, the assembly name is the root level in the namespace hierarchy. If namespaces are declared within the assembly, they are subnames to the assembly name. For example, the `MyApp` assembly defines `MyForms` and `MyReports` namespaces. You access the `Form1` class within the `MyForms` namespace by using the following statement:

```
MyApp.MyForms.Form1
```

Tip

You might look at a Visual Basic .NET application source file and wonder how it's getting access with no apparent `Imports` statement. This situation can get confusing and send you looking for classes that you have no clue where they are defined. An imports setting in the project setting enables you to add your imports there without specifying them in the source code. As shown in Figure 9.3, using this setting makes the imported namespaces available to all source files within the project instead of just the file in which the `Imports` statement is defined.

Note

If you want more information on .NET namespaces, a good book to check out is *Visual Basic Programmer's Guide to the .NET Framework Class Library* by Lars Powers and Mike Snell (Sams Publishing, ISBN 0-672-32232-3).

FIGURE 9.3

*Namespaces in the
project properties are
available to all files.*

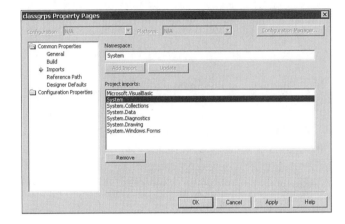

Creating Namespaces

You declare namespaces in your Visual Basic .NET applications with the Namespace
keyword, which defines a block of code to be located within the declared namespace.
You can have as many different namespaces in your application as you need. The code in
Listing 9.1 shows namespace declarations within the MyApp assembly.

LISTING 9.1   Namespaces Declared in the MyApp Assembly

```
'Declare the MyForms namespace
Namespace MyForms

'Define classes to be included in the MyForms namespace
Public Class Form1
End Class

'More classes...

End Namespace 'End of MyForms namespace

'Declare the MyForms.Transactions namespace
Namespace MyForms.Transactions

'Define classes to be included in the MyForms.Transactions namespace
Public class Form2
End Class

'More classes...

End Namespace 'End of MyForms.Transactions namespace
```

ANALYSIS The code in Listing 9.1 declares a `MyForms` namespace that contains a `Form1` class and a `Transactions` namespace. The `MyForms.Transaction` namespace contains the `Form2` class, which is fully referenced as `MyApp.MyForms.Transactions.Form2`.

You can declare the same namespace several times within your Visual Basic .NET application. The contents of each declaration are the result of the namespace contents. Listing 9.2 shows a namespace declared twice.

LISTING 9.2 Declaring the Same Namespace Twice

```
Namespace MyForms
    Public Class Form1
    End Class
End Namespace

Namespace MyForms
    Public Class Form2
    End Class
End Namespace
```

ANALYSIS With the declarations shown in Listing 9.2, both `Form1` and `Form2` are in the `MyForms` namespace. Declaring the namespace around each class definition is useful when you're breaking class definitions into multiple source files. This way, each class can have its own source file and still be included in a namespace.

You declare namespaces within namespaces by declaring the namespace with the full reference, as shown in the `MyForms.Transactions` namespace declaration in Listing 9.1. This method makes it very clear which namespace a class is defined within. A second method is to declare the namespaces within a namespace declaration. For example, both namespace declarations shown in Listing 9.3 accomplish the same result.

LISTING 9.3 Declaring a Namespace Within a Namespace in Different Ways

```
Namespace MyForms
    Namespace Transactions
        Public Class Form1
        End Class
    End Namespace
End Namespace

Namespace MyForms.Transactions
    Public Class Form1
    End Class
End Namespace
```

Summary

Today, you learned how to use namespaces to group related classes, structures, and namespaces together. Namespaces add organization to large applications and minimize naming conflicts with other modules. You also learned how to declare namespaces within your Visual Basic .NET applications and the different ways to make the declarations.

As you learned, all assemblies, including applications, have a default namespace that equals the assembly or application name.

Q&A

Q **Are the namespaces declared within an assembly visible to other assemblies?**

A Yes. Namespaces are visible to other assemblies if classes, structures, or other namespaces with classes or structures are available for use. For example, as long as a public structure or class is defined within a namespace, it's visible to other assemblies.

Q **You mention that assemblies contain metadata that describes their contents. If the code is compiled, how do I find out what is inside and available for use by other programs?**

A The .NET Framework includes a tool called the IL Disassembler (ILDASM) that lets you peek into the intermediate language and manifest of a .NET executable or DLL. Figure 9.4 shows the contents of the Visual Basic .NET sample application called Calc. Run ILDASM from the Visual Studio .NET command line and open the file you want to interrogate.

FIGURE 9.4

The .NET Framework IL Disassembler lets you view an assembly's manifest.

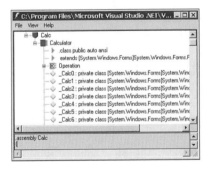

Workshop

The Workshop provides quiz questions and an exercise to help solidify your understanding of namespaces and provide you with experience in using what you've learned. Answers are provided in Appendix A, "Answers to Quizzes."

Quiz

1. What two root namespaces are shipped with the .NET Framework?

2. Can a namespace include another namespace?

3. What are the primary benefits from using namespaces?

Exercise

Create three levels of namespaces with classes defined in each level. The name of the classes or namespaces isn't important; however, you need to define a root namespace with three namespace levels. Each level should have classes defined.

DAY **10**

Creating a User Interface

When you're designing Visual Basic .NET applications that require a user interface, you have two choices with distinct differences: Windows Forms and Web Forms. Both forms have design-time environments to create rich user interfaces and provide similar functionality. Deciding which type of form to use within a particular application requires you to make decisions on the type of use the form will have.

Both Windows Forms and Web Forms have their own namespaces that contain all the classes, controls, enumerations, and structures required to create and use the forms. Windows Forms are implemented with the classes and namespaces found in `System.Windows.Forms`, whereas Web Forms are found in the `System.Web.UI` namespace.

Today's lesson covers choosing the right form for the application and implementing the two form types with the classes provided within the .NET Framework. By the end of the day, you will learn the following about user interfaces in Visual Basic .NET:

- Choosing the correct form for the application task
- Creating a Windows Form

- Enhancing a Windows Form with additional functionality
- Creating a Web Form
- Using a Web Form with an ASP.NET application

Choosing the Form for the Task

When you're designing an application, which type of form to create might be obvious to you. For example, an e-commerce application will use Web Forms because it's an Internet application and the user interface is Web based. In contrast, if you're building an application that requires a highly responsive user interface and runs entirely on the client machine such as an application like Microsoft Word, the choice should be a Windows Form.

In other situations, the decision of what form to use isn't as straightforward. You can have a standard Windows application that uses Web Forms or a combination of Windows and Web Forms. However, when you're designing an application that must exclusively run on the Internet and be platform independent, the only choice is Web Forms.

Windows applications that use Windows Forms are built on the Windows framework the same as applications written in previous versions of Visual Basic and C++. The compiled program has access to system resources on the client computer and can take advantage of the .NET GDI+ classes to create graphic user interfaces on the client. This requirement is common for productivity applications and games.

You might need a text-intensive user interface within a standard Windows application. In this case, it's better to use a Web Form that's well suited for text-intensive applications of any sort when text formatting is important. Using Web Forms in this manner provides your application with features that would otherwise be difficult to implement with Windows Forms. The same application may use Windows Forms for other areas of the application that aren't text intensive.

You can find a good example of Web Form usage in the Visual Studio .NET IDE's Start Page (see Figure 10.1). The Start Page is a Web Form, whereas the application itself uses Windows Forms for most of the user interface.

FIGURE 10.1

*The Visual Studio .NET
Start Page as a Web
Form.*

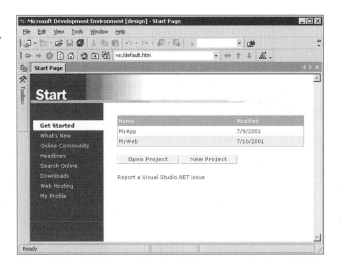

Using Windows Forms

Windows Forms are used in applications in which the client executes a significant amount of those applications on the client PC. These types of applications are traditional Win32 desktop applications, which were previously developed in Visual Basic and C++. For example, they include Microsoft Office products, games, graphics applications, even the Visual Studio .NET IDE.

Most applications don't have a single Windows Form; they have several. Windows Forms provide several UI aspects to your applications. They are used for the main application window, dialogs, MDI frame windows, MDI child windows, and so on.

If you developed applications using previous versions of Visual Basic, you are familiar with Visual Basic forms. Windows Forms are similar to Visual Basic forms, with some differences. The most important difference is that Windows Forms are built at runtime by the source code, whereas Visual Basic forms were stored in the compiled module as resources.

Understanding Windows Forms

If you haven't done so already, open Visual Basic .NET and create a new Windows application called `myFormApp`.

As I indicated earlier, all Windows Forms–related classes, structures, and enumerations are found in the `System.Windows.Forms` namespace. This namespace includes the `Form` class, the base class of all Windows Forms.

When you create a new Windows application, a default Windows Form (see Figure 10.2) is created for you to start building your application's user interface. The default form, given the class name Form1, is generally used as the main form of your application.

FIGURE **10.2**

The Visual Basic .NET default Windows Form, Form1.

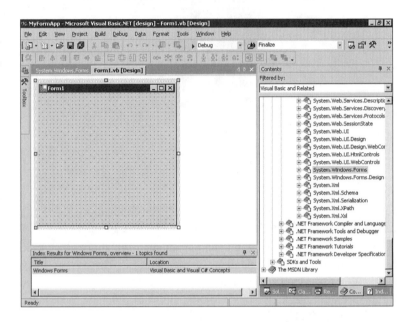

You can rename the default form so that it better fits the purpose it has in your application and change its characteristics to match the desired use. For example, the default form is set up for a dialog application, as shown in Figure 10.2. By adding a menu and toolbar and changing the form's background color, you set it up to be an application with a single document interface (SDI), as shown in Figure 10.3. Changing the form's IsMdiContainer property makes it a multiple document interface (MDI) frame window (see Figure 10.4).

FIGURE **10.3**

Form1 *as an SDI Form with menu, toolbar, and status bar.*

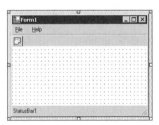

FIGURE 10.4

Form1 as an MDI Form with menu, toolbar, and status bar.

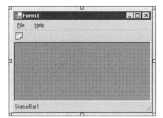

Unlike forms in previous versions of Visual Basic, Windows Forms are built in the source code. Through the form designer, the Visual Studio .NET IDE modifies the source code in your project to build the Windows Form you design. Listing 10.1 shows the source for the MDI version of the Form1 class. All the boldfaced code is added as a result of using the form designer to add the menu, toolbar, and status bar and change the style to an MDI container.

LISTING 10.1   Form1 Class with MDI Modifications as Shown in Figure 10.4

```
Public Class Form1
    Inherits System.Windows.Forms.Form

#Region " Windows Form Designer generated code "

    Public Sub New()
        MyBase.New()

        'This call is required by the Windows Form Designer.
        InitializeComponent()

        'Add any initialization after the InitializeComponent() call

    End Sub

    'Form overrides dispose to clean up the component list.
    Protected Overloads Overrides Sub Dispose(ByVal disposing As Boolean)
        If disposing Then
            If Not (components Is Nothing) Then
                components.Dispose()
            End If
        End If
        MyBase.Dispose(disposing)
    End Sub

    Friend WithEvents MainMenu1 As System.Windows.Forms.MainMenu
    Friend WithEvents MenuItem1 As System.Windows.Forms.MenuItem
    Friend WithEvents MenuItem2 As System.Windows.Forms.MenuItem
    Friend WithEvents MenuItem3 As System.Windows.Forms.MenuItem
```

10

LISTING 10.1 continued

```
Friend WithEvents ImageList1 As System.Windows.Forms.ImageList
Friend WithEvents StatusBar1 As System.Windows.Forms.StatusBar
Friend WithEvents ToolBar1 As System.Windows.Forms.ToolBar
Friend WithEvents ToolBarButton1 As System.Windows.Forms.ToolBarButton
Friend WithEvents MdiClient1 As System.Windows.Forms.MdiClient

Private components As System.ComponentModel.IContainer

'Required by the Windows Form Designer

'NOTE: The following procedure is required by the Windows Form Designer
'It can be modified using the Windows Form Designer.
'Do not modify it using the code editor.
<System.Diagnostics.DebuggerStepThrough()> _
Private Sub InitializeComponent()
    Me.components = New System.ComponentModel.Container()
    Me.StatusBar1 = New System.Windows.Forms.StatusBar()
    Me.ToolBar1 = New System.Windows.Forms.ToolBar()
    Me.ToolBarButton1 = New System.Windows.Forms.ToolBarButton()
    Me.ImageList1 = New System.Windows.Forms.ImageList(Me.components)
    Me.MainMenu1 = New System.Windows.Forms.MainMenu()
    Me.MenuItem1 = New System.Windows.Forms.MenuItem()
    Me.MenuItem3 = New System.Windows.Forms.MenuItem()
    Me.MenuItem2 = New System.Windows.Forms.MenuItem()
    Me.MdiClient1 = New System.Windows.Forms.MdiClient()
    Me.SuspendLayout()
    '
    'StatusBar1
    '
    Me.StatusBar1.Location = New System.Drawing.Point(0, 149)
    Me.StatusBar1.Name = "StatusBar1"
    Me.StatusBar1.Size = New System.Drawing.Size(292, 20)
    Me.StatusBar1.TabIndex = 0
    Me.StatusBar1.Text = "StatusBar1"
    '
    'ToolBar1
    '
    Me.ToolBar1.Appearance = System.Windows.Forms.ToolBarAppearance.Flat
    Me.ToolBar1.Buttons.AddRange _
    (New System.Windows.Forms.ToolBarButton() {Me.ToolBarButton1})
    Me.ToolBar1.DropDownArrows = True
    Me.ToolBar1.ImageList = Me.ImageList1
    Me.ToolBar1.Name = "ToolBar1"
    Me.ToolBar1.ShowToolTips = True
    Me.ToolBar1.Size = New System.Drawing.Size(292, 25)
    Me.ToolBar1.TabIndex = 1
    '
    'ToolBarButton1
    '
```

LISTING 10.1   continued

```
Me.ToolBarButton1.ImageIndex = 0
'
'ImageList1
'
Me.ImageList1.ColorDepth = System.Windows.Forms.ColorDepth.Depth8Bit
Me.ImageList1.ImageSize = New System.Drawing.Size(16, 16)
Me.ImageList1.TransparentColor = System.Drawing.Color.Transparent
'
'MainMenu1
'
Me.MainMenu1.MenuItems.AddRange _
(New System.Windows.Forms.MenuItem() {Me.MenuItem1, Me.MenuItem2})
'
'MenuItem1
'
Me.MenuItem1.Index = 0
Me.MenuItem1.MenuItems.AddRange _
  (New System.Windows.Forms.MenuItem() {Me.MenuItem3})
Me.MenuItem1.Text = "&File"
'
'MenuItem3
'
Me.MenuItem3.Index = 0
Me.MenuItem3.Text = "E&xit"
'
'MenuItem2
'
Me.MenuItem2.Index = 1
Me.MenuItem2.Text = "&Help"
'
'MdiClient1
'
Me.MdiClient1.Dock = System.Windows.Forms.DockStyle.Fill
Me.MdiClient1.Location = New System.Drawing.Point(0, 25)
Me.MdiClient1.Name = "MdiClient1"
Me.MdiClient1.TabIndex = 2
'
'Form1
'
Me.AutoScaleBaseSize = New System.Drawing.Size(5, 13)
Me.ClientSize = New System.Drawing.Size(292, 169)
Me.Controls.AddRange _
  (New System.Windows.Forms.Control() {Me.ToolBar1, _
  Me.StatusBar1, Me.MdiClient1})
Me.IsMdiContainer = True
Me.Menu = Me.MainMenu1
Me.Name = "Form1"
Me.Text = "Form1"
Me.TransparencyKey = System.Drawing.Color.LightPink
Me.ResumeLayout(False)
```

10

LISTING 10.1   continued

```
      End Sub

#End Region

      Private Sub MenuItem3_Click(ByVal sender As System.Object, _
        ByVal e As System.EventArgs) Handles MenuItem3.Click
          End
      End Sub
End Class
```

As you can see, without the form designer for Windows Forms, hand-coding the Windows Form layout would be tedious. It's strongly recommended that you don't tweak the Windows Form code by hand. Use the form designer only to work with Windows Forms. With that said, sometimes you can get things right more easily by manually tweaking it when you know what you're doing.

 Note   Any changes you make by hand can cause the form designer to stop working with a form. If you create an error or do something the form designer can't work with, you get an error when trying to load the form in the designer.

Creating a Windows Form

Applications often require Windows Forms in addition to the default form created by the Application Wizard. The easiest way to create a new Windows Form for an application is to add a new class to your project with the Solution Explorer window. Follow these steps:

1. Right-click the project and select Add and then Add Class to display the dialog shown in Figure 10.5.

2. Select the Windows Form class type and accept the default name Form2.vb.

3. Click OK. A new file is added to your project, and the new blank form is displayed and ready to edit in the Windows form designer.

This basic Windows Form has no controls or characteristics other than its name. You create a Windows Form with controls for use as a dialog by dragging items from the control toolbox onto the form. Each control has corresponding code associated with it that the form designer generates. To see an example, drag a new button object onto the form, as shown in Figure 10.6.

FIGURE 10.5

The Add New Item dialog to add new Windows Form classes.

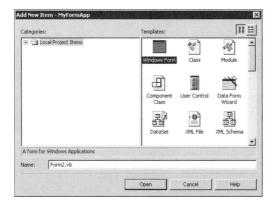

FIGURE 10.6

A new Windows Form with a button control.

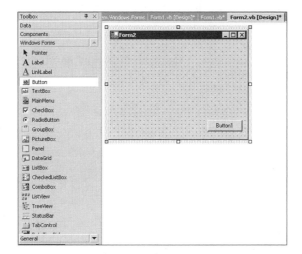

10

The boldfaced code in Listing 10.2 creates the new push button control. Also, notice that the new class inherits `System.Windows.Forms.Form`, the base class for Windows Forms.

LISTING 10.2   Code Added to Create a New Button on a Windows Form

```
Public Class Form2
    Inherits System.Windows.Forms.Form

#Region " Windows Form Designer generated code "

    Public Sub New()
        MyBase.New()
        InitializeComponent()
    End Sub
```

LISTING **10.2**   continued

```
Protected Overloads Overrides Sub Dispose _
  (ByVal disposing As Boolean)
    If disposing Then
        If Not (components Is Nothing) Then
            components.Dispose()
        End If
    End If
    MyBase.Dispose(disposing)
End Sub
Friend WithEvents Button1 As System.Windows.Forms.Button

Private components As System.ComponentModel.IContainer

<System.Diagnostics.DebuggerStepThrough()> _
Private Sub InitializeComponent()
    Me.Button1 = New System.Windows.Forms.Button()
    Me.SuspendLayout()
    Me.Button1.Location = New System.Drawing.Point(224, 200)
    Me.Button1.Name = "Button1"
    Me.Button1.TabIndex = 0
    Me.Button1.Text = "Button1"
    Me.AutoScaleBaseSize = New System.Drawing.Size(5, 13)
    Me.ClientSize = New System.Drawing.Size(312, 245)
    Me.Controls.AddRange _
      (New System.Windows.Forms.Control() {Me.Button1})
    Me.Name = "Form2"
    Me.Text = "Form2"
    Me.ResumeLayout(False)
End Sub

#End Region
End Class
```

As you add controls to the Windows Form, the designer adds the appropriate code in the
InitializeComponent() subroutine to create the controls on the Windows Form at runtime.

When you actually want to create the Windows Form in response to user or program
actions, you simply create a new instance of the Windows Form class you defined and
call the ShowDialog() function to use it as a dialog or Show() subroutine to use it as a
normal window. Listing 10.3 shows how to create the instance of the Form2 class and use
it as a dialog in response to the user clicking a toolbar button.

LISTING 10.3   Launching a Second Form When the Toolbar Button Is Clicked

```
Private Sub ToolBar1_ButtonClick(ByVal sender As System.Object, _
    ByVal e As System.Windows.Forms.ToolBarButtonClickEventArgs) _
    Handles ToolBar1.ButtonClick
  If CType(e.Button.Tag(), String) = "101" Then
     Dim NewForm As Form2 = New Form2()

     If NewForm.ShowDialog(Me) = DialogResult.OK Then
        ' OK was pressed on the Dialog Box
     End If
  End If
End Sub
```

Enhancing a Windows Form

Besides creating new Windows Forms by creating a new class that inherits from the `System.Windows.Forms.Form` class, you can also create a new Windows Form from an already existing Windows Form class. Support for doing so is built into the Add New Item dialog box shown in Figure 10.5. Rather than select the Windows Form as your new class type, select Inherited Form to open the dialog shown in Figure 10.7 when you create the new class. Here, you can select from which form to inherit.

FIGURE 10.7

The Inheritance Picker dialog box.

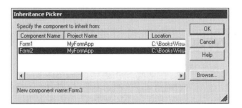

After you select the form to inherit from (in this case, `Form2`), the new form is displayed in the form designer. Any controls from the inherited form are also shown on the new form with an indicator showing that the control is from an inherited form, as shown in Figure 10.8. All characteristics of the form being inherited are also the characteristics of the new form.

Adding any new controls or changing any of the characteristics on the new form enhances and adds to what's already defined in the base class, `Form2`. As you add controls to the new form, the tab order of the controls must follow the tab order of the controls added in the base class because all the controls are created in the base class first and then the controls in the derived class are created. You can overcome this limitation with some hand coding and tweaking.

FIGURE 10.8

A new form with an inherited control and characteristics.

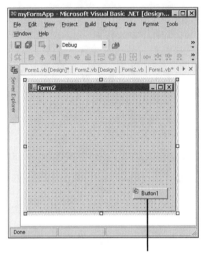

Indicator for an inherited form

The trick is to set the button's TabIndex property on Form2 to a relatively high number, such as 10. On Form3, set the TabIndex properties of any controls to values lower than 10. When Form3 loads, the control with the lowest TabIndex value will get the focus and tabbing continues to the control with the next higher value.

Using Web Forms

Applications accessible via a Web browser or text-intensive content use Web Forms in the user interface. For strictly Web-based applications, the user interface is created with Web Forms and HTML. Client-side applications can use a mix of Windows Forms and Web Forms or the Rich Text control.

Web Forms vary from Windows Forms in that they are based on Microsoft's ASP.NET technology. The Web Form's functionality is dynamically generated by the Web server, and the appropriate HTML file is created to represent the Web Form to users within their Web browsers or client devices.

Web Forms are compatible on any browser or mobile device because the Web server can generate the correct browser-specific HTML to represent the Web Form. Developers don't have to write different versions of their code as they had to do with ASP to work on different browsers. ASP.NET can take advantage of all a browser's features to provide the best possible rendition and functionality. For example, when you run Internet Explorer 5, ASP.NET takes advantage of DHTML to cut down on roundtrips to the Web server.

Because Web Forms are built on the .NET Framework, they provide all the benefits that come with it. They run in a managed execution environment, have strong type safety, and are fully object-oriented. They are also flexible and allow custom controls to be used alongside the standard Web Form controls.

Working with Web Forms and ASP.NET

A Web Forms page is divided into two pieces. The first defines the visual component, and the second provides the logic. The visual element, the Web Forms page, consists of a file with an .aspx extension that contains the Web Form's visual definition.

The code behind the user interface consists of the Visual Basic .NET code that you create to react to user events and initialization. The logic code also resides in a separate file—in this case, with the extension .aspx.vb. Keep in mind that some of the files that Visual Basic .NET creates for you inside the development environment might be hidden. A toolbar button toggles the show/hide state for these special files.

The Web server uses the two files, .aspx and .aspx.vb, together to provide a complete Web Form. To optimize the usage of the two files, the server compiles the logic file into a dynamic link library (DLL) file. The .aspx file is compiled in a different fashion. The Web server waits to compile the .aspx file until the first time it's used. When it's accessed, ASP.NET automatically generates a .NET class file that represents the page and compiles it with the DLL that contains the logic. When the user requests the Web Form, the DLL runs on the server and dynamically produces the HTML output for the Web Form.

Creating an ASP.NET Web Form

To create a new Web Form, you must have an ASP.NET application. You create a new ASP.NET application using Visual Basic .NET from the New Project dialog, as shown in Figure 10.9.

When you create a Web application, it has a default Web Form the same as a new Windows application has a default Windows Form. As you do with the default Windows Form, you can use the default Web Form as your first form in your project. You create additional Web Forms in the same fashion as you created new Windows Forms earlier. The only difference is that Web Forms don't have the option of creating a new Web Form by inheriting another.

The Web Form has its own designer (see Figure 10.10) that allows you to lay out the design of the form as it should appear when users view it through their Web browsers. Some of the same controls are available on Web Forms that were available on Windows Forms. Some additional Web-specific controls are available, but other Windows Form–specific controls aren't available.

FIGURE 10.9

Using the New Project dialog to create a new ASP.NET application with Visual Basic .NET.

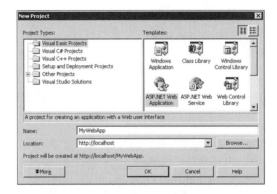

FIGURE 10.10

The Web form designer in Visual Studio .NET.

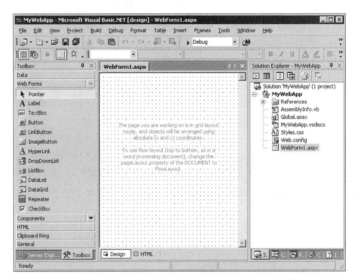

Building a Web Form in the designer is the same as building a Windows Form. From the toolbox, drag the fields and controls you want on the Web Form and drop them where you want them. After you design the controls that you want on your page, as shown in Figure 10.11, the application is compiled. At this point, the logic portion of the page is compiled. When you view your page by running the application, the visual portion of the Web Form is compiled and then displayed in the browser (see Figure 10.12).

You add logic to the Web Form in the corresponding .vb file to the particular Web Form. Listing 10.4 shows the code for the WebForm1 class shown in Figure 10.11 without any added logic. Listing 10.5 shows the corresponding .aspx file, which controls the layout of the Web Form.

FIGURE 10.11

A Designed Web Form ready to compile and run.

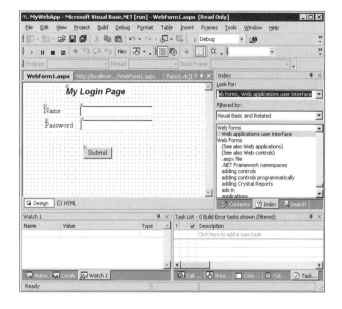

FIGURE 10.12

A Web Form running within Internet Explorer.

LISTING 10.4 WebForm1 Class Without Added Logic

```
Public Class WebForm1
    Inherits System.Web.UI.Page
    Protected WithEvents btnSubmit As System.Web.UI.WebControls.Button
    Protected WithEvents stName As System.Web.UI.WebControls.Label
    Protected WithEvents edtName As System.Web.UI.WebControls.TextBox
    Protected WithEvents stPassword As System.Web.UI.WebControls.Label
    Protected WithEvents stTitle As System.Web.UI.WebControls.Label
    Protected WithEvents edtPassword As System.Web.UI.WebControls.TextBox
```

LISTING 10.4   continued

```
'This call is required by the Web Form Designer.
<System.Diagnostics.DebuggerStepThrough()> _
Private Sub InitializeComponent()

End Sub

Private Sub Page_Init _
(ByVal sender As System.Object, ByVal e As System.EventArgs) Handles _
MyBase.Init
    InitializeComponent()
End Sub

#End Region

Private Sub Page_Load _
(ByVal sender As System.Object, ByVal e As System.EventArgs) Handles _
MyBase.Load
End Sub

End Class
```

LISTING 10.5   Visual Layout of WebForm1 in the .aspx File

```
<%@ Page Language="vb" AutoEventWireup="false"
    Codebehind="WebForm1.aspx.vb" Inherits="MyWebApp.WebForm1"%>
<!DOCTYPE HTML PUBLIC "-//W3C//DTD HTML 4.0 Transitional//EN">
<HTML>
<HEAD>
<title></title>
</HEAD>
<body MS_POSITIONING="GridLayout">
<form id="Form1" method="post" runat="server">
  <asp:Button id="btnSubmit" style="Z-INDEX: 101; LEFT: 129px;
  POSITION: absolute; TOP: 135px" runat="server" Text="Submit"></asp:Button>
  <asp:Label id="stName" style="Z-INDEX: 102; LEFT: 44px;
  POSITION: absolute; TOP: 49px" runat="server">Name</asp:Label>
  <asp:TextBox id="edtName" style="Z-INDEX: 103; LEFT: 122px;
  POSITION: absolute; TOP: 48px" runat="server"></asp:TextBox>
  <asp:Label id="stPassword" style="Z-INDEX: 104; LEFT: 47px;
  POSITION: absolute; TOP: 79px" runat="server">Password</asp:Label>
  <asp:TextBox id="edtPassword" style="Z-INDEX: 105; LEFT: 123px;
  POSITION: absolute; TOP: 77px" runat="server"
  ToolTip="Enter your password" TextMode="Password"></asp:TextBox>
  <asp:Label id="stTitle" style="Z-INDEX: 106; LEFT: 91px;
  POSITION: absolute; TOP: 8px" runat="server" Width="135px" Height="21px"
```

LISTING 10.5 continued

```
    Font-Bold="True" Font-Names="Arial" Font-Size="Larger"
    Font-Italic="True">My Login Page</asp:Label>
</form>
</body>
</HTML>
```

To do some processing when users click the Submit button, such as display a message, you need to add an event handler for the Submit button. Within the event handler shown in the following subroutine, you can perform any required coding. In this case, users are redirected to another Web Form.

```
Private Sub btnSubmit_Click _
    (ByVal sender As System.Object, ByVal e As System.EventArgs) _
    Handles btnSubmit.Click
  Response.Redirect("webform2.aspx")
End Sub
```

10

Summary

Today you learned how to create user interfaces for your Visual Basic .NET applications and decide which types of interface objects to use. You learned the difference between Windows Forms and Web Forms and how to create and use them. Windows Forms are the basis of the user interface for traditional applications and can be combined with Web Forms that provide text-intensive user interfaces. ASP.NET applications exclusively use Web Forms and HTML to provide a platform-independent user interface.

After today, you should be able to create Visual Basic .NET applications and determine the best type of user interface to use for your design. You also have enough knowledge to start using the classes provided in the .NET Framework to create and enhance your user interface using object-oriented techniques.

Q&A

Q Can I create a Web Form class within a Windows Application that uses Windows Forms?

A No. Web Forms require a Web server to host the form and to dynamically create the script. You can use Web Forms within a Windows Form by using a Web Browser control on your Windows Form and pointing it to the URL that contains the Web Forms.

Q Can I use controls other than the standard Web controls and Windows controls provided?

A Yes. You can add ActiveX controls to either Web Forms or Windows Forms. You can also create your own custom Web controls and Windows controls and use them or a third party's controls. Therefore, you aren't limited to the default set of controls provided by Microsoft.

Workshop

The Workshop provides quiz questions and an exercise to help solidify your understanding and provide you with experience in using what you've learned. Answers are provided in Appendix A, "Answers to Quizzes."

Quiz

1. What's the base class of a Windows Form?
2. What's the base class of a Web Form?
3. What two file extensions are created for each Web Form?
4. Are all Windows Forms data-entry related?

Exercise

Create a new Web Form, WebForm2, in the MyWebApp application. Include a welcome message with the name of the user who logs in and clicks the Submit button on WebForm1. The handler for the button's click event in WebForm1 was added at the end of the lesson, so the only task left in WebForm1 is to assign the name value to the Session object inside the handler.

The other task, in WebForm2, is to add a Label control to the page and display the Session variable's value entered for the Name field as part of the welcome message.

DAY 11

Creating and Using Components

Components contain objects in a reusable form that other applications written in .NET can use in building other applications. You can use components in the same assembly as they are created or in other assemblies. The entire .NET Framework is designed and implemented through components that your Visual Basic .NET applications can incorporate by using the components' objects and calling their methods.

Today you will learn how to create your own components in Visual Basic .NET and design them for use in other .NET languages. Another feature covered today is the ability to use components that aren't bound to a project until runtime. This process, known as *late binding*, allows an application to dynamically decide which components it needs and then load them. By the end of today, you will learn how to

- Create a custom component using Visual Basic .NET.
- Create component classes that allow late binding.
- Understand reflection and how it relates to components.
- Work with unknown object types.

Creating Visual Basic .NET Component Classes

In previous versions of Visual Basic, you could use classes to expose component functionality. Standard modules couldn't be exposed outside the project; user-defined types could be exposed but provided only complex data types with no functionality. Visual Basic .NET removes these restrictions, and with full object-oriented development, components are more useful than before.

What's the difference between a class and a component if a component is a class? A class becomes a component when it provides the appropriate interfaces for component interaction. A component in .NET either implements the `System.ComponentModel.IComponent` interface or has the `System.ComponentModel.Component` class somewhere in the inheritance chain. This interface and class make it easy to use components and author them so that they work well in design mode.

The process of creating components should be well thought out before you actually program the components. Consider the following while authoring a component:

- Decide what the component should provide and accomplish within your application or others that it's used within.
- Outline complex object models to decide what's exposed and how access is controlled.
- Determine how to divide the functionality between the component and subobjects in the object model.
- Decide on the best class or component to use as the base class for the component, which should already implement most of the properties and methods you need.
- Decide the best base class for all subobjects within the component.
- Determine what functionality your component can provide from the .NET Framework classes.
- If interfaces are necessary, determine which classes will implement them.
- Ensure that functionality is provided through properties, methods, and events of the component and subobjects.
- Determine appropriate access levels for the component. For example, what should be `Public`, `Private`, and so on?

- Be sure the component is solid and well tested. A major factor in components is that they should be solid and reliable additions to a project.

When you create a new component, choose short and descriptive class names, using individually capitalized whole words.

Creating a Component Project

You create a new component class library with Visual Studio .NET the same as you do with a standard Visual Basic .NET application—by using the New Project dialog. The exception is that rather than pick a Windows application or another type of application, you select the Class Library option. Choose the name of your library carefully because it will be the default root namespace where your components reside. For the purposes of this exercise, create a new class library with the name MyComponents.

After the class library is created, a default object class, Class1, is created. Use the Solution Explorer to delete the Class1.vb file to remove this default class. Use the Solution Explorer again and right-click the MyComponents project. Select Add and then Add Component to display the dialog box shown in Figure 11.1. From the available templates, select Component Class.

FIGURE 11.1

Using the Add New Item dialog to create a Visual Basic .NET component.

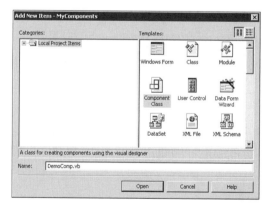

Choose the name of the component class you want to create by naming the file. For this exercise, use the name DemoComp.vb, which will create a component named DemoComp. After the component is created, a blank component designer is displayed (see Figure 11.2). Listing 11.1 shows the default code generated for the component.

FIGURE 11.2

After you add a component class, Visual Basic .NET defaults to a blank design view.

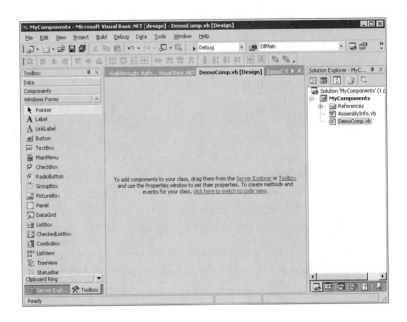

LISTING 11.1   Default Code for the DemoComp Component Class

```
Public Class DemoComp
    Inherits System.ComponentModel.Component

#Region " Component Designer generated code "

    Public Sub New(Container As System.ComponentModel.IContainer)
        MyClass.New()

        'Required for Windows.Forms Class Composition Designer support
        Container.Add(me)
    End Sub

    Public Sub New()
        MyBase.New()

        'This call is required by the Component Designer.
        InitializeComponent()

        'Add any initialization after the InitializeComponent() call

    End Sub

    'Required by the Component Designer
    Private components As System.ComponentModel.Container
```

LISTING 11.1 continued

```
        'NOTE: The following procedure is required by the Component Designer
        'It can be modified using the Component Designer.
        'Do not modify it using the code editor.
        <System.Diagnostics.DebuggerStepThrough()> _
         Private Sub InitializeComponent()
            components = New System.ComponentModel.Container()
        End Sub

    #End Region

    End Class
```

As you can see, the `DemoComp` class inherits the `System.ComponentModel.Component` class, which is a primary requirement for a class to be a component.

Designing and Implementing the Component

The component designer enables you to easily incorporate other components within your new component. All the .NET controls and other components available within the Windows form designer can be used within a component. However, a component isn't visual, and therefore any visual object added is invisible when the component is used. Visual components are built as control libraries.

Although it's not a requirement for a component to include other components, in this exercise a timer is required. From the Components section of the Toolbox (not the Windows Forms section), drag the timer control to the component designer. The component class is changed accordingly, as shown by the boldfaced code in Listing 11.2.

LISTING 11.2 DemoComp Component Class with the `Timer1` Control Added

```
Public Class DemoComp
    Inherits System.ComponentModel.Component

#Region " Component Designer generated code "

    Public Sub New(Container As System.ComponentModel.IContainer)
        MyClass.New()

        'Required for Windows.Forms Class Composition Designer support
        Container.Add(me)
    End Sub

    Friend WithEvents Timer1 As System.Timers.Timer
```

LISTING 11.2   continued

```
Public Sub New()
    MyBase.New()

        'This call is required by the Component Designer.
        InitializeComponent()

        'Add any initialization after the InitializeComponent() call
    End Sub

    'Required by the Component Designer
    Private components As System.ComponentModel.Container

    'NOTE: The following procedure is required by the Component Designer
    'It can be modified using the Component Designer.
    'Do not modify it using the code editor.
    <System.Diagnostics.DebuggerStepThrough()> _
      Private Sub InitializeComponent()
    Me.Timer1 = New System.Timers.Timer()
      CType(Me.Timer1, System.ComponentModel.ISupportInitialize).BeginInit()
      '
      'Timer1
      '
    Me.Timer1.Enabled = True
    CType(Me.Timer1, System.ComponentModel.ISupportInitialize).EndInit()
    End Sub

#End Region

End Class
```

The purpose of this component is to beep every two seconds; therefore, you need to set the timer interval to 2000 milliseconds. You can do so in Design view by selecting the Timer component that you added previously and setting its Interval property to 2000, as shown in Figure 11.3.

FIGURE 11.3

Setting the Timer1 interval to 2000 milliseconds in the Properties page.

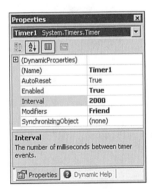

Setting the timer values adds the following line of code to the `InitializeComponent()` subroutine:

```
Me.Timer1.Interval = 2000
```

All that's left for the component is to handle the `Elapsed` event from the timer control. Add the following `OnTimer()` subroutine, which is called after two seconds have elapsed and `Beep()` is called:

```
Private Sub OnTimer _
   (ByVal source As Object, ByVal e As _
    System.Timers.ElapsedEventArgs) Handles Timer1.Elapsed
    Beep()
End Sub
```

Save your work and build the component. You've just created the `MyComponents`. `DemoComp` component. There's not much more you can do with the component at the moment, but keep it available because you'll use it later today as part of the exercise. Whenever this component is added to a Windows Form or used within your application, it will beep every two seconds. Although this component isn't very useful, it demonstrates the lifetime of a component because it continues to beep until it's no longer in memory.

Programming Classes for Runtime

Sometimes applications need to use classes that aren't known at compile time. For example, an application made up of installable components that may or may not exist at runtime can load the installed components and adjust itself based on the components actually installed.

NEW TERM Visual Basic .NET uses a feature known as *reflection* to provide the infrastructure and features that allow the use of components at runtime. Here's the official definition for reflection as provided by Microsoft:

> The process of obtaining information about assemblies and the types defined within them, and creating, invoking, and accessing type instances at runtime.

This delayed use of components is known as *late binding*, and this use can occur in two ways in Visual Basic .NET.

The first late binding method is implicitly done for you by the compiler. The Visual Basic .NET compiler uses reflection to determine the methods and to determine arguments of methods invoked on objects that aren't bound to the application at compile time. However, the compiler must be set to allow this operation to occur, which involves turning off `Option Strict`. To turn off `Option Strict` in Solution Explorer, right-click the project name and select Properties. On the properties page, select Build and adjust the combo boxes as required.

Listing 11.3 shows an example using implicit late binding. Notice that the code declares the variable as an `Object`, without specifying which one. Late binding occurs when the method is actually invoked.

LISTING 11.3   Implicit Late Binding Use in Visual Basic .NET

```
Imports System

Module MyModule
    Sub Main()
        ' Set up variable
        Dim MyUnknownObject As Object

        ' Create the object
        MyUnknownObject = New MyObject()

        ' Invoke a method as if the object was already bound
        ' even though it is late bound
        MyUnknownObject.MyMethod()
    End Sub
End Module
```

NEW TERM The other method of late binding, known as *custom binding*, is to use the reflection classes explicitly in your code. Custom binding allows you to load an assembly at runtime, determine information about the types in the assembly, specify the type you want, and invoke methods and access the type.

Understanding the Reflection Classes

Reflection in the .NET Framework is managed with the classes found in the `System.Reflection` namespace. Another namespace, `System.Reflection.Emit`, allows you to build new types at runtime.

You need to follow a hierarchy in discovering information at runtime. Assemblies are the root level, and they contain modules. Modules contain types, and types contain members. The reflection classes encapsulate assemblies, modules, and types. By using the reflection classes, you can dynamically create an instance of a type, bind the type to an object, or get the type from an existing object. You also can invoke the type's methods and access its member data and properties. Table 11.1 shows the reflection classes and their use in performing custom binding.

TABLE 11.1 Reflection Classes and Their Use

Class	Description and Use
Assembly	Defines and loads assemblies, loads modules listed within the assembly, and locates a type from an assembly and creates an instance of it.
Module	Specifies information such as the assembly that contains the module and the classes within the module. You can also retrieve global methods or other nonglobal methods defined in the module.
ConstructorInfo	Specifies information such as the name, parameters, access modifiers, and implementation details of a constructor.
MethodInfo	Specifies the name, return type, parameters, access modifiers, and implementation details of a method.
FieldInfo	Specifies the name, access modifiers, and implementation details of a field and gets or sets field values.
EventInfo	Specifies the name, event handler data type, declaring type, and reflected type of an event and adds or removes event handlers.
PropertyInfo	Specifies the name, data type, declaring type, reflected type, and read-only or writable status of a property and gets or sets property values.
ParameterInfo	Specifies the parameter's name, data type, whether the parameter is an input or output parameter, and the position of the parameter in a method signature.

Programming Unknown Objects

This next example uses reflection to perform late binding. First, add a class module to your MyComponents project and name the file HelloWorld.vb. Listing 11.4 shows the complete code that you need as your HelloWorld class.

LISTING 11.4 The HelloWorld Class in HelloWorld.vb

```
Public Class HelloWorld
   ' Default public constructor.
   Public Sub New()

   End Sub

   ' Print "Hello World" plus the passed text.
   Public Sub PrintHello(ByVal txt As String)
      System.Windows.Forms.MessageBox.Show("Hello " & txt)
   End Sub
End Class
```

The next step is to late bind the `HelloWorld` class into an application. Add a new class module file to the `MyComponents` project and use the default name, Module1.vb. In this module, remove the default code and insert the `Imports` statement and the `Main()` subroutine as shown in Listing 11.5.

LISTING 11.5   Using Reflection to Add Late Binding to the `MyComponents.HelloWorld` Class

```
Imports System.Reflection

Module Main
    Sub Main()
        ' Set up the variables.
        Dim MyAssembly As System.Reflection.Assembly
        Dim MyObject As Object
        Dim MyHelloType As Type
        Dim PrintHello As MethodInfo

        ' Load the assembly to use.
        MyAssembly = System.Reflection.Assembly.Load("MyComponents")

        ' Get the type to use from the assembly.
        MyHelloType = MyAssembly.GetType("MyComponents.HelloWorld")

        ' Get the method to use from the type.
        PrintHello = MyHelloType.GetMethod("PrintHello")

        ' Create an instance of the type.
        MyObject = Activator.CreateInstance(MyHelloType)

        ' Create an array to hold the arguments.
        Dim args(0) As Object

        ' Set the arguments.
        args(0) = "Reflection Example."

        ' Invoke the method.
        PrintHello.Invoke(MyObject, args)
    End Sub
End Module
```

At this point, you have all the code you need, but the project isn't set up correctly to use the reflection example. To set up the project, follow these steps:

1. In Solution Explorer, right-click the project name (MyComponents) and select Properties.

2. On the Property dialog's General page, set the Output type as Windows Application and the Startup object as Sub Main (see Figure 11.4). Click OK.

3. From the Build menu, choose Build MyComponents to compile your project.

4. Run the program. The output appears in a message box, as shown in Figure 11.5.

FIGURE 11.4

Setting the MyComponents project as a Windows application.

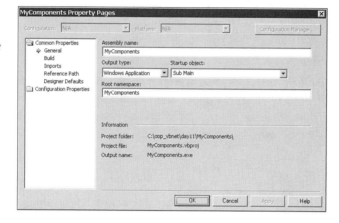

FIGURE 11.5

Output of the MyComponents project using reflection.

Note

To keep this example simple, you don't perform error checking. In production code, you should error check and make sure that you use exception handling to catch any errors that occur within the component to which you are late binding.

This example uses many of the reflection classes described previously. The first, `Assembly`, loads the `MyComponents` assembly. When the assembly is loaded, the `HelloWorld` type is located, and a reference to the type is kept for later use.

Now that the `HelloWorld` type is found, you can find the `PrintHello()` method you want to call. This example makes the assumption that the application already knows what method it's going to call and how many parameters it has. Therefore, an instance of the HelloWorld class is created, and the PrintHello() method is called with the Invoke() method and appropriate argument.

Summary

Today you learned how to create components and use reflection to work with unknown objects using late binding. Creating your own components allows you to reuse not only your own components but others as well. Creating components allows you to bundle objects into libraries that you can use in several applications and even share with other developers.

Late binding is useful in dynamic applications that need to use components based on runtime need. You can create entire applications that dynamically load installed features by using the reflection classes. Reflection allows you to easily deal with unknown class types and use them in your applications.

Q&A

Q Can I use components developed in other .NET languages?

A Yes. Components created with other .NET languages are compatible with Visual Basic .NET and can be used as though they were written in Visual Basic .NET.

Q Can I enumerate which assemblies are installed on a machine?

A Not directly, but you can search a directory or computer for all DLL files and determine whether they implement a .NET assembly. You then can get information about the assembly and its implemented types by using the reflection classes.

Workshop

The Workshop provides quiz questions and an exercise to help solidify your understanding of components and reflection and provide you with experience in using what you've learned. Answers are provided in Appendix A, "Answers to Quizzes."

Quiz

1. What does reflection allow an application to do?
2. What types of items are stored in a component?
3. Can a component be used at design time?
4. What reflection class retrieves information about an assembly?

Exercise

The goal of this exercise is to become familiar with using a component in your own Windows application. For this simple exercise, use the `DemoComp` component that you created today (in Listing 11.1) in a Windows application.

Add a form to the MyComponents project, being sure to change the application's properties to Windows Application with `Form1` as the startup object instead of `Sub Main`. (If you forget the preceding step, you'll invoke the `HelloWorld` module instead of your form.)

Place two buttons on the form: one to start the beep and the other to stop the beep and exit the application.

11

DAY **12**

Building Web Applications

Visual Studio .NET allows you to create Web-based applications with the .NET Framework and Visual Basic .NET. The types of Web-based applications can range from the traditional Web site with HTML pages, to fully featured business applications, to business-to-business applications that use XML to exchange information.

Today's lesson will cover how to use Visual Basic .NET and object-oriented techniques with ASP.NET to create Web pages and Web Services. Today you will learn how to do the following with Web applications and Visual Basic .NET:

- Create an ASP.NET application in Visual Basic .NET.
- Create multiple Web forms and handle generated events.
- Pass data from one Web Form to another.
- Create a Web Service and use it from a Web application.

Object-Oriented ASP.NET with Visual Basic .NET

Web applications written for ASP.NET are based on .NET Framework classes; therefore, object-oriented techniques are employed as they are with Windows applications and the .NET Framework. ASP.NET applications involve many of the same elements used in desktop applications, including the user interface, components, data, security, and project management.

Creating a Web Project

Creating an ASP.NET application in Visual Basic .NET is similar to creating desktop applications in Visual Basic .NET, except that you select the ASP.NET Web Application template for the project template. When the application is created, Visual Studio creates the files necessary on the Web server and locally, sets the security on the files, and creates the application. After the project is created, you use the same Solution Explorer to add new files and new objects to the project.

In Visual Studio for this first example, create a new ASP.NET Web project for Visual Basic .NET and name it MyWebSite, as shown in Figure 12.1.

FIGURE 12.1

Creating a new ASP.NET Web site in Visual Studio using Visual Basic .NET.

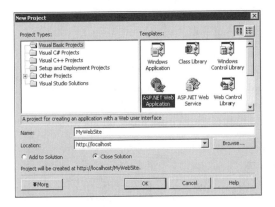

Creating a User Interface

The user interface of the Web site is created with HTML pages and Web Forms. By using HTML for the static information and Web Forms for the dynamic programmable interface, you get the best of both worlds when creating the Web site user interface.

Most sites have some sort of introduction page with a selection list of items that take you to different locations within the Web site. This type of page is best implemented with a typical HTML page. In the Solution Explorer, create a new HTML page, Welcome.htm, for your application by selecting Add and then Add HTML Page from the right-click menu.

Now, using the HTML controls, create a page that has the elements you want for the opening page of your site. After you add what you want on your welcome page, add a hyperlink control to send the users to the WebForm1.aspx file. Because the method for adding a hyperlink with the HTML Form designer isn't clear and entering it directly in the HTML editor is easier, edit the hyperlink by hand in the HTML editor. Listing 12.1 shows the HTML code for the HTML page shown in Figure 12.2.

LISTING 12.1   Welcome Page in HTML for MyWebSite

```
<!DOCTYPE HTML PUBLIC "-//W3C//DTD HTML 4.0 Transitional//EN">
<html>
<head>
  <title>Welcome</title>
  <script id="clientEventHandlersJS" language="javascript">
    <!—

    //—>
  </script>
</head>
<body>
  <DIV style="DISPLAY: inline; FONT-WEIGHT: bold;
      FONT-SIZE: large; Z-INDEX: 101; LEFT: 159px;
          WIDTH: 373px; COLOR: green; FONT-STYLE: italic;
          FONT-FAMILY: Arial; POSITION: absolute;
          TOP: 90px; HEIGHT: 19px; TEXT-ALIGN: center"
          ms_positioning="FlowLayout">
      Welcome to my Web Site
  </DIV>
  <DIV style="DISPLAY: inline; Z-INDEX: 102; LEFT: 292px;
      WIDTH: 104px; POSITION: absolute;
      TOP: 162px; HEIGHT: 20px" align="center"
      ms_positioning="FlowLayout">
      <a href="WebForm1.aspx">Enter my site</a>
  </DIV>
</body>
</html>
```

12

Now when users visit your Web site, they will see the welcome page. Up to this point, everything has basically been the same as a traditional Web site. After users view the WebForm1.aspx file, ASP.NET and object-oriented development will take over.

FIGURE 12.2

HTML welcome page for MyWebSite.

> **Note**
>
> This example uses the pubs database that comes loaded by default with Microsoft SQL Server. You can easily modify the source to make it work with other database types and databases.

You typically design a Web Form, as shown in Figure 12.3, for ASP.NET through a combination of using the form designer and the HTML editor. Some controls, such as the Repeater, simply require the HTML editor to design the control's layout.

To begin, drag OleDBConnection, OleDBDataAdapter, and OleDBCommand controls on the WebForm1 Web Form. You'll find the data controls on the Data tab of the Toolbox. If you don't want to use the wizards to configure your data connections, just cancel out and make the changes in the code as shown in the following listings.

You also need to drag a Repeater control to display a list of data from the database. Editing the code for the controls directly is easier than modifying them through the form designer, so select Code from the View menu to view the WebForm1.aspx.vb file.

First, notice that the WebForm1 class is nothing more than a Visual Basic .NET class. It inherits the System.Web.UI.Page class, which gives it the characteristics of a Web Form. The controls you added in the form designer are already added to the class. Make the appropriate name changes to the objects, as shown in Listing 12.2.

FIGURE 12.3

Completed WebForm1 *in the Web Form designer.*

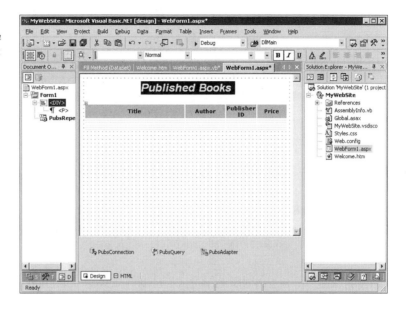

LISTING 12.2 WebForm1 Class with Newly Renamed Objects

```
Public Class WebForm1
    Inherits System.Web.UI.Page

    Protected WithEvents PubsAdapter As System.Data.OleDb.OleDbDataAdapter
    Protected WithEvents PubsQuery As System.Data.OleDb.OleDbCommand
    Protected WithEvents PubsRepeater As System.Web.UI.WebControls.Repeater
    Protected WithEvents PubsConnection As System.Data.OleDb.OleDbConnection

#Region " Web Form Designer Generated Code "

    'This call is required by the Web Form Designer.
    <System.Diagnostics.DebuggerStepThrough()> _
    Private Sub InitializeComponent()
        Me.PubsAdapter = New System.Data.OleDb.OleDbDataAdapter()
        Me.PubsQuery = New System.Data.OleDb.OleDbCommand()
        Me.PubsConnection = New System.Data.OleDb.OleDbConnection()
    End Sub

    Private Sub Page_Init _
      (ByVal sender As System.Object, ByVal e As System.EventArgs) _
      Handles MyBase.Init
        'CODEGEN: This method call is required by the Web Form Designer
        'Do not modify it using the code editor.
        InitializeComponent()
    End Sub
```

12

LISTING 12.2   continued

```
#End Region

    Private Sub Page_Init _
      (ByVal sender As System.Object, ByVal e As System.EventArgs) _
      Handles MyBase.Init
    End Sub

End Class
```

To connect to the database and build a query that will return results to display on the Web Form, you need to provide the initialization code for the OleDb objects. Listing 12.3 shows the additional code needed to initialize the connection, query, and data adapter. Again, you can assign these values through the Form designer and the object properties; however, for this example, entering the code is simpler.

LISTING 12.3   WebForm1 Object with Database Initialization Code

```
Public Class WebForm1
    Inherits System.Web.UI.Page

    Protected WithEvents PubsAdapter As System.Data.OleDb.OleDbDataAdapter
    Protected WithEvents PubsQuery As System.Data.OleDb.OleDbCommand
    Protected WithEvents PubsRepeater As System.Web.UI.WebControls.Repeater
    Protected WithEvents PubsConnection As System.Data.OleDb.OleDbConnection

#Region " Web Form Designer Generated Code "

    'This call is required by the Web Form Designer.
    <System.Diagnostics.DebuggerStepThrough()> _
      Private Sub InitializeComponent()
        Me.PubsAdapter = New System.Data.OleDb.OleDbDataAdapter()
        Me.PubsQuery = New System.Data.OleDb.OleDbCommand()
        Me.PubsConnection = New System.Data.OleDb.OleDbConnection()
        '
        'PubsAdapter
        '
    Me.PubsAdapter.SelectCommand = Me.PubsQuery
    Me.PubsAdapter.TableMappings.AddRange _
     (New System.Data.Common.DataTableMapping() _
     {New System.Data.Common.DataTableMapping("Table", "titleview", _
     New System.Data.Common.DataColumnMapping() _
     {New System.Data.Common.DataColumnMapping("title", "title"), _
     New System.Data.Common.DataColumnMapping("au_ord", "au_ord"), _
     New System.Data.Common.DataColumnMapping("au_lname", "au_lname"), _
     New System.Data.Common.DataColumnMapping("price", "price"), _
```

LISTING 12.3   continued

```
      New System.Data.Common.DataColumnMapping("ytd_sales", "ytd_sales"), _
      New System.Data.Common.DataColumnMapping("pub_id", "pub_id")}})
      '
      'PubsQuery
      '
      Me.PubsQuery.CommandText = "SELECT title, au_ord, au_lname, " & _
      "price, ytd_sales, pub_id FROM titleview"
      Me.PubsQuery.Connection = Me.PubsConnection
      '
      'PubsConnection
      '
      Me.PubsConnection.ConnectionString = _
        "Provider=SQLOLEDB.1;Persist Security Info=False;" & _
        "User ID=sa;Password=;" & _
        "Initial Catalog=pubs;Data Source=(local)"
   End Sub

   Private Sub Page_Init _
   (ByVal sender As System.Object, ByVal e As System.EventArgs) _
   Handles MyBase.Init
         'CODEGEN: This method call is required by the Web Form Designer
         'Do not modify it using the code editor.
         InitializeComponent()
   End Sub

#End Region

End Class
```

ANALYSIS   The PubsAdapter object is assigned the PubsQuery object, which ties the two objects together. The PubsAdapter object also is initialized with the table mappings for the table that will be queried, titleview. The PubsQuery object actually contains the SQL select statement to execute against the database. When the query is executed, the PubsAdapter object is used to map the results.

For the PubsQuery object to execute its select statement, it must know what connection to use. Therefore, the Connection property is assigned to the PubsConnection object. The PubsConnection.ConnectionString property is set to the connection string needed to connect to the database. You need to make sure that the login name and password reflect your SQL server. The actual connection isn't made until the object is used for the first time by the PubsQuery object.

The final step to getting the data into the Web Form is to bind it to the PubsRepeater control on WebForm1. This process is done when ASP.NET loads the WebForm1 object and

12

prepares it for display, which triggers the Load event defined by the System.Web.UI. Page class. Now add the Page_Load() subroutine as shown in Listing 12.4.

LISTING 12.4   Page_Load() Subroutine as It's Defined in the WebForm1 Class

```
Private Sub Page_Load _
  (ByVal sender As System.Object, ByVal e As System.EventArgs) _
  Handles MyBase.Load
    'Declare and initialize a DataSet
    Dim DS As DataSet = New DataSet()

    PubsAdapter.Fill(DS)

    'Bind PubsRepeater to the DataSet
    PubsRepeater.DataSource = DS.Tables("titleview").DefaultView
    PubsRepeater.DataBind()
End Sub
```

ANALYSIS   The Page_Load() subroutine creates a DataSet object, DS, and fills it with the PubsAdapter object. This causes the query to execute in PubsQuery, and all the returned records are stored in the DS DataSet object. The PubsRepeater.DataSource property is set to the appropriate view in the dataset and then told to bind itself. This causes PubsRepeater to iterate through all the returned records and render itself for display.

Switching out of object-oriented mode and going back to HTML mode, you now can define what the Web Form page will look like. The Repeater control requires you to use the HTML editor to define its layout. Switch to the Web Form designer and choose HTML Source from the View menu. The code for the form at this point has nothing more than a Repeater control with no display elements, as shown in Listing 12.5.

LISTING 12.5   WebForm1 with Repeater Control and No Visual Elements

```
<%@ Page Language="vb" AutoEventWireup="false"
  Codebehind="WebForm1.aspx.vb"
  Inherits="MyWebSite.WebForm1"%>
<!DOCTYPE HTML PUBLIC "-//W3C//DTD HTML 4.0 Transitional//EN">
<HTML>
    <HEAD>
        <title></title>
        <meta content="JavaScript" name="vs_defaultClientScript">
    </HEAD>
    <body MS_POSITIONING="GridLayout">
        <form id="Form1" method="post" runat="server">
            <asp:repeater id="PubsRepeater" runat="server">
```

LISTING 12.5 continued

```
                </asp:repeater>
            </form>
        </body>
</HTML>
```

ANALYSIS The Repeater control allows you to design a `HeaderTemplate`, `FooterTemplate`, and `ItemTemplate`. The `ItemTemplate` section is repeated for each record to which it's bound. The header and footer use standard HTML tags to define what they should look like. Listing 12.6 shows the visual definition for the Repeater control.

LISTING 12.6 WebForm1.aspx File with Repeater Content Included

```
<%@ Page Language="vb" AutoEventWireup="false"
 Codebehind="WebForm1.aspx.vb"
 Inherits="MyWebSite.WebForm1"%>
<!DOCTYPE HTML PUBLIC "-//W3C//DTD HTML 4.0 Transitional//EN">
<HTML>
    <HEAD>
        <title></title>
        <meta content="JavaScript" name="vs_defaultClientScript">
    </HEAD>

    <body MS_POSITIONING="GridLayout">
     <form id="Form1" method="post" runat="server">
        <asp:repeater id="PubsRepeater" runat="server">
          <HeaderTemplate>
            <table width="100%" style="font: 8pt verdana">
                <tr style="background-color:DFA894">
                    <th width="50%">
                        Title
                    </th>
                    <th width="20%">
                        Author
                    </th>
                    <th width="15%">
                        Publisher ID
                    </th>
                    <th width="15%">
                        Price
                    </th>
                </tr>
            </table>
          </HeaderTemplate>
          <ItemTemplate>
        <table width="100%" style="font: 8pt verdana">
          <tr style="background-color:FFECD8">
```

12

LISTING 12.6   continued

```
                <td width="50%">
                 <%# DataBinder.Eval(Container.DataItem, "title") %>
                </td>
                <td width="20%">
                  <%# DataBinder.Eval(Container.DataItem, "au_lname") %>
                </td>
                <td width="15%">
                  <%# DataBinder.Eval(Container.DataItem, "pub_id") %>
                </td>
                <td width="15%" align="right">
                  <%# DataBinder.Eval(Container.DataItem, "price", "$ {0}")%>
                  </td>
               </tr>
             </table>
          </ItemTemplate>
          <FooterTemplate></FooterTemplate>
      </asp:repeater>
    </form>
   </body>
  </HTML>
```

ANALYSIS For Listing 12.6, only header and item sections are defined with tables to define columns that float with the page when sized. The header's definition is straightforward; the item section uses a server-side object, DataBinder, which retrieves the results from each column. The column names must match the ones used with the PubsAdapter object created earlier.

One item added to the Web Form is a title. Other objects and visual items can also be placed on the Web page. The only limit is your creativity because HTML tags work as you would expect on a Web Form. Figure 12.4 shows the finished Web page.

FIGURE 12.4

WebForm1 displayed in a Web browser.

Published Books

Title	Author	Publisher ID	Price
The Busy Executive's Database Guide	Bennet	1389	$ 19.99
Fifty Years in Buckingham Palace Kitchens	Blotchet-Halls	0877	$ 11.95
But Is It User Friendly?	Carson	1389	$ 22.95
The Gourmet Microwave	DeFrance	0877	$ 2.99
Silicon Valley Gastronomic Treats	del Castillo	0877	$ 19.99
Secrets of Silicon Valley	Dull	1389	$ 20
The Busy Executive's Database Guide	Green	1389	$ 19.99
You Can Combat Computer Stress!	Green	0736	$ 2.99
Sushi, Anyone?	Gringlesby	0877	$ 14.99
Secrets of Silicon Valley	Hunter	1389	$ 20
Computer Phobic AND Non-Phobic Individuals: Behavior Variations	Karsen	0877	$ 21.59
Net Etiquette	Locksley	1389	
Emotional Security: A New Algorithm	Locksley	0736	$ 7.99
Cooking with Computers: Surreptitious Balance Sheets	MacFeather	1389	$ 11.95
Computer Phobic AND Non-Phobic Individuals: Behavior Variations	MacFeather	0877	$ 21.59
Cooking with Computers: Surreptitious Balance Sheets	O'Leary	1389	$ 11.95
Sushi, Anyone?	O'Leary	0877	$ 14.99

Understanding Web Services

Yesterday you learned about components and how to use them in other applications. In simple terms, a Web Service is a Web-based component that's called over a TCP/IP network by the applications instead of directly. Web Services are the same as components in that they perform a specific function, are modular, and facilitate code reuse.

The real difference between a component and a Web Service is that a Web Service is called over the Internet. Web Services are invoked using HTTP or SOAP requests and exchange data with XML. Because they are Web-based, they form an integral part of ASP.NET applications and provide services to any applications that have Web access. This feature makes Web Services ideal for business-to-business transactions.

Although the concept of exchanging data and logic isn't new, Web Services are unique in that they don't require tight integration with user applications. They require only that the user applications understand the messages they receive. Because these messages use common transports such as HTTP and a common format such as XML, Web Services are accessible to any applications running on any operating system as long as they understand and can work with these common technologies.

Creating a Web Service

Web Services are created using the ASP.NET environment, allowing them to access the .NET Framework's features the same as other components. The .NET Framework provides the infrastructure code to create Web Services. Therefore, developers don't have to spend time developing the groundwork; they can focus on building the solution.

Web Forms in ASP.NET have the .aspx file extension, and Web Services have the .asmx extension, which differentiates the two types of ASP.NET applications. Creating a Web Service exposes functionality to Web Service clients in the same way that building components exposes functionality to applications.

For this next example, the new Web Service will provide the current date and time in displayable format. Start by creating a new ASP.NET Web Service in Visual Basic .NET using the New Project dialog as you've done with previous projects. Name the Web Service MyWebService. Visual Studio will create the Web Service on the Web server and open the Web Service designer. It is the same designer that components use. Select the link on the designer to view the code.

The default code created for the Web Service doesn't supply a namespace, so the service falls under a default namespace. Placing the following declaration in front of the class declaration defines the namespace of the Web Service:

```
<WebService(Namespace:="http://www.server.com/webservices/")>
```

The Web Service in this example is simple in that it provides only a single interface to supply a string with the current date and time. You create this interface by declaring a DateTime() function within the service class, as shown in the following code segment:

```
<WebMethod()> Public Function DateTime() As String
    DateTime = Date.Now.ToString("M/dd/yyyy hh:mm:ss")
End Function
```

The <WebMethod()> declaration signifies that the method is for Web use and is available via the Web. With its method defined in the Service1 class, the Web Service is ready to be compiled and used.

Using a Web Service

As I stated earlier, you can use Web Services in any application or any operating system. Web Services are commonly used with Web sites to perform tasks such as validating credit card transactions.

In this example, use the ASP.NET application you created earlier. To use the new Web Service, you add a Web reference with the Solution Explorer by selecting Add Web Reference from the right-click menu. The Add Web Reference dialog appears (see Figure 12.5). Using this dialog, you can browse for external Web Services or Web Services on the local computer.

FIGURE 12.5

*The Add Web
Reference dialog.*

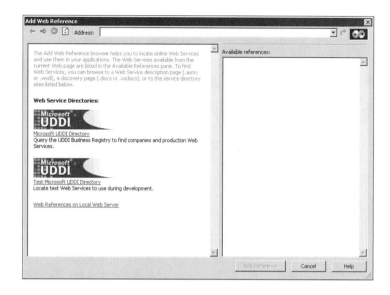

Because the Web Service you want to use for this example is on the local computer,
select the appropriate hyperlink to display all Web Services you have. Then select the
hyperlink that corresponds to MyWebService in the linked reference group list. Clicking
the Add Reference button adds the Web Service reference to your ASP.NET project,
which allows it to use the Web Service. The Solution Explorer now lists Web References
for localhost, as shown in Figure 12.6.

FIGURE 12.6

*The Solution Explorer
showing Web
References.*

To use the Web Reference to display the date and time on your Web Form, add a Label
control set to the result of the DateTime() method provided by the Service1 Web
Service. Listing 12.7 shows the code needed to add the Label control, DateTimeLabel, to

the Web Form, along with the corresponding changes to the WebForm1.aspx.vb file
shown in Listing 12.8.

LISTING 12.7   DateTimeLabel Control Added to the Web Form

```
<%@ Page Language="vb" AutoEventWireup="false"
 Codebehind="WebForm1.aspx.vb"
 Inherits="MyWebSite.WebForm1"%>
<!DOCTYPE HTML PUBLIC "-//W3C//DTD HTML 4.0 Transitional//EN">
<HTML>
    <HEAD>
        <title></title>
        <meta content="JavaScript" name="vs_defaultClientScript">
    </HEAD>
    <body>
        <form id="Form1" method="post" runat="server">
            <div align="right">
                <asp:Label id="DateTimeLabel" runat="server" Width="200px"
                           Height="19px">Label</asp:Label>
            </div>
    ...
```

LISTING 12.8   Additions to WebForm1.aspx.vb to Support the DateTimeLabel Control

```
Public Class WebForm1
    Inherits System.Web.UI.Page

    Protected WithEvents PubsAdapter As System.Data.OleDb.OleDbDataAdapter
    Protected WithEvents PubsQuery As System.Data.OleDb.OleDbCommand
    Protected WithEvents PubsRepeater As System.Web.UI.WebControls.Repeater
    Protected WithEvents PubsConnection As System.Data.OleDb.OleDbConnection

    Protected WithEvents DateTimeLabel As System.Web.UI.WebControls.Label

#Region " Web Form Designer Generated Code "

'This call is required by the Web Form Designer.
<System.Diagnostics.DebuggerStepThrough()> _
Private Sub InitializeComponent()
  Me.PubsAdapter = New System.Data.OleDb.OleDbDataAdapter()
  Me.PubsQuery = New System.Data.OleDb.OleDbCommand()
  Me.PubsConnection = New System.Data.OleDb.OleDbConnection()
  '
  'PubsAdapter
  '
  Me.PubsAdapter.SelectCommand = Me.PubsQuery
    Me.PubsAdapter.TableMappings.AddRange _
```

LISTING 12.8 continued

```
    (New System.Data.Common.DataTableMapping() _
    {New System.Data.Common.DataTableMapping("Table", "titleview", _
    New System.Data.Common.DataColumnMapping() _
    {New System.Data.Common.DataColumnMapping("title", "title"), _
    New System.Data.Common.DataColumnMapping("au_ord", "au_ord"), _
    New System.Data.Common.DataColumnMapping("au_lname", "au_lname"), _
    New System.Data.Common.DataColumnMapping("price", "price"), _
    New System.Data.Common.DataColumnMapping("ytd_sales", "ytd_sales"), _
    New System.Data.Common.DataColumnMapping("pub_id", "pub_id")})}) _
    '
    'PubsQuery
    '
    Me.PubsQuery.CommandText = "SELECT title, " & _
    " au_ord, au_lname, price, ytd_sales, pub_id FROM titleview"
Me.PubsQuery.Connection = Me.PubsConnection
    '
    'PubsConnection
    '
    Me.PubsConnection.ConnectionString = "Provider=SQLOLEDB.1;" & _
    "Persist Security Info=False; User ID=sa;Password=;" & _
    "Initial Catalog=pubs;Data Source=(local)"
    End Sub

    Private Sub Page_Init _
    (ByVal sender As System.Object, _
    ByVal e As System.EventArgs) Handles MyBase.Init
    InitializeComponent()
    End Sub

#End Region

    Private Sub Page_Load _
    (ByVal sender As System.Object, _
    ByVal e As System.EventArgs) Handles MyBase.Load
    'Declare and initialize a DataSet
    Dim DS As DataSet = New DataSet()

    PubsAdapter.Fill(DS)

    'Bind PubsRepeater to the DataSet
    PubsRepeater.DataSource = DS.Tables("titleview").DefaultView
    PubsRepeater.DataBind()

    'Retrieve the date and time from the Web Service
    Dim DateTimeService As New localhost.Service1()
    DateTimeLabel.Text = DateTimeService.DateTime()
    End Sub
End Class
```

12

Summary

Today you learned how to create ASP.NET applications and Web Services using Visual Basic .NET and object-oriented development. Although the visual side of ASP.NET development isn't much different from previous ASP development, the code behind it is strictly object-oriented, starting with the class that represents the Web Form.

You can use Web Services as components with your ASP.NET applications or from any other application. The platform or operating system the applications are running on doesn't matter because Web Services use standard protocols and data formats for communication.

By using ASP.NET and Visual Basic .NET together, you can create complex Web applications in far less time than was possible before Microsoft introduced .NET. By learning how to use object-oriented techniques in that development, you are even more efficient through code reuse, and the applications are more robust.

Q&A

Q Can all classes in the .NET Framework be used with ASP.NET?

A No. Many classes are specific to certain types of client applications. For example, Windows Forms classes don't have a purpose in ASP.NET applications.

Q Can I publish my Web Service someplace where other companies or individuals can use it?

A Yes. You can actually make your Web Service available to the public by allowing access to its Web address. Microsoft is working to build a method to list Web Services that you provide so that others can find your Web Services without knowing who you are. By allowing others to use your Web Services, you can provide an API to your company, which is what makes this feature so useful for business-to-business applications.

Workshop

The Workshop provides quiz questions and an exercise to help solidify your understanding of developing ASP.NET with Visual Basic .NET and provide you with experience in using what you've learned. Answers are provided in Appendix A, "Answers to Quizzes."

Quiz

1. How is a Web Service included into a .NET application?

2. When a Web Form is viewed within a Web browser, what renders the HTML file the user sees?

3. Can an ASP.NET application use standard HTML tags?

4. How are Web Reference objects referenced within your code?

Exercise

Add `CurrentTime()` and `CurrentDate()` methods to the `Service1` service in `MyWebService`. Return the results as a string as the `DateTime()` method did. (`DateTime()` was discussed in the section "Creating a Web Service.")

12

DAY 13

Deploying Visual Basic .NET Projects

Deploying traditional Windows applications presented developers with several issues. Deploying the applications could be very complex and involve checking for DLL conflicts and other software on the machine that could cause the application to fail. With applications written in the .NET Framework, you can install applications by simply copying the files to your machine. In fact, you might be able to install all the files with the Xcopy utility. You can easily uninstall by deleting the files from the machine. Also, conflicting DLLs aren't an issue with .NET applications, as you will learn today.

Does this mean that .NET applications don't have install programs? No, they still have install programs to make it easy to copy files to the machine. The install programs are just simpler and easier to develop.

Today's lesson will cover deploying your Visual Basic .NET projects and understanding how the .NET Framework accomplishes versioning to eliminate DLL conflicts. In working through today's lesson, you will learn the following:

- What an assembly is and how it works
- How to version with assemblies
- How to build an installer for a project
- How to deploy an ASP.NET application to a Web server

Understanding Assemblies

NEW TERM   Recall from Day 9, "Organizing Classes into Groups," that components in .NET are packaged in assemblies. Assemblies are fundamental units of deployment and are versionable, self-describing, and reusable. All assemblies describe themselves through the metadata of the assemblies. This metadata, known as the *manifest* for the assemblies, contains the information about what the assemblies include.

Assemblies can include multiple executable files, resource files, and DLLs. When this is the case, the manifest is typically a separate file; however, it can be included in one of the executable files. With the assembly manifest, the common language runtime (CLR) can locate and securely execute code.

A primary purpose of assemblies is to provide versioning information. This information provides a method for developers to specify version rules between different software components that are enforced at runtime. Because each assembly has a specific version number as part of its identity, you can specify that an application works only with that specific assembly version. Even if another assembly of the same name is installed on a computer, the application can find the correct version and use it. This feature is key to eliminating the DLL conflicts that plague traditional Windows applications.

Typically, a static assembly consists of a manifest, type information, Microsoft intermediate language (MSIL) code that implements the types, and a set of resources. Technically, only the manifest is required, however; the other information is needed for the assembly to have any functionality.

What Is Microsoft Intermediate Language (MSIL)?

MSIL is the intermediate language to which all .NET language compilers compile. When you write an application using Visual Basic .NET and then compile it, MSIL code is generated to represent the Visual Basic .NET code. MSIL code is a CPU-independent set of code that's easily compiled to native code. Before execution, the MSIL code is compiled with the just-in-time (JIT) compiler to machine-specific code.

The MSIL makes it possible for all .NET languages to share their code. Because all .NET language compilers create MSIL code, multiple .NET languages can be used together as native code. You can even write MSIL code directly or create your own custom .NET language. As long as the result is MSIL code, it will work with .NET and other .NET languages.

Assemblies can group elements as a single file, such as an executable file or DLL. Grouping an assembly into one file is the most common approach and produces a nice self-contained file. Alternatively, assembly elements can be spread out over several files. This capability is useful when you want to combine modules written in different languages and optimize downloading an application by placing the lesser-used types in a separate module that isn't downloaded until it's needed. The only glue that binds the separate files together is the assembly manifest.

The assembly manifest includes the assembly's name and version, a file table describing all the other files that make up the assembly, and an assembly reference that describes all the external dependencies for the assembly. The external references are typically DLL files and are created externally to the assembly that references them.

Using Assemblies

You use an assembly in Visual Basic .NET by adding a reference to the external assembly you want to use. After you add the reference, the `Imports` statement works with the different namespaces contained within the assembly.

When you reference an assembly, the exact assembly is added to your assembly's manifest with the version information you are using. By storing the exact information of the referenced assembly, your application can use the appropriate assembly when it executes and doesn't get confused by duplicate assembly names. Figure 13.1 shows in the Intermediate Language Disassembler (ILDASM) utility an external `MyWebApp` assembly as used in the project from Day 10.

FIGURE 13.1

Use the ILDASM utility to view assembly information.

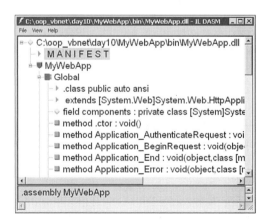

13

You run ILDASM from the command line and then navigate to the assembly that you want to explore. When you double-click a node, the utility displays detailed information about the assemblies, including their exact names and versions. Figure 13.2 shows an example of the information about assemblies.

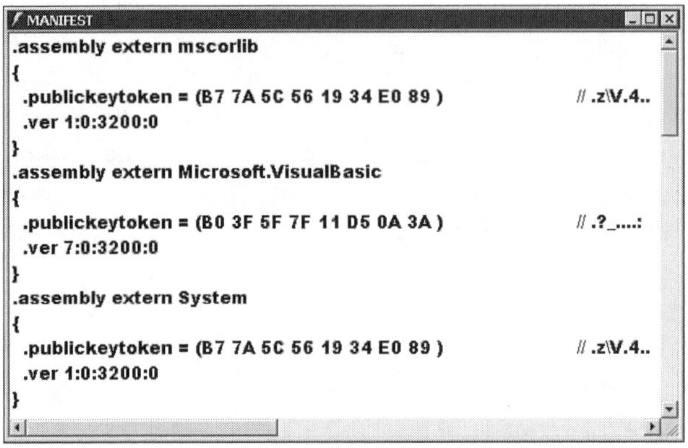

FIGURE 13.2

Double-click a node in the ILDASM utility to view assembly version details.

```
MANIFEST                                                              _ □ X
.assembly extern mscorlib
{
  .publickeytoken = (B7 7A 5C 56 19 34 E0 89 )              // .z\V.4..
  .ver 1:0:3200:0
}
.assembly extern Microsoft.VisualBasic
{
  .publickeytoken = (B0 3F 5F 7F 11 D5 0A 3A )              // .?_....:
  .ver 7:0:3200:0
}
.assembly extern System
{
  .publickeytoken = (B7 7A 5C 56 19 34 E0 89 )              // .z\V.4..
  .ver 1:0:3200:0
}
```

After an assembly is referenced in your application, all namespaces declared within the assembly, starting at the root namespace, are available to your assembly. By using the Imports keyword, you can import the namespaces you want to use the same as you would with the .NET Framework namespaces. At runtime, your assembly will find the referenced assembly and dynamically bind it for use.

Deploying Assemblies

Every time you compile your application project, whether it be a desktop application or Web application, the compiler deploys the assemblies to your local machine. When an application is finished, the best way to deploy assemblies is to use an installer that installs the assembly to the target machine or Web server.

The installer installs the assemblies to the appropriate location on the target machine and knows how to deal with the assemblies. This installer is based on Windows Installer 2.0, so the install programs created are up to standards and easy to create.

Local Assemblies

Applications are installed on local machines and typically copy the files to the local machines in the appropriate directories. The installer provides several customizations so that you can perform more advanced installations if necessary.

Successful deployment of a .NET Framework application requires an understanding of how the runtime locates referenced assemblies that make up your application. The default is to bind to the exact version of the assembly referenced by your application; however, you can override the default by changing the configuration settings.

When an application binds to an assembly at runtime, the first step in resolving the assembly is to determine the correct assembly version by examining configuration files. Then the system checks to see whether the assembly has been bound to before and uses that assembly if found. If the assembly hasn't been bound before, the Global Assembly Cache is checked for the assembly. If one is found, it is used. Finally, if an assembly isn't found, the system probes for the assembly by checking for a codebase declaration in the configuration file, the application root directory, and any subdirectories of the application root directory.

If the assembly is still not located after all the searching and probing, the application fails because it can't find the required assembly.

Defining a codebase

The best way to ensure that your application will find the correct assembly is to specifically indicate the codebase in the configuration file. For applications, this file isn't a default item within your project. Therefore, use the Solution Explorer to add the configuration file item by choosing Add and then Add New Item from the Context menu and select the Application Configuration File type. This action creates an app.config file in your project.

Listing 13.1 shows how to define a codebase value in the app.config file.

LISTING 13.1   Configuration File with codebase Declaration

```
<?xml version="1.0" encoding="utf-8" ?>
<configuration>
 <runtime>
  <assemblyBinding xmlns="urn:schemas-microsoft-com:asm.v1">
   <dependentAssembly>
   <assemblyIdentity name="MyComponents" culture="en-us" />
   <codeBase version="1.0.*" href="file:///d:/Components/MyComponents.dll" />
   </dependentAssembly>
   </assemblyBinding>
 </runtime>
</configuration>
```

13

Understanding the Global Assembly Cache

If an assembly is shared by two or more applications, it should be installed in the Global Assembly Cache (GAC). This area on the local machine is the place where all shared assemblies are installed and the first place an application searches for assemblies.

 NEW TERM Any assembly stored in the Global Assembly Cache must have a *strong name* assembly. The strong name is an ID that consists of the information that uniquely identifies that assembly, such as name, version, culture, and any public key or digital signature.

When you want to deploy assemblies to the global cache, it's best to use Windows Installer 2.0. Use the application installer with Visual Studio .NET to take care of installing the files to the appropriate locations. The only downside to installing global assemblies is that users must have administrator privileges on the computer. This could be a positive feature also, depending on your situation.

The .NET Framework SDK provides a utility, the Global Assembly Cache tool (GACUTIL.EXE), that you can use to work with the Global Assembly Cache. The SDK also provides an Assembly Cache Viewer (SHFUSION.DLL), which works with Windows Explorer to allow you to view the Global Assembly Cache (see Figure 13.3).

FIGURE 13.3

The Assembly Cache Viewer in Windows Explorer.

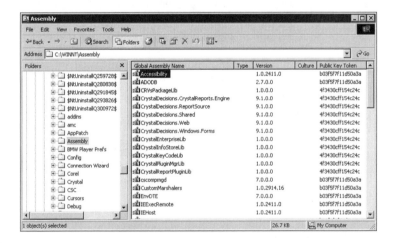

> **Tip**
>
> You can install and uninstall assemblies in the global cache by simply dragging items to and from the Global Assembly Cache. Although using an installer is preferred, this method works well for your own machine.

Web Assemblies

As with client .NET assemblies, Web .NET assemblies are deployed whenever you compile your projects with Visual Studio .NET. When you're deploying to another server, the .NET Web assemblies can be copied to the new server. Because everything is URL based, you don't have to configure any Registry settings or other settings outside the files that you copy.

An ASP.NET project generally has a web.config file to configure the assembly settings, including the `codebase` of referenced assemblies. The configuration file allows you to configure session state information, security, debug settings, and so on. Because the web.config file is text and not compiled into the assembly, you configure customization information for each site by editing this file when it's deployed to other Web servers.

You create a new installer for a Web assembly by adding a new project to a solution that contains the Web assembly or assemblies to deploy. Follow these steps:

1. Open the `MyWebSite` project you previously created.

2. In Solution Explorer, select the solution name, right-click, and then select Add and then New Project.

3. From the Project Types list on the left, select Setup and Deployment Projects. From the Templates list on the right, click Web Setup Project. Finally, name your project `MyWebSetup`, as shown in Figure 13.4.

FIGURE 13.4

Adding a Web setup project to your solution.

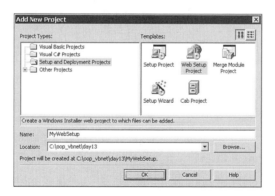

4. Click OK. The new project is added to your environment, as shown in Figure 13.5.

5. Right-click the MyWebSetup project name and select Properties.

6. Configure the setup project to package the files in the setup file, use the Windows Installer Bootstrapper, and use a compression system optimized for size, as shown in Figure 13.6. Click OK.

13

FIGURE 13.5

A Web setup project uses a split window for configuration.

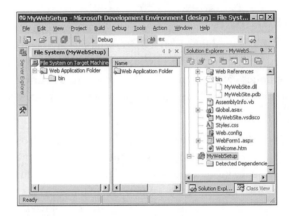

FIGURE 13.6

Configuring the Web setup project to use the Windows Installer.

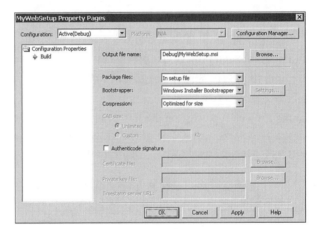

7. From the Build menu, click Build Configuration and make sure that the MyWebSetup project is checked in the Build column (see Figure 13.7). Click Close when you're done.

8. In the File System editor (see Figure 13.8), right-click the Web Application Folder node and select Add and then Project Output.

9. In the Add Project Output Group dialog, Ctrl+click to select Primary Output and Content Files (see Figure 13.9). Click OK.

FIGURE 13.7

Ensure that the Web Setup Project is included in the Build.

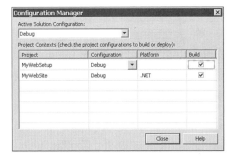

FIGURE 13.8

Selecting the Web Application Folder in the Web setup project.

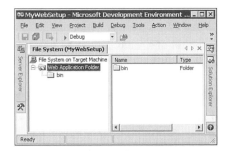

FIGURE 13.9

Including the output and content files in the Web setup project.

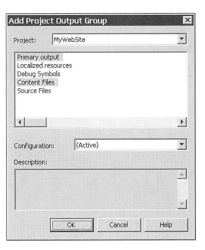

13

10. From the Build menu, choose Rebuild Solution. The rebuild process can take a few minutes. Watch the Output window for progress.

At the end of the build, your directory should include all the files necessary for setup on another computer. Figure 13.10 shows a sample of the built files as they appear in Windows Explorer.

FIGURE 13.10

The Web setup project builds all the files required to replicate the site on another server.

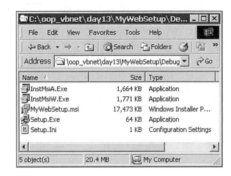

To deploy a Web application to a Web server, copy the installation files to a temporary directory on the Web server and run the setup. Figure 13.11 shows a startup screen from the installer you've created.

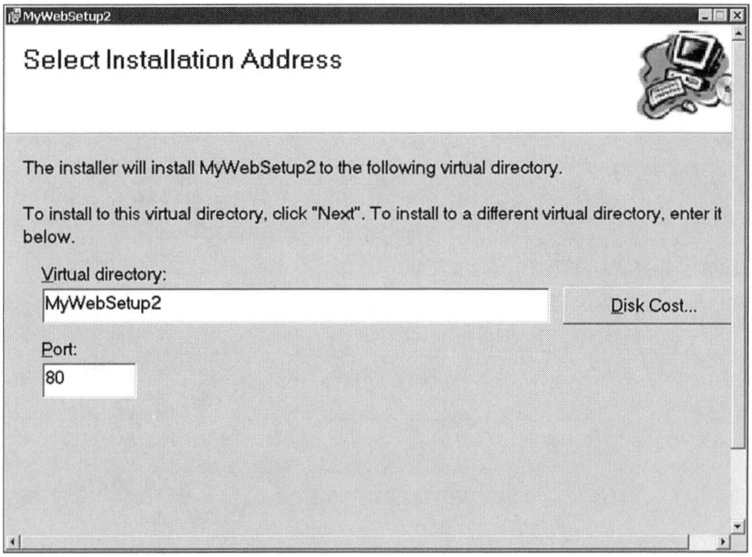

FIGURE 13.11

A sample installation screen created by the Web Setup project.

Summary

NEW TERM Today you learned how Visual Basic .NET and the .NET Framework have built-in mechanisms that prevent version conflicts among components, also known as *DLL hell*. The section on versions and assemblies explained how assemblies are self-documenting through the inclusion of a manifest and metadata. By using the ILDASM utility, you can investigate the manifest. You saw how easily you can deploy a Visual Basic .NET project by simply copying the files and subdirectories to the target machine. For a more sophisticated and user-friendly setup, you created a Web setup project that generates a full-scale installer with all the executables and required components.

Q&A

Q Can I use assemblies remotely from another Web server? If so, how does my application find them?

A By using the `codebase` declaration, you can specify the exact URL where an assembly resides. The URL can point to a DLL file or a Web service, depending on the type of assembly you are referencing.

Q What happens if an assembly isn't available when my application needs it?

A The answer depends on how your application binds to the component. If the component is bound at compile time, the application won't execute at all because it can't find the assembly it needs to load. If the assembly was late bound, the application will load and work correctly until the assembly is required and can't be found. The application, if handling errors correctly, should gracefully display a message that an assembly couldn't be found and then continue executing without it if possible.

Workshop

The Workshop provides quiz questions and an exercise to help solidify your understanding of deploying assemblies and provide you with experience in using what you've learned. Answers are provided in Appendix A, "Answers to Quizzes."

Quiz

1. What do all assemblies have?
2. What is the recommended way to deploy assemblies?

Exercise

Create a setup kit for the `MyFormApp` that installs the `MyFormApp` assembly. Use the Setup Projects Template. Compile, build, and test the installer.

13

DAY 14

Working with Object Interfaces

Interfaces available in previous versions of Visual Basic provided polymorphic characteristics within Visual Basic. Now Visual Basic .NET has inheritance to provide polymorphism in addition to interfaces. Using interfaces or inheritance is a decision that you have to make based on your specific requirements. Inheritance is generally used when baseline functionality is established in a base class, which you can extend through other classes. Interfaces are best used in situations in which similar functionality is needed with different implementations in several classes that have little in common.

Today's lesson covers the role of Visual Basic .NET interfaces and how to best use them in .NET applications. Because you are already somewhat familiar with interfaces from previous lessons, this lesson focuses on how to decide when to use them and how to work with the interfaces. Today you will learn how to

- Define an interface.
- Derive interfaces from other interfaces.
- Implement interfaces within class definitions.
- Know when it's best to use interfaces.
- Use interfaces for callbacks.

Revisiting Interfaces and OOP

Interfaces are like classes in that they define a set of properties, methods, and events. Interfaces and classes vary in that interfaces don't provide an implementation; however, classes provide the implementation for interfaces when they implement them.

Interfaces have an added advantage: They allow systems to be built with software components described by interfaces in which the underlying implementation can change without breaking the existing code. In fact, whole classes can change and, as long as they still implement an interface, can be used as though they were never changed, thus making your code future proof.

Multiple Inheritance

You can inherit interfaces from other interfaces and build a completely object-oriented interface design that's then implemented by classes. With interfaces, you also can inherit from more than one other interface. This feature isn't available to classes and is sometimes desirable in object-oriented development.

For example, a combo box consists of a text box and a list box. Implementing a combo box with classes requires you to use composition, as you learned in Day 6, "Building Complex Objects by Combining Objects," because you can't derive a combo box from both a text box and a list box. With interfaces, you could define a combo box as in Listing 14.1.

LISTING 14.1 Sample Interfaces for a Combo Box Control

```
Interface IUIControl
    Sub Paint()
End Interface

Interface ITextBox
    Inherits IUIControl

    Sub SetText( value As String )
End Interface
```

LISTING 14.1   continued

```
Interface IListBox
    Inherits IUIControl

    Sub SetItems( items() As String )
End Interface

Interface IComboBox
    Inherits ITextBox, IListBox
End Interface
```

Interfaces inherit all members of their base interfaces. Therefore, both the `ITextBox` and `IListBox` interfaces have a `Paint()` subroutine. The `IComboBox` interface has the `SetText()`, `SetItems()`, and `Paint()` subroutines. Although the `Paint()` subroutine is brought in from both base interfaces, the `IComboBox` interface has only one `Paint()` implemented by the class.

Polymorphism Through Interfaces

Interfaces provide another way to accomplish polymorphism in Visual Basic .NET. Polymorphism is actually an inherent feature of interfaces because they provide no implementation. Therefore, each class that implements the interface will have a different implementation and thus polymorphic characteristics.

An example of polymorphism is to define several classes that all implement the same interface. By using the interface instead of the classes for parameter types and calling the interface methods implemented by the classes, you can see how interfaces foster polymorphism. Listing 14.2 shows how to use interfaces with a series of shape objects.

LISTING 14.2   Polymorphism with Interfaces

```
Public Interface Shape
    Function IsPtInShape(ByVal Pt As System.Drawing.Point) As Boolean
End Interface

Public Class Rectangle
    Implements Shape

    Private rect As Drawing.Rectangle

    Public Function PtInRect(ByVal Pt As System.Drawing.Point) As Boolean _
        Implements Shape.IsPtInShape
        PtInRect = Pt.Equals(rect)
    End Function
End Class
```

14

LISTING 14.2   continued

```
Public Class Circle
    Implements Shape

    Private rgn As Drawing.Region

    Public Function PtInCircle(ByVal Pt As System.Drawing.Point) As Boolean _
        Implements Shape.IsPtInShape
        PtInCircle = Pt.Equals(rgn)
    End Function
End Class

Sub CheckPoint(ByVal ShapeObject As Shape, ByVal Pt As System.Drawing.Point)
    If (ShapeObject.IsPtInShape(Pt)) Then
        Beep()
    End If
End Sub

Sub Test()
    Dim Pt As System.Drawing.Point
    Dim RectObject As Rectangle
    Dim CircleObject As Circle

    CheckPoint(RectObject, Pt)
    CheckPoint(CircleObject, Pt)
End Sub
```

ANALYSIS   Notice how the CheckPoint() subroutine takes a Shape as the parameter and then uses the interface's method. In turn, the method that implemented the interface function is actually called, which varies for each object type. You can name the class method whatever you like and implement it in whatever way necessary as long as the parameters are the same. This way, a class can implement an interface and have meaningful names within the class. You could also substitute any object that implements the Shape interface as a parameter to the CheckPoint() subroutine.

Creating the Interface Contract

Interfaces represent a contract with a class. A class agrees to the contract by saying it will implement an interface with the Implements keyword. After the class agrees to implement an interface, it's bound by that contract to implement the entire interface. The class can't implement a piece of the interface and fulfill the contract. Therefore, if a class implements an interface, the class's user is assured that it can use any method defined within the interface because it must have an implementation.

The flip side is that a class can fulfill the contract agreement by providing any method, even one that doesn't do anything, that implements an interface method. The only requirement is that the method's parameters and the return value (if it's a function) match the interface. Everything else is up to the class to decide how the interface is implemented. This is actually a benefit of using interfaces; the class can decide what's an appropriate implementation for its particular design.

Implementing interfaces within classes is fairly straightforward; however, be careful to implement all the methods, properties, and events that an interface defines. Remember that if an interface is derived from another interface, a class must implement whatever the base interface or interfaces define. The class example in Listing 14.3 implements three different interfaces.

LISTING 14.3 Implementing Several Interfaces Within a Class and Using the Class Object as Each Implemented Interface

```
Public Interface IEmployee
    Function GetSalary() As Decimal
End Interface

Public Interface IParent
    Function HasChildren() As Boolean
End Interface

Public Interface IFriend
    Function NumberOfFriends() As Integer
End Interface

Public Class Person
    Implements IEmployee
    Implements IParent
    Implements IFriend

    Private m_dSalary As Decimal
    Private m_bChildren As Boolean
    Private m_nFriends As Integer

    Public Function Salary() As Decimal Implements IEmployee.GetSalary
        Salary = m_dSalary
    End Function

    Public Function HasChildren() As Boolean Implements IParent.HasChildren
        HasChildren = m_bChildren
    End Function
```

14

LISTING 14.3 continued

```
    Public Function HowManyFriends() _
    As Integer Implements IFriend.NumberOfFriends
        HowManyFriends = m_nFriends
    End Function
End Class

Module PersonUser
    Sub CheckSalary(ByVal Employee As IEmployee)
        ' Code here.. Only GetSalary() is usable for this object
    End Sub

    Sub CheckFamily(ByVal Parent As IParent)
        ' Code here.. Only HasChildren() is usable for this object
    End Sub

    Sub CheckFriends(ByVal MyFriend As IFriend)
        ' Code here.. Only NumberOfFriends() is usable for this object
    End Sub

    Sub TestPerson()
        Dim Person As Person = New Person()

        CheckSalary(Person)
        CheckFamily(Person)
        CheckFriends(Person)
    End Sub
End Module
```

For the Person class definition to be complete, it has to provide implementations for each method defined in the IEmployee, IParent, and IFriend interfaces. Also, the Person class can define its own characteristics; however, those methods, properties, and events aren't available for use when the class is being used via one of its interfaces.

In any of the three interfaces shown in the TestPerson() subroutine, you can use the Person class. This capability is useful when you're designing applications that have several unrelated or loosely related classes that you need to use interchangeably. When using interface types as parameters, users can see only the methods, properties, events, and so on defined by the interface. The rest of the implementation within the class isn't visible to users of the interface.

Programming for Interfaces

Up to this point, you have seen some examples of how interfaces work and how to use them in object-oriented programming. Programming for interfaces can be somewhat different from programming with classes alone.

The first apparent issue when designing the interfaces that you will later implement is that interface methods don't have scope. All methods are visible and available for use by the public. For example, with classes, you can define a method to be available to the public, protected, or private to the class. Interfaces don't have this capability. Any method you declare within an interface is available to the public as though you declare the method public. Even if the implementing class implements a method as `Private`, when a user uses the interface, the method is still available as though it were `Public`.

Having all methods within an interface declared as public makes sense if you think about why you define interfaces in the first place. Interfaces are defined to describe a common interface that can be used. If something is defined as private, why would that be in an interface? Such a method would have no practical purpose other than to force a class to implement a private method that could be used only by the class itself.

A second issue—which may at first seem like a problem but really isn't—is that interfaces don't define member data items. An interface's purpose is to define only a public interface of methods, events, and properties. Again, because the interface has no implementation, it has no purpose defining member data. Any access to data should be done through an interface's methods and properties.

The final issue covered in this lesson and a somewhat frustrating issue that you will face when designing interfaces occurs when two interfaces contain the same method. When both interfaces are inherited into a new interface, the interface's user is forced to specify which method to call. Listing 14.4 shows an example of this issue.

LISTING 14.4   Interface Method Name Collision and Using `CType()` to Indicate Proper Usage

```
Public Interface IArray
    Function Count() As Integer
End Interface

Public Interface ICounter
    Function Count() As Integer
End Interface

Public Interface ICountArray
    Inherits IArray
    Inherits ICounter
End Interface

Module CountArrayTest
    Sub Test(ByVal x As ICountArray)
        Dim nCount = CType(x, ICounter).Count()
        Dim nArrayCount = CType(x, IArray).Count()
```

14

LISTING 14.4   continued

```
          'Other code..
        End Sub
    End Module
```

ANALYSIS   In Listing 14.4, the CType() function converts the expression specified in the first argument (in this case, x) to the type named in the second argument. Therefore, when the code executes, the desired interface is selected, and the correct Count method is used.

Earlier you learned that if the same method is included within an interface from the same base interface, it's implemented only once and therefore doesn't have the problem illustrated in Listing 14.4.

Implementing Interfaces

Because interfaces don't contain an implementation, they must be implemented to provide functionality for the methods, events, and properties within the interface before they can be used. Interfaces are implemented either by a class or structure definition with the Implements keyword.

As you've learned so far, a class can implement one or more interfaces. Structures have the same capability to implement one or more interfaces. The following code segment shows how a structure implements interfaces in a similar manner as classes:

```
Structure MyStructure
    Implements IMyInterface

    Public Function InterfaceFunction() _
    As Integer Implements IMyInterface.MyFunction
    End Function
End Structure
```

As I stated earlier, interfaces can declare methods (subroutines and functions), events, and properties. Also, remember that interfaces can't declare member data.

Methods

To implement an interface method within a class or structure, you declare the method within the class or structure by using the Implements keyword and assigning the interface method to implement. The only requirement to implement a method is that the class or structure method must have the same parameters and return value as the declared interface method.

You also can implement multiple interface methods with a single class or structure method, as long as the parameters and return types match. For example, the following code shows how to implement the two Count() methods defined in Listing 14.4 with a single function:

```
Public Function Count() As Integer Implements IArray.Count(), ICounter.Count()
   Count = m_nCount
End Function
```

By implementing multiple interface methods with the same class or structure method, you can tie multiple interface methods to the same functionality without writing extra code.

Properties

Implementing interface properties is similar to implementing methods in that the class or structure declares a property and assigns it to the interface property with the Implements keyword. The property that implements the interface property must be the same type as the interface property and have the same read/write modifiers. Listing 14.5 shows the implementation of an interface property.

LISTING 14.5   Implementation of an Interface Property

```
Public Interface ICompany
   Property Name() As String
End Interface

Public Class Business
   Implements ICompany

   Dim m_sCompanyName As String

   Public Property CompanyName() As String Implements ICompany.Name
   Get
      CompanyName = m_sCompanyName
   End Get
   Set(ByVal Value As String)
      m_sCompanyName = Value
   End Set
   End Property

End Class
```

14

If the property is declared as ReadOnly or WriteOnly in the interface, the implementing class or structure must also implement the property with ReadOnly or WriteOnly.

Events

As with methods and properties, events are implemented within a class or structure with the Implements keyword. As you recall from Day 2, "Learning to Speak OOP," events in class definitions don't have code associated with them in the class. As a result, the Implements keyword literally ties the interface event to the class or structure event. Listing 14.6 shows how to implement and use an event through an interface.

LISTING 14.6   Implementation and Usage of Interface Events

```
Public Interface ICompany
    Property Name() As String
    Event NameChanged()
End Interface

Public Class Business
    Implements ICompany

    Dim m_sCompanyName As String

    Public Property CompanyName() As String Implements ICompany.Name
    Get
        CompanyName = m_sCompanyName
    End Get
    Set(ByVal Value As String)
        m_sCompanyName = Value

        'Signal event now that the name has changed
        RaiseEvent NameChanged()
    End Set
    End Property

    Public Event NameChanged() Implements ICompany.NameChanged

End Class

Module CompanyTest
    Sub OnNameChanged()
        Beep()
    End Sub

    Sub Test(ByVal Company As ICompany)
        'Add handler for interface event NameChanged
        AddHandler Company.NameChanged, AddressOf OnNameChanged

        'This will cause the event to be signaled
        Company.Name = "My Company"
    End Sub
End Module
```

Using Interfaces as Callbacks

Interfaces provide many advantages if used properly. They allow you to develop an interface that's free of problems encountered when changing the underlying code. They also provide flexibility in implementation.

Another use for interfaces is as callback definitions. For example, if several object types implement the same interface, the interface could be used as a callback method when a single callback method isn't sufficient. Using interfaces allows the callback to contain several methods, properties, and events. Listing 14.7 shows how to use an interface defined for use as a callback. Whenever this interface is implemented, the object that implements the interface has a known interface for calling back into the object. Instead of a single function or subroutine, the callback is the entire interface.

LISTING 14.7   Callback Interface Declaration for a User Interface Control

```
Public Interface IUIControl
    Sub Paint()
    Sub ControlPressed()
    Function IsPtInControl(ByVal Pt As Drawing.Point) As Boolean
    Property ControlRect() As Drawing.Rectangle
    Event ControlHit()
End Interface
```

Implementing the IUIControl interface with different classes provides a common interface to use when you're working with user interface controls. Listing 14.8 shows a simple implementation for a push button and radio control.

LISTING 14.8   Implementation of the IUIControl Interface in PushButton and RadioButton Classes

```
Public Class PushButton
    Implements IUIControl

    Dim m_rcRect As Drawing.Rectangle

    'Interface implementation
    '......................
    Public Sub Paint() Implements IUIControl.Paint
        ' Paint the control
    End Sub

    Public Function IsPtInControl(ByVal Pt As Drawing.Point) _
        As Boolean Implements IUIControl.IsPtInControl
```

14

LISTING **14.8**   continued

```vbnet
         IsPtInControl = Pt.Equals(ControlRect())
      End Function

   Public Property ControlRect() As Drawing.Rectangle _
     Implements IUIControl.ControlRect
     Get
        ControlRect = m_rcRect
     End Get
     Set(ByVal Value As Drawing.Rectangle)
        m_rcRect = Value
     End Set
     End Property

     Public Sub ControlPressed() Implements IUIControl.ControlPressed
        RaiseEvent ControlHit()
     End Sub

     Public Event ControlHit() Implements IUIControl.ControlHit

     'Other class specific code
     '.......................

End Class

Public Class RadioButton
   Implements IUIControl

   Dim m_rcRect As Drawing.Rectangle

   'Interface implementation
   '.......................
   Public Sub Paint() Implements IUIControl.Paint
      ' Paint the control
   End Sub

   Public Function IsPtInControl(ByVal Pt As Drawing.Point) _
   As Boolean Implements IUIControl.IsPtInControl
      IsPtInControl = Pt.Equals(ControlRect())
   End Function

   Public Property ControlRect() As Drawing.Rectangle _
   Implements IUIControl.ControlRect
   Get
      ControlRect = m_rcRect
   End Get
   Set(ByVal Value As Drawing.Rectangle)
      m_rcRect = Value
   End Set
```

LISTING 14.8   continued

```
    End Property

    Public Sub ControlPressed() Implements IUIControl.ControlPressed
        RaiseEvent ControlHit()
    End Sub

    Public Event ControlHit() Implements IUIControl.ControlHit

    'Other class specific code
    '......................

End Class
```

The implementation for the IUIControl interface depends on the control, and each control can have its own implementation. Using the controls is now simplified because users deal only with the interface when needing to call back into the control, as shown in Listing 14.9.

LISTING 14.9   Using the IUIControl Interface for Calling Back into the Classes When an Event Occurs

```
Public Class MyForm
      Inherits System.Windows.Forms.Form

   Dim UIControls(2) As Object

  Public Sub OnMouseClick(ByVal sender As Object, _
   ByVal e As EventArgs) Handles MyBase.Click
       Dim i As Integer

    For i = 0 To 2
      If CType(UIControls(i), IUIControl).IsPtInControl(MousePosition()) Then
         CType(UIControls(i), IUIControl).ControlPressed()
         CType(UIControls(i), IUIControl).Paint()
      End If
    Next
  End Sub
End Class
```

Also, you can interfaces to deal with asynchronous callbacks for network communications, file I/O, or any other situation in which a complex callback is needed.

14

Summary

Today you learned how to use interfaces as part of your object-oriented programming in Visual Basic .NET. You learned that interfaces have certain advantages over classes, such as multiple inheritance and flexibility in the implementation of the interface. You also learned that interfaces are polymorphic by nature because each class or structure that implements an interface has a different implementation. Classes and structures can implement more than a single interface, which gives the class or structure multiple uses in an application.

Q&A

Q Why user interfaces at all? Can't I do everything with classes that I do with interfaces now that classes support inheritance and polymorphism in Visual Basic .NET?

A It's true that interfaces aren't used as often as they may have been in previous versions of Visual Basic, where inheritance and polymorphism weren't available in classes. However, interfaces still have an advantage over classes in that they can define generic interfaces that unrelated objects can implement, provide multiple inheritance, and future-proof components by providing a common interface that frees up the underlying implementation.

Q Are interfaces in .NET the same as they were before? In other words, are they usable outside the application and exportable?

A Yes. The interfaces are essentially the same in Visual Basic .NET as they were in previous versions of Visual Basic. The .NET Framework hides much of the implementation details on the interface, but in reality it still has an interface identity (based on a GUID) and data is still marshaled when passed to an interface.

Workshop

The Workshop provides quiz questions and an exercise to help solidify your understanding of interfaces and provide you with experience in using what you've learned. Answers are provided in Appendix A, "Answers to Quizzes."

Quiz

1. What keyword declares an interface?
2. What keyword ties a method, event, or property to an interface?
3. Can a class selectively implement parts of an interface?

4. How many interfaces can a class implement?

5. What type other than a class can implement an interface?

Exercise

Design an `IError` interface that has a method for displaying an error message named `DisplayError()`. Then declare a class, `MyClass`, that implements the `IError` interface and displays the error message passed as a parameter to the `DisplayError()` method.

14

WEEK 2

In Review

You might find it hard to believe, but you are two-thirds of the way through the book and making great progress. Let's look at some of the accomplishments and issues from your second week.

In addition to having a good grasp of the data types in the common language runtime (CLR), you now can manipulate arrays and collections. After completing Day 9, you now realize why Microsoft had no choice but to organize the myriad .NET Framework classes into namespaces. As you look through the online documentation that ships with Visual Studio .NET, you can see the rich, impressive, and mind-boggling range of classes available to you. Even when the classes are grouped into namespaces, pinpointing the .NET class that does exactly what you want may take awhile. When you're not sure, try using an index keyword that relates to the task. For example, type **file** to speed your way toward the list of file-access functions.

Part of the enjoyment of programming is developing a graphical user interface (GUI) that's intuitive, visually appealing, and functional. During the past week, you had a chance to practice this task by building Windows Forms and Web pages. With Visual Basic .NET's drag-and-drop capabilities and features such as IntelliSense and code completion, you've seen how it can really make page design a pleasure.

Near the end of the week, you had a chance to create a deployment project and explore various configuration options. The goal of deployment is to make the software install and run as well on the end user's computer as it does on your development machine. That's not always an easy task because the computing environment out in the real world often doesn't resemble your lab.

You've seen how to create interfaces to components. Interfaces are intriguing because there's an implicit rule that you must not do anything that breaks an existing consumer's application. You can always change the way you you implement the logic inside your component. After you publish a function's parameters and return types, however, you can't change it. Of course, nothing prevents you from allowing overrides for flexibility.

WEEK 3

At a Glance

Here you are in the home stretch toward your goal of learning object-oriented programming in 21 days. The upcoming week will polish your skills in Visual Basic .NET programming and then put those skills to the test in a real project.

Day 15, "Handling Events, Messages, and Notifications," explores how programs in the Windows environments react to events. As you'll see, events are generated from many sources, including user interactions, changes to a value, and updates to the file system. You'll learn about delegates and asynchronous operations. This lesson features some very useful code for monitoring changes to a file directory.

On Day 16, "Gracefully Capturing Errors," you'll encounter the `Try...Catch...Finally` statements that are new to this version of Visual Basic. This lesson takes you through structured exception handling, which is a technique for ensuring that your program behaves properly even when it encounters an error or unexpected situation. As you'll see, the .NET Framework has a wide range of `Exception` classes that let you pinpoint what went wrong so that your code can cope with it.

The whole area of remoting is tackled on Day 17, "Developing and Using Remote Objects." This is a fascinating and valuable lesson in the age of the Internet. You'll see that in your local program you can employ objects that are found wherever you can make a TCP connection. The hands-on portion of this lesson will walk you through the creation of a program that acts as a remote object's server. Then you'll build a client that uses this powerful technology.

On Day 18, "Designing a Project Management Application," you'll design a real-world program that starts to put into practice the object-oriented theory that you have acquired since Day 1. In this architectural lesson, you'll analyze what has to be done to solve a business problem. Then you'll create the diagrams that you or another developer will use to build the objects that go into the application.

Days 19, 20, and 21 convert the Day 18 plan into code. On each of these days, you'll build and walk through the code that reflects the classes you've designed. All the key elements of object-oriented programming will be employed and demonstrated in this practical project management application.

This week will be challenging and exciting. Finally—the theory and the practice unite to create a concrete product!

DAY **15**

Handling Events, Messages, and Notifications

Windows applications aren't the typical top-down applications of old, where an application started at the top and finished executing when it got to the bottom. Those applications were linear in their execution path and weren't event driven. Windows applications, on the other hand, are entirely event driven. In fact, Windows applications are based around a simple monitor that waits for an event to occur; it then dispatches that event to the appropriate code within the application to process.

To effectively write a Windows or Web application with Visual Basic .NET, you write code that reacts to events. In fact, you've already done so in previous lessons. Today's lesson will teach you more details about handling events, messages, and notifications that occur within Windows and Web applications and how to work with them. You will also learn how to work with events to build more efficient applications with threads and asynchronous operations. In this lesson, you will learn how to

- Write code to handle event notifications.
- Use asynchronous operations with events.
- Use events to synchronize operations between threads.
- Write synchronous code with events.
- Create and use custom events and delegates.

Revisiting Events and Delegates

On Day 2, "Learning to Speak OOP," you learned what an event is and how delegates are used to handle events. Reviewing what events are and what they represent is important because you need to understand how to work with them and the role delegates play.

In review, events are signals generally triggered by a user action, such as clicking with a mouse button. Events can also be triggered within an application for purposes of sending a signal to other areas of the program. For example, a class can use the RaiseEvent statement to signal an event when something happens within the application about which a form needs to alert the user.

NEW TERM Because Windows and Web applications are event driven, they are written to execute code in response to events. When you're writing code to respond to events, delegates then fit into the picture. *Delegates* are basically object-oriented pointers to functions. Because delegates are object-oriented, they can be bound to one or more methods. Binding a delegate to more than one method is referred to as *multicasting*.

Events are bound to delegates with the AddHandler keyword. If an event is no longer handled by a delegate, the application removes the binding with the RemoveHandler keyword. After an event is bound to a delegate, when that event is signaled within the program, the delegate is invoked. The delegate then calls the one or more bound methods in response to the event.

Delegates also allow multiple events to be bound to the same method. By using this feature, you can write a single method to respond to multiple events and reduce the amount of redundant code in an application. For example, a single delegate method could respond to both button clicks and menu commands.

Simple Event Handling

The most common use of events within an application is in the code that responds to user interaction with the application. For example, Windows applications deal with users through Windows Forms; Web applications deal with them through Web Forms.

All classes in the .NET Framework that represent objects with which users interact define a set of events that are signaled as users interact with the objects. A simple method of handling those events uses the Handles keyword, which allows you to bind one or more events to a class method that matches the required parameters for an event handler. Listing 15.1 shows an event handler in a Windows Form that is run when a user clicks a button.

LISTING 15.1 Using the Handles Keyword to Handle an Event Within a Windows Form

```
Public Class Form1
    Inherits System.Windows.Forms.Form

    'Windows Form Designer generated code

    Private Sub Button1_Click _
    (ByVal sender As System.Object, ByVal e As System.EventArgs) _
    Handles Button1.Click
        MsgBox("Button Pushed")
    End Sub
End Class
```

If you have a single method that can handle multiple events within an object, you can bind more than one event to the method by adding other object events, as shown in the following code segment:

```
Private Sub Button1_Click _
(ByVal sender As System.Object, ByVal e As System.EventArgs) _
Handles Button1.Click, Button2.Click
    MsgBox("Button Pushed")
End Sub
```

This method of handling events is useful and easy to code when the events and event handlers are all known at design time. However, events bound with the Handles keyword can't be changed at runtime as they can with the AddHandler keyword.

Dynamic Event Handling with Delegates

The use of delegates and the AddHandler and RemoveHandler keywords allows applications to dynamically set up and remove event handlers at runtime. This capability can be useful when an application must dynamically decide how and when to handle an event based on some unknown criteria at design time.

For example, if a button is clicked in an application, the application may then need to handle events for another control. The events are handled until the user chooses another option, in which case the events are no longer handled for the other control or are handled differently. The possibilities are endless and very flexible when dynamically handling events. Listing 15.2 shows how to dynamically add an event handler and remove it for a Windows Form push button.

LISTING 15.2   Choosing to Handle Events for Another Control

```
Public Class Form2
    Inherits System.Windows.Forms.Form

    Dim m_bButton2Handled As Boolean = False

    'Windows Form Designer generated code

    Private Sub Button_Click _
    (ByVal sender As System.Object, ByVal e As System.EventArgs) _
        Handles Button1.Click
        'If there is no handler for Button2, then add one, otherwise remove it
        If Not m_bButton2Handled Then
          AddHandler Button2.Click, AddressOf Button2_Click

          m_bButton2Handled = True
          MsgBox("Button2 Handled")
        Else
          RemoveHandler Button2.Click, AddressOf Button2_Click

          m_bButton2Handled = False
          MsgBox("Button2 is not Handled")
        End If
    End Sub

    Private Sub Button2_Click _
    (ByVal sender As System.Object, ByVal e As System.EventArgs)
        MsgBox("Button2 Pressed")
    End Sub
End Class
```

ANALYSIS   The code in Listing 15.2 handles the Click event for Button1 and then decides whether the Click event of Button2 should be toggled on or off. When you use the AddHandler and RemoveHandler keywords, the event handler for Button2.Click is added and removed.

Using Asynchronous Operations with Events

NEW TERM Visual Basic .NET is fully capable of multithreaded operations and therefore capable of asynchronous execution. This feature allows you to create applications that perform more efficiently by taking advantage of background processing. *Background processing* allows an application to offload long calculations or operations to a background thread while freeing up the primary application thread for other operations, including user interaction.

Asynchrony and Threads

Asynchronous means that an event can happen intermittently rather than at a predetermined or regular intervals. For example, a telephone conversation is asynchronous because either party can interrupt the speaker or contribute a comment at any time. Either can react to the interruption and change the subject of conversation. Synchronous communication would require one party to remain silent until the speaker announced that he or she was now prepared to be silent and listen. As you can see, asynchronous communication is far more flexible.

In simple terms, a *thread* is a code sequence that uses computer resources such as CPU time. In a multithreading computer scenario, a modern operating system "time-slices" its CPU time by attending to each thread in short bursts that effectively simulate continuous operation. Also, one thread can be given a higher priority so that it can preempt other threads that continue to run in the background.

For example, if an application has to process a large dataset to come up with results and freezing the user interface for that period of time is not reasonable, creating a background thread to process the dataset is the answer. Applications can use events to synchronize asynchronous operations. Signaling an event when a thread completes its task or hits a milestone allows the main application or other threads to synchronize themselves.

Figure 15.1 shows a unified modeling language (UML) activity diagram for the sample application in Listing 15.3; this figure demonstrates the use of a background thread with a custom event to signal the main thread when the background process is done.

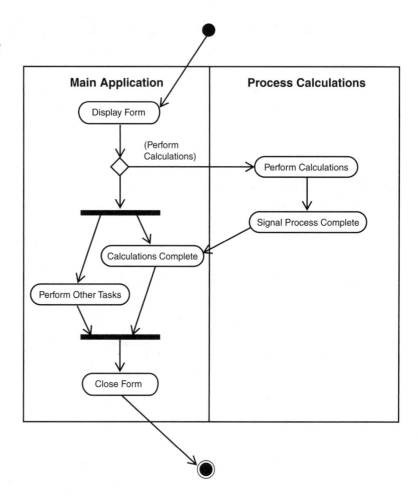

FIGURE 15.1

*UML diagram showing
the activity between
the main thread and
background thread.*

Main Application

Display Form

(Perform
Calculations)

Perform Calculations

Signal Process Complete

Process Calculations

Calculations Complete

Perform Other Tasks

Close Form

LISTING 15.3 Using Events to Synchronize Asynchronous Operations

```
Public Class ProcessCalculations
    Public Event ThreadDone()

    Public Sub Process()
        'Process Calculations

        'Signal that the thread is complete
        RaiseEvent ThreadDone()
    End Sub
End Class

Public Class Form1
    Inherits System.Windows.Forms.Form
```

LISTING 15.3   continued

```
        Dim m_Thread As System.Threading.Thread
        Dim WithEvents m_Process As ProcessCalculations

        'Windows Form Designer generated code

    Private Sub Button_Click _
    (ByVal sender As System.Object, ByVal e As System.EventArgs) _
    Handles Button.Click
        m_Process = New ProcessCalculations()

        'Create and start a thread to do background processing
        m_Thread = New System.Threading.Thread(AddressOf m_Process.Process)

        m_Thread.Start()
    End Sub

    Private Sub ProcessCompleted() Handles m_Process.ThreadDone
        'Calculation process is complete,

        Beep()
    End Sub
End Class
```

ANALYSIS   In Listing 15.3, when users click a button to start the calculation process, a thread is created to perform the calculations. When the thread is finished calculating, it raises an event that is handled by the calling object so it knows when the thread processing is complete.

Using the `IAsyncResult` Interface

Another way to perform synchronization within an application is to use the `IAsyncResult` interface. Several .NET Framework calls that allow asynchronous operation take a parameter as an asynchronous callback. The `IAsyncResult` interface is returned from such functions and used to determine the state of the asynchronous call.

By using the `IAsyncResult` interface, you can determine the operation's state and whether it has completed. You can also get a wait handle that can be used to wait on the operation if necessary. For example, if an application is waiting on two separate file I/O operations that must be completed before continuing, the application can wait on both wait handles with the `WaitHandle` object. When both file operations are completed, the handles are signaled and the application proceeds.

Creating and Using Custom Events and Delegates

When a custom application event requires that parameters be passed when they are raised, a delegate is required to be associated with the event. Up to this point, any events you've added to a class haven't been declared with a delegate and therefore don't have defined parameters.

Creating Custom Events Using .NET Framework Delegates

Most events in the .NET Framework are declared with delegates that take parameters. For example, most events in the .NET Framework are declared as type EventHandler. You can create your own custom events with several other delegates defined within the .NET Framework.

Listing 15.4 shows how to create a custom event in your application that uses a .NET Framework delegate to describe its parameters.

LISTING 15.4   Declaring a Custom Event by Using the .NET Framework EventHandler Delegate

```
Public Class MyClass
   Public Event MyEvent As EventHandler

   'Other class code
End Class

Dim WithEvents MyObject As New MyClass()
  Sub MyEventHandler _
  (ByVal sender As Object, ByVal e As EventArgs) Handles _
  MyObject.MyEvent
   'Event handler code
End Sub
```

MyEvent is of type EventHandler, which means that any handler bound to the event must match the parameters of the EventHandler delegate. The declaration of the EventHandler delegate within the .NET Framework is shown in the following code statement:

```
Public Delegate Sub EventHandler(ByVal sender As Object, ByVal e As EventArgs)
```

Declaring and Using Custom Delegates

The delegates defined in the .NET Framework won't work for all events in a complex application. Often, an event will produce specific information when raised that only a custom delegate can handle.

Declaring a custom delegate is similar to declaring a normal subroutine. The difference is that the `Delegate` keyword is placed in front of the subroutine declaration, as follows:

```
Public Delegate Sub MyDelegate(ByVal value As String)
```

Delegates are typically declared within the namespace and class that define the event with which they are used. For example, if you declare a class with a custom event that relies on a custom delegate, you should declare the delegate within the same class as the event. Listing 15.5 shows how to declare a custom event and delegate within a class.

LISTING 15.5   Custom Delegate and Event Declaration and Usage

```
Public Class MyClass
    Public Delegate Sub MyDelegate(ByVal Value As String)
    Public Event MyEvent As MyDelegate

    Public Sub ProcessWithEvent()
      'Subroutine Functionality

      RaiseEvent MyEvent("Event Triggered")
    End Sub
End Class

Dim WithEvents MyObject As New MyClass()
Sub MyEventHandler(ByVal Value As String) Handles MyObject.MyEvent
    MsgBox(Value)
End Sub

Sub main()
    'Other code
    '...

    MyObject.ProcessWithEvent()

    'Other code
    '...
End Sub
```

ANALYSIS   MyClass now declares a `MyEvent` event of type `MyDelegate`. Whenever `MyEvent` is raised, it must provide a string as a parameter that is passed to the event handler. The example in Listing 15.5 simply displays the string value in a message box;

however, you can define a delegate with any parameters necessary for a particular situation and use them however they are needed in the handler.

 Note

> Although you can declare delegates as functions with a return value, you can't use them with events. Because events are raised and there's no way to handle a return value, only subroutine delegates are used with events.

Understanding the **Delegate** Class

Whenever you declare a delegate subroutine or function, the .NET language compiler actually builds a new class that inherits the Delegate class. For example, the following delegate declaration encapsulates a method that takes a string parameter:

```
Public Delegate Sub MyDelegate(ByVal Value As String)
```

When this declaration is compiled, a new class named MyDelegate is created. This new class has two members: a constructor and an Invoke() method. The compiler builds these members with metadata to indicate that no implementation is provided. Listing 15.6 shows code the compiler creates for a class that the compiler generates. Because the compiler generates this class directly, there's no true Visual Basic .NET representation of this class.

LISTING 15.6   Compiler Code for Generated Delegate Class

```
Public Class MyDelegate
    Inherits Delegate

    Public Sub New(ByVal obj as Object, ByVal ptr As Long)
    Public Sub Invoke(ByVal Value As String)
End Class
```

ANALYSIS   The first member generated is the class constructor. This constructor is called when using the AddHandler keyword. The first parameter is the target object, which, in the case of handling events, is the event object to handle. The second parameter is the address of the subroutine called for the delegate. For example, this subroutine is used with the AddressOf keyword when adding a handler.

The second method, Invoke(), has the same parameters as those declared with the delegate. When the bound function is called for this delegate, it uses the Invoke() method, passing the single String value as its parameter.

Using Events for Notification

15

Events effectively provide notification when something occurs. Classes in the .NET Framework, such as the `FileSystemWatcher` class, rely on using events to notify the application when selected items change within a directory.

For example, an application that acts like the Windows Explorer uses events with the `FileSystemWatcher` class to receive notifications when any file changes within the directory. This application displays the current list of files within a directory. Continuously querying the files within a directory isn't efficient, so instead you use the `FileSystemWatcher` class and handle the events that it signals when a file changes.

To write an application that displays an updated list of files and monitors them with the `FileSystemWatcher` class, you start by creating a Windows application and designing the default form, as shown in Figure 15.2.

For this project, add these controls to `Form1`:

- A ListBox control named `lbDirectory`
- A TextBox control named `tbCurDirectory`
- A Button control name `btnChangeDir`
- A FileSystemWatcher control (from the Components tab) named `DirectoryWatcher`

FIGURE 15.2

Directory Monitor Form in the Windows form designer.

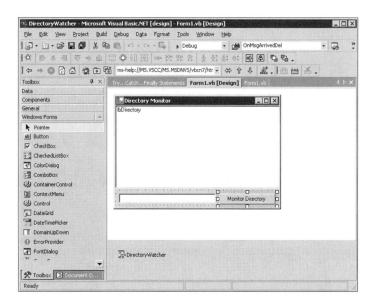

After you design the form, open the code for the `Form1` class and make the modifications necessary until your code is the same as shown in Listing 15.7.

LISTING 15.7   Source Code for a Directory Watcher Application

```
Public Class Form1
    Inherits System.Windows.Forms.Form

#Region " Windows Form Designer generated code "

    Public Sub New()
        MyBase.New()

        'This call is required by the Windows Form Designer.
        InitializeComponent()

        'Initialize with the current directory and start the process.
        tbCurDirectory.Text = CurDir()
        SetupWatcher()
    End Sub

    'Form overrides dispose to clean up the component list.
    Protected Overloads Overrides Sub Dispose(ByVal disposing As Boolean)
        If disposing Then
            If Not (components Is Nothing) Then
                components.Dispose()
            End If
        End If
        MyBase.Dispose(disposing)
    End Sub

    Friend WithEvents lbDirectory As System.Windows.Forms.ListBox
    Friend WithEvents btnChangeDir As System.Windows.Forms.Button
    Friend WithEvents DirectoryWatcher As System.IO.FileSystemWatcher
    Friend WithEvents tbCurDirectory As System.Windows.Forms.TextBox

    'Required by the Windows Form Designer
    Private components As System.ComponentModel.Container

    'NOTE: The following procedure is required by the Windows Form Designer
    'It can be modified using the Windows Form Designer.
    'Do not modify it using the code editor.
    <System.Diagnostics.DebuggerStepThrough()> _
    Private Sub InitializeComponent()
        Me.tbCurDirectory = New System.Windows.Forms.TextBox()
        Me.lbDirectory = New System.Windows.Forms.ListBox()
        Me.btnChangeDir = New System.Windows.Forms.Button()
        Me.DirectoryWatcher = New System.IO.FileSystemWatcher()
        CType(Me.DirectoryWatcher, _
```

LISTING 15.7 continued

```
System.ComponentModel.ISupportInitialize).BeginInit()
Me.SuspendLayout()
'
'tbCurDirectory
'
Me.tbCurDirectory.Anchor _
 = ((System.Windows.Forms.AnchorStyles.Bottom Or _
 System.Windows.Forms.AnchorStyles.Left) _
 Or System.Windows.Forms.AnchorStyles.Right)
Me.tbCurDirectory.Location = New System.Drawing.Point(8, 184)
Me.tbCurDirectory.Name = "tbCurDirectory"
Me.tbCurDirectory.Size = New System.Drawing.Size(208, 20)
Me.tbCurDirectory.TabIndex = 2
Me.tbCurDirectory.Text = ""
'
'lbDirectory
'
Me.lbDirectory.Anchor = (((System.Windows.Forms.AnchorStyles.Top Or _
                          System.Windows.Forms.AnchorStyles.Bottom) _
            Or System.Windows.Forms.AnchorStyles.Left) _
            Or System.Windows.Forms.AnchorStyles.Right)
Me.lbDirectory.Name = "lbDirectory"
Me.lbDirectory.Size = New System.Drawing.Size(356, 173)
Me.lbDirectory.TabIndex = 0
'
'btnChangeDir
'
Me.btnChangeDir.Anchor _
 = (System.Windows.Forms.AnchorStyles.Bottom Or _
 System.Windows.Forms.AnchorStyles.Right)
Me.btnChangeDir.Location = New System.Drawing.Point(224, 184)
Me.btnChangeDir.Name = "btnChangeDir"
Me.btnChangeDir.Size = New System.Drawing.Size(120, 23)
Me.btnChangeDir.TabIndex = 1
Me.btnChangeDir.Text = "Monitor Directory"
'
'DirectoryWatcher
'
Me.DirectoryWatcher.EnableRaisingEvents = True
Me.DirectoryWatcher.NotifyFilter _
= ((System.IO.NotifyFilters.FileName Or _
 System.IO.NotifyFilters.DirectoryName) _
 Or System.IO.NotifyFilters.LastWrite)
Me.DirectoryWatcher.SynchronizingObject = Me
'
'Form1
'
Me.AutoScaleBaseSize = New System.Drawing.Size(5, 13)
Me.ClientSize = New System.Drawing.Size(352, 213)
```

LISTING 15.7   continued

```
            Me.Controls.AddRange(New System.Windows.Forms.Control() _
                    {Me.tbCurDirectory, Me.btnChangeDir, Me.lbDirectory})
            Me.Name = "Form1"
            Me.Text = "Directory Monitor"
            CType(Me.DirectoryWatcher, System.ComponentModel. _
            ISupportInitialize).EndInit()
            Me.ResumeLayout(False)

    End Sub

#End Region

    Private Sub btnChangeDir_Click _
    (ByVal sender As System.Object, ByVal e As System.EventArgs) _
    Handles btnChangeDir.Click
        SetupWatcher()
    End Sub

    Private Sub DirectoryChanged(ByVal sender As Object, _
    ByVal e As System.IO.FileSystemEventArgs) _
    Handles DirectoryWatcher.Changed, _
    DirectoryWatcher.Created, DirectoryWatcher.Deleted
        FillList()
    End Sub

    Private Sub SetupWatcher()
        Try
            DirectoryWatcher.Path = tbCurDirectory.Text()
            DirectoryWatcher.EnableRaisingEvents = True
            FillList()
        Catch BadArg As ArgumentException
            lbDirectory.Items.Clear()
            lbDirectory.Items.Add("Bad Directory")
        End Try
    End Sub

    Private Sub FillList()
        lbDirectory.Items.Clear()
        lbDirectory.Items.AddRange _
        (System.IO.Directory.GetFiles(DirectoryWatcher.Path))
    End Sub

End Class
```

ANALYSIS   When the application first starts, it begins by monitoring the current directory. The current directory contents are loaded, and the FileSystemWatcher class is initialized with the SetupWatcher() method. Figure 15.3 shows the application as it appears monitoring the Windows subdirectory.

FIGURE 15.3

Directory Monitor monitoring the Windows subdirectory.

When a user clicks the btnChangeDir button, whatever directory is entered in the tbCurDirectory text box is used as the new directory to monitor, and the SetupWatcher() method is called again to initialize the FileSystemWatcher class with the new directory.

Whenever the Changed, Created, or Deleted events occur within the directory being watched, the DirectoryChanged() method is called, and the list box, lbDirectory, is reloaded with the latest contents from the directory.

Summary

Today you learned how to use and create events and delegates for receiving notifications of user interactions, completion of processes, and changes within a file system. Events and delegates have broad uses within your applications and are essential to writing Windows and Web applications that rely on event-oriented processing.

Events are also useful in threads with asynchronous operation and places where you need to pass values back from the thread after execution. An event can use a system-defined or custom delegate to define what type of data is passed as parameters when an event is raised, thus giving you complete flexibility.

Q&A

Q What's the difference between events in .NET and the event handles in Win32? Can I use both of them in my .NET applications?

A Events in the .NET Framework are separately managed and relate more closely to Windows messages than true Win32 events. Raising a .NET event is like posting a message that's handled by a function defined by a delegate. Win32 events, on the other hand, are true events that are part of the Windows operating system. These Win32 events are accessible through the .NET Framework and usable with the WaitHandle class. Win32 events are much more efficient than .NET events and are the only true events.

Q If .NET events are more like Windows messages than Win32 events, can I still receive Windows messages in my .NET application?

A Not directly. The .NET Framework encapsulates the Windows messages and replaces them with .NET events, thus eliminating the need for message maps and handlers for the messages.

Workshop

The Workshop provides quiz questions and an exercise to help solidify your understanding of events, notifications, and delegates and provide you with experience in using what you've learned. Answers are provided in Appendix A, "Answers to Quizzes."

Quiz

1. What keyword declares an event?
2. What's the purpose of a delegate as it relates to events?
3. What's the keyword to bind an event to a method?
4. Can an event be bound to a function?

Exercise

Design a class that encapsulates two events, Event1 and Event2, that have different delegates. The first delegate takes an Integer as a parameter, whereas the second delegate takes an Object and a String. Then write another class that has a subroutine for each event and bind the events to them. Finally, write another subroutine in the same class in which the events are declared to raise the events passing the current object as the parameter for the event that takes an object.

15

DAY 16

Gracefully Capturing Errors

Current Windows and Web applications are generally complex applications with several thousand lines of code. Inevitably, coding errors occur and situations that can cause runtime errors arise. If these errors aren't handled, the applications exit with unhandled exceptions. In the case of a desktop application, users are notified and have to restart the application. With Web applications, users might see embarrassing script syntax or Page not found errors. However, in severe cases, server-side errors can cause the Web site to become unstable.

Until Visual Basic .NET, applications written in Visual Basic had only unstructured error handling. With Visual Basic .NET, structured exception handling is added to the language. Structured exception handling gives you greater control over handling exceptions and even designing classes to generate exceptions. This capability is key to writing robust applications. If you use structured exception handling, there's little reason for an application to exit with an unhandled exception.

Today's lesson teaches you how to write Visual Basic .NET applications with structured exception handling. As a result, you can build robust applications that gracefully deal with unexpected errors. In today's lesson, you will learn how to

- Write `Try...Catch...Finally` statements to catch exceptions.
- Create exceptions with the `Throw` statement.
- Create custom exception classes.
- Handle exceptions generated by the .NET Framework and your own classes.

Understanding Structured Exception Handling

Starting with Visual Basic .NET, two types of exception handling are supported:

- *Unstructured* exception handling is what previous versions of Visual Basic used with the `On Error` statement.
- *Structured* exception handling, new with Visual Basic .NET, uses the `Try...Catch...Finally` statements.

Using structured exception handling is generally better when you're writing applications because it gives more support for handling different types of errors and uses an `Exception` class to provide error information. Therefore, it's enough to say that unstructured exception handling is still supported in Visual Basic .NET, but it shouldn't be used. If you want to use it, keep in mind that you can't mix unstructured exception handling and structured exception handling within the same procedure.

Using the `Try` and `Catch` Statements

In structured exception handling, the `Try...End Try` statements mark a code block protected by error handlers. The `Catch` statement declares the error handlers with an optional exception filter. When an exception is raised, the error handlers are searched to find a handler for the raised exception. If a handler has no exception filter, it catches all exceptions not handled by other exception handlers. If no exception filter matches the raised exception, the exception is unhandled.

The code shown in Listing 16.1 shows a `Try...Catch...End Try` block within a subroutine. This block checks for a divide-by-zero error and array index out of range while calculating an average.

LISTING 16.1   Structured Exception Handling to Check for Exceptions While Calculating an Average Value from an Array

```
Public Function CalculateAverage(ByVal Values() As Integer) As Integer
    Dim i As Integer
    Dim Sum As Integer

    Try
        For i = Values.GetLowerBound(0) To Values.GetUpperBound(0)
            Sum += Values(i)
        Next

        CalculateAverage = Sum \ _
        (Values.GetUpperBound(0) - Values.GetLowerBound(0))

    Catch e As IndexOutOfRangeException
        'Index was out of range, calculate average now
        Try
            CalculateAverage = Sum \ (i - Values.GetLowerBound(0))
        Catch
            CalculateAverage = 0
        End Try

    Catch e As DivideByZeroException
        'Must have had only 1 value
        CalculateAverage = Sum

    Catch
        'Unknown exception
        CalculateAverage = 0

    End Try
End Function
```

ANALYSIS   In Listing 16.1, each error type is handled differently. This is the advantage of using structured exception handling. Within an exception handler, you also can use another Try...Catch block to protect that code. This approach is shown in the IndexOutOfRangeException block in Listing 16.1. Table 16.1 lists some of the common exception classes and describes the conditions that cause the error to occur.

TABLE 16.1   Some Common Exception Classes and When They Are Thrown

Exception	Thrown When
ArgumentException	One argument provided to a method isn't valid.
ArgumentNullException	A null reference (Nothing in Visual Basic) is passed to a method that doesn't accept it as a valid argument.

TABLE 16.1   continued

Exception	Thrown When
ArgumentOutOfRangeException	The value of an argument is outside the allowable range as defined by the called method.
ArithmeticException	There is an error in an arithmetic, casting, or conversion operation.
ArrayTypeMismatchException	An attempt is made to store an element of the wrong type within an array.
BadImageFormatException	The file image of a DLL or an executable program is invalid.
CannotUnloadAppDomainException	An attempt to unload an application domain fails.
DivideByZeroException	An attempt to divide an integral or decimal value by zero.
DllNotFoundException	A DLL to be imported can't be found.
ExecutionEngineException	An internal error in the execution engine of the common language runtime.
FieldAccessException	There's an illegal attempt to access a private or protected field inside a class.
FormatException	The format of an argument doesn't meet the parameter specifications of the invoked method.
IndexOutOfRangeException	An attempt is made to access an element of an array with an index outside the bounds of the array.
InvalidCastException	There has been an invalid casting or explicit conversion.
InvalidOperationException	A method call is invalid for the object's current state.
InvalidProgramException	The program contains invalid Microsoft intermediate language (MSIL) or metadata.
MemberAccessException	An attempt to access a class member fails.
MethodAccessException	An illegal attempt is made to access a private or protected method inside a class.
MissingFieldException	An attempt is made to dynamically access a field that doesn't exist.
MissingMemberException	An attempt is made to dynamically access a class member that doesn't exist.
MissingMethodException	An attempt is made to dynamically access a method that doesn't exist.
NotFiniteNumberException	A floating-point value is positive infinity, negative infinity, or Not-a-Number (NaN).
NotImplementedException	A requested method or operation isn't implemented.

TABLE 16.1   continued

Exception	Thrown When
NotSupportedException	An invoked method isn't supported, or when there's an attempt to read, seek, or write to a stream that doesn't support the invoked functionality.
NullReferenceException	There's an attempt to dereference a null object reference.
OutOfMemoryException	There isn't enough memory to continue program execution.
OverflowException	An arithmetic, casting, or conversion operation in a checked context results in an overflow.
PlatformNotSupportedException	A feature doesn't run on a particular platform.
RankException	An array with the wrong number of dimensions is passed to a method.
StackOverflowException	The execution stack overflows by having too many pending method calls.
TypeLoadException	The Common Language Runtime can't find the assembly or the type within the assembly, nor can it load the type.
TypeUnloadedException	There is an attempt to access an unloaded class.
UnauthorizedAccessException	The operating system denies access because of an I/O error or a specific type of security error.

Nesting Error Handling

You also can nest structured exception handling within a single procedure or across multiple procedures. When an application has nested exception handling coded and an exception occurs, the innermost Try...Catch block has the first chance to handle the exception. Each exception handler is checked within the block the exception occurred. If no acceptable exception handler is found, the exception falls out to the next Try...Catch block to look for an appropriate exception handler. This process continues until an exception handler is found or there are no more levels of Try...Catch blocks to check. If the exception is unhandled, the application exits with an unhandled exception.

Consider the code shown in Listing 16.2. It has two levels of exception handling within the same Calculate() procedure and another level of exception handling in the Test() subroutine.

LISTING **16.2**   Nested Exception Handling

```
Public Function Calculate(ByVal A As Integer, _
ByVal B As Integer, ByVal Values() As Integer) As Integer
    Dim i As Integer
    Dim Value As Integer

    Try

        Value = A \ B

        Try
            For i = Values.GetLowerBound(0) To Values.GetUpperBound(0)
                Value += Value \ (A + B)
            Next
        Catch e As IndexOutOfRangeException
            'don't do or change anything
        End Try

    Catch e As DivideByZeroException
        Value = 0
    End Try

    Calculate = Value
End Function

Public Function Test(ByVal Values() As Integer) As Integer
    Try
        Test = Calculate(10, 20, Values)
    Catch
        ' If any error occurs, return 0
        Test = 0
    End Try
End Function
```

The flow diagram in Figure 16.1 shows how an exception is handled in this example.

Using `Finally`

`Finally` is an optional block that you can define within a `Try...Catch` block. A `Finally` block is always executed after the code in the `Try` block, even if an exception occurs. If an exception occurs, the `Finally` block is called after the exception is processed or before leaving the block for an unhandled exception. Listing 16.3 shows a `Try...Catch...Finally` block.

FIGURE 16.1

Exception handling in the sample from Listing 16.2.

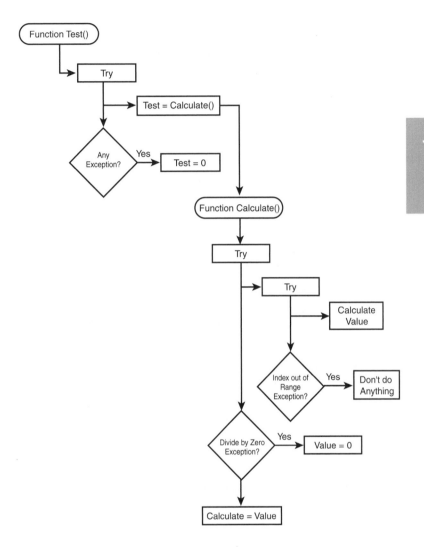

16

LISTING 16.3 A Try...Catch...Finally Block

```
Public Function TestFinally() As Boolean
    Dim gr As Graphics
    Dim br As SolidBrush

    Try
        gr = Graphics.FromHwnd(Handle())
        br = New System.Drawing.SolidBrush(System.Drawing.Color.Blue)

        gr.FillRectangle(br, New Drawing.Rectangle(0, 0, 10, 10))
```

LISTING 16.3   continued

```
                TestFinally = True
            Catch
                'Something happened
                TestFinally = False
            Finally
                'Cleanup
                br.Dispose()
                gr.Dispose()
            End Try
        End Function
```

By using the Finally block, you can write code to clean up or perform tasks that are always necessary even if an exception occurs.

Throwing Exceptions

Besides handling exceptions, structured exception handling allows you to write code that specifically generates exceptions. You generate exceptions in code by using the Throw keyword, which allows you to specify the exception that you're throwing.

Why would you ever want to generate an exception? The following few examples illustrate why generating exceptions is a good practice. First, say you're writing an encapsulated class and want to provide a way to pass errors out of your object to the object's user. If a predefined set of exceptions is generated when errors occur within the class, any code using the object can catch those exceptions. You also can use return values as errors; however, if a return value is needed for a function's result or more error information is available than a return value can provide, exceptions are the answer. The function in Listing 16.4 throws an exception to pass an error string to the exception handler if an error occurs (see Figure 16.2).

LISTING 16.4   Using Throw to Return an Error String

```
Public Function CalcResult(ByVal A As Integer, ByVal B As Integer) As Integer
    Try
        CalcResult = A \ B
    Catch e As DivideByZeroException
        CalcResult = 0
        Throw New Exception("You Tried To Divide By Zero")
    End Try
End Function

Public Sub TestCalcResult()
    Try
```

LISTING 16.4   continued

```
      MsgBox(CalcResult(5, 0).ToString())
   Catch e As Exception
      MsgBox(e.ToString())
   End Try
End Sub
```

Note

You might not always get the predefined exception that you expect. For example, notice the third line of Listing 16.4, CalcResult = A \ B. In this case, if you use the floating-point division operator (/) rather than the integer division operator (\), the exception thrown is OverflowException rather than DivideByZeroException.

FIGURE 16.2

Custom error message after exception thrown in Listing 16.4 during a debug session.

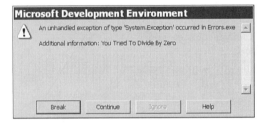

Another reason to generate exceptions is to eliminate the use of the goto statement and nested If statements that check the success before continuing in the code. It's easier and much cleaner to throw an exception if something fails in a process and is then caught by your process and handled appropriately. Also, when you might be tempted to use a goto, throwing an exception allows you not only to jump to a new location within a process, but also to jump out of the current method and into the calling method where the exception is caught. Listing 16.5 shows how to use a Throw statement to eliminate nested If statements.

Note

In this example, the program continues running and doesn't crash on encountering unacceptable values. Figure 16.3 shows a simple form that calls the functions and passes inappropriate values. Figure 16.4 shows the result of passing the values 6 and 7. Figure 16.5 shows how the CalcCompxResult() function responds to the values 0 and 0.

LISTING 16.5   Using `Throw` in Place of Nested `If` Statements

```
Public Function CalcCompxResult _
(ByVal A As Integer, ByVal B As Integer) As Integer
 Try
    If A < B Then
       Throw New Exception("A must be greater than B")
    End If

    'Some dumb calculation
    A += 10 * B
    B += 20

    'Re-check before doing another calculation
    If A - B < 10 Then
       Throw New Exception("A - B is not greater than 10")
    End If

    CalcCompxResult = A + B

 Catch e As DivideByZeroException
    CalcCompxResult = 0

 Catch e As Exception
    MsgBox(e.ToSTring())

 End Try
End Function
```

FIGURE 16.3

A Windows Form with sample values passed to Listing 16.5.

FIGURE 16.4

Error handler message caused by calling `CalcCompxResult(6, 7)` *in Listing 16.5.*

FIGURE 16.5

Error handler message caused by calling `CalcCompxResult(0, 0)` *in Listing 16.5.*

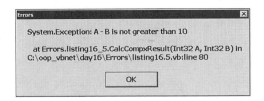

16

NEW TERM   Your code also might throw an exception within the catch of an exception. For example, if you write code that catches an exception, such as `DivideByZeroException`, your code might do something on that exception; then you might want to reflect the exception to the caller. Listing 16.6 shows an example of *reflecting*, or rethrowing, an exception.

LISTING 16.6   Using `Throw` to Rethrow an Already-Caught Exception

```
Public Function CalcResult(ByVal A As Integer, ByVal B As Integer) As Integer
   Try
      CalcResult = A \ B

   Catch e As DivideByZeroException
      CalcResult = 0

      'Re-throw the divide-by-zero error
      Throw e

   End Try
End Function
```

Creating and Using Custom Exception Classes

The .NET Framework defines a common set of exceptions that you can use within your applications to handle most types of errors. Sometimes an application requires a special exception that doesn't fit into one of the exceptions defined in the .NET Framework. In this case, an application can define custom exception classes by creating a class and deriving it from Exception.

In reality, an application can throw an exception of any object type derived from Object. However, this practice isn't recommended because the exception logic isn't present unless you derive from the Exception class. This class provides a stack trace, message string, a help link, and other useful features usually needed for dealing with errors.

When you're declaring a new exception class, it's best practice to declare the class with Exception as the last part of the class name. For example, the exception name MyCustomException follows best practices.

When you declare a custom exception class, it can hold whatever information you need to carry with the exception to help your application deal with the exception correctly. For example, an exception class can hold different member data items, methods, and properties that are all custom to the exception you're creating. One design consideration in custom exception classes should be to include all information in the exception class's constructor. This way, the exception can be thrown with a single statement as follows:

```
Throw New MyCustomException(10, "Error Occurred", Me)
```

If the exception class doesn't take the parameters on the constructor, you have to instantiate the class and then set the properties for the class before throwing the exception. That method works, but using a single statement is much easier. Listing 16.7 shows the definition of the MyCustomException class.

LISTING 16.7   MyCustomException Class Definition

```
Public Class MyCustomException
   Inherits Exception

   Private m_nCondition As Integer
   Private m_source As Object

   Public Sub New(ByVal nCondition As Integer, _
   ByVal sMsg As String, ByVal source As Object)
      MyBase.New(sMsg)

      m_nCondition = nCondition
      m_source = source
   End Sub

   Public ReadOnly Property Condition() As Integer
   Get
      Condition = m_nCondition
   End Get
```

LISTING 16.7 continued

```
    End Property

    Public ReadOnly Property SourceObject() As Object
    Get
        SourceObject = m_source
    End Get
    End Property
End Class
```

16

Unless you have functionality to perform in an exception class, the class is primarily composed of a constructor, member data, and properties to access the member data.

Summary

Today you learned how to write code to handle exceptions and use them to your advantage in creating robust applications. You also learned how to create custom exceptions for use in your applications. You can use these exceptions, combined with the Throw statement, to generate your own custom exceptions to simplify your code.

Exception handling is key to writing robust applications that can withstand unforeseen errors and even coding errors that would normally cause an application to terminate. By handling all exceptions, you can write applications that should never exit uncontrollably, which is a nuisance for desktop applications and can be fatal for Web sites.

Q&A

Q What type of performance difference does exception handling cause?

A Exception handling causes some performance loss because of the overhead. However, the advantages outweigh the minimal performance hit that exception handling causes.

Q If unmanaged code or a COM object throws an exception, can Visual Basic .NET catch the exception and handle it?

A Yes. Managed code can catch exceptions thrown from unmanaged code. Unmanaged code also can catch exceptions thrown in managed code.

Workshop

The Workshop provides quiz questions and an exercise to help solidify your understanding of exceptions and error handling and provide you with experience in using what you've learned. Answers are provided in Appendix A, "Answers to Quizzes."

Quiz

1. What are the three blocks within structured exception logic?
2. What's the keyword to generate an exception?
3. When is the code within the `Finally` block executed?

Exercise

Write a custom exception class that has three constructors. The first one should take no parameters, the second one should take a message as a parameter, and the third one should take a message and an `Object` as parameters. Create a property to return the `Object` if one was provided.

DAY 17

Developing and Using Remote Objects

The .NET Framework runtime allows objects to call other object methods and access properties and members within other objects. This process usually occurs within the same application boundary. However, the runtime also provides for calling methods of objects that cross the application boundaries. When this situation occurs, the remoting features within the .NET Framework are used. With the remoting features, objects can call other objects across contexts, application processes, and even machines.

Today's lesson will teach you more about the remoting capabilities of the .NET Framework runtime and how to design objects usable from remote clients. In this lesson, you will learn the following:

- The fundamentals of the remoting architecture
- How to use objects remotely
- How to create objects for remote use
- How data is marshaled between client and server objects
- How to dynamically publish objects for remote use

Understanding the Fundamentals of Remote Objects

.NET remoting features can be used to enable different applications to communicate with each other. The applications can reside on the same computer or on different computers connected with a local network or even the Internet. You can even connect applications running on different operating systems through .NET remoting.

The .NET Framework provides support for remote objects by providing services for activation, lifetime of object control, and communications. Either binary or XML communication is supported, which gives the application developer a choice between performance and interoperability. Security is also a strong feature of .NET remoting, which provides the capability to access serialized data before it's transmitted to validate security.

As you'll see in the sample project later in the section "Building a Host and Client for TCP," the .NET Framework makes using remote objects almost as easy as using locally installed objects. The benefits of .NET remoting include the capability to enable communication between objects in different applications by using different transport protocols, serialization formats, object creation modes, and lifetimes. Figure 17.1 shows an overview of the remoting architecture and how the communication occurs.

Remote Objects

The primary goal of the .NET remoting infrastructure is to hide the complexities of calling methods on remote objects and returning the results. This includes any object that is outside the primary physical application known as the application domain. All objects used by an application that are outside the application domain are considered remote even when the objects are executing on the same machine.

Within a .NET application, all objects are passed by reference, and data types are passed by value. When dealing with objects outside the application domain, object references are no longer valid because they refer to memory within an application domain. Therefore, all objects passing outside the application domain must be serialized in a transmittable form. Classes passed as values outside the application domain need to be declared with the [serializable] attribute or need to implement the ISerializable interface.

Whenever an object is passed outside the application domain, the framework serializes the object into either a binary format or an XML format that is transportable. The framework then sends it to the destination application domain, where the object is deserialized and reconstructed.

FIGURE **17.1**

*.NET remoting com-
munication overview.*

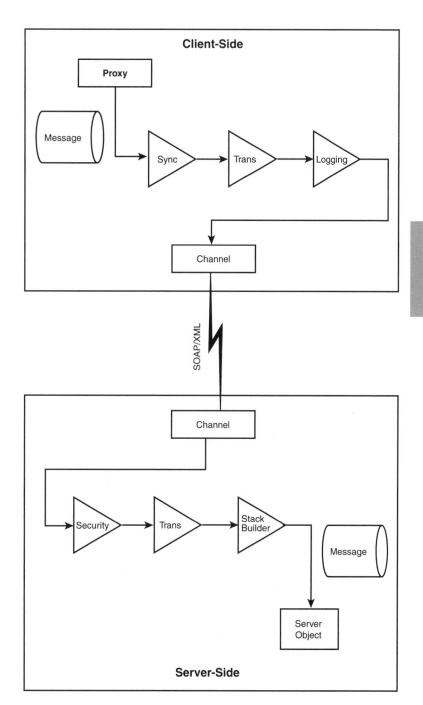

17

The `MarshalByRefObject` class allows a class to be passed by reference and handles the tasks required to make an object usable by remote applications. By inheriting the `MarshalByRefObject` class, the new object can be used remotely by other application domains. When a client activates a remote object, it receives a proxy to that object. Any operations on this proxy are handled and forwarded onto the remote object. There is a small performance hit on objects even when they're used within the local application domain; however, the compiler and runtime are optimized to help minimize the impact.

Listing 17.1 shows a sample definition of a remotable class that inherits the `MarshalByRefObject` class.

LISTING 17.1 Remotable Class Definition

```
Public Class HelloService
    Inherits MarshalByRefObject

    Public Function ReturnGreeting(name As String) As String
        ReturnGreeting = "Hi " + name +"!"
    End Function

End Class 'HelloService
```

Proxy Objects

A proxy object is created when a client activates a remote object. It acts as a representative of the remote object to ensure that all calls made on the proxy are forwarded to the correct remote object instance.

Proxy objects work by creating a local instance of the `TransparentProxy` class, which contains a list of all classes and interface methods within a remote object. When a client accesses the remote object through the proxy object, the common language runtime (CLR) intercepts the call and determines whether the call is valid and whether the object resides in the same application domain as the proxy. If the object is within the same application domain, the method call is routed to the actual object (hence the performance hit discussed earlier). If the object is within a different application domain, the parameters are packaged into an `IMessage` object and passed with the `Invoke()` method to the `RealProxy` class, which is responsible for forwarding the messages to the remote object.

Object Activation

The .NET remoting features support server and client activation of remote objects. Server activation is usually used when remote objects aren't required to maintain state between method calls. However, it can also be used when multiple clients call methods on the same object instance and the remote object maintains state information between calls. Client-activated objects are instantiated on the client, and the client manages the lifetime of the remote object by using a lease-based system the remoting framework provides.

Before remote objects can be accessed, they must be registered with the remoting framework. The hosting application usually handles registration when it starts. After starting, the hosting application registers one or more channels, followed by one or more remote objects. When the hosting application exits, the remote objects and channels are removed from the remoting services.

You activate an object on the server by using GetObject or New. The object isn't actually instantiated at the point the call is made. Instead, the object is instantiated when a client connects and makes a method call into the object. If the object is registered as SingleCall, it's destroyed after the method call is completed. A new instance of the object is then created for each method call.

You activate an object on the client side by using CreateInstance or New. Both methods allow you to instantiate an object with constructor parameters. The lifetime of the client-activated object is controlled by the leasing service within the .NET remoting framework.

Remote Object Lifetime

The lifetimes of remote objects activated on the client are controlled by a lease manager that all application domains contain. The lease manager watches the leases and checks for expired lease times to decide when the objects should be destroyed. However, before an object is destroyed, the client that activated the object is given a chance to renew the lease. If the lease isn't renewed, the garbage collector destroys the object and frees its memory.

The lease manager has a list of sponsors, which implement the ISponsor interface, for each client-activated object. When a sponsor is needed to renew a lease, the lease manager polls the sponsor list until one of the sponsors renews the lease time. If a sponsor doesn't respond to the lease manager, it's removed from the list. When the RemotingServices.GetLifetimeService() method is called, a lease for an object is obtained.

Objects can provide their own leases and control their own lifetimes by overriding the InitializeLifetimeService() method within the MarshalByRefObject class. The implementation of this method normally calls the corresponding method of the base class to retrieve the existing lease for the remote object. The lease can be extended by calling the Renew() method, requesting a renewal from a sponsor, or by invoking a method on the object. When the client invokes a method on the object, the lease is automatically renewed.

Dynamically Published Remote Objects

For the most part, the default remoting architecture and transport channels should provide what most applications will require. However, an application might require more explicit control over the remoting process. When this control is required, you can extend or replace the remoting features at a low level.

.NET's remoting infrastructure supports the capability to create an object at runtime and publish it for use. You do so by using the `RemotingServices.Marshal()` method after the object is created. This way, you also can create the object using whatever constructor is appropriate and initialize the object before it's published for use. When the object is no longer appropriate for use, you can use the `RemotingServices.Disconnect()` method to remove it.

Choosing Between Copies and References

Remote objects are used by clients in two ways. One way is to make a complete copy of an object, bring it into the client application domain, and call its methods directly. This approach works well for small utility objects that don't need to be executed on the server. Performance on the initial copy can be a problem if the object is large, so this method may not be practical and shouldn't be used for such objects.

For objects that can't or shouldn't be copied into the client application domain, the remote object is used as a reference. Usually, clients need to access only a few of the methods for very large objects while most of the features are encapsulated within the remote object. Remote objects that aren't copied should be well encapsulated with a concise interface for the client.

NEW TERM   Also, some types of objects simply can't be copied. For example, an object that maintains a `FileInfo` object to a local server-based file would have no meaning if copied to the client application domain. In these situations, the server process passes the client process a reference to the server object. Because the method calls don't execute in the client application domain, they are marshaled to the server object, where they are executed on the server and the results returned. *Marshalling*, if you'll recall, is the packaging and sending of method calls across thread or process boundaries. This process greatly reduces bandwidth because it requires only the most critical of information to be transmitted and also keeps private information within the server-based object truly private from the client application.

Using Channels for Communication

NEW TERM *Channels* are objects that transport messages between applications across remote boundaries. The boundaries can be simple, such as cross-application domains running on the same machine, to complex, such as a remote object running on another machine in another country connected only by the Internet.

Channels listen for inbound messages and send outbound messages to other listeners. They enable you to use a wide range of protocols, including platform-independent protocols based on XML. All channels implement the IChannel interface, which provides information such as the channel name and priority.

Channels designed to listen are assigned a particular protocol and port and implement the IChannelReceiver interface. Channels sending information implement the IChannelSender interface. Two channels defined within the .NET Framework already implement both of these interfaces: TcpChannel and HttpChannel.

As shown earlier in Figure 17.1, the client side hands messages off to the client channel sink chain. The first channel sink typically formats the message by serializing it into a stream. That stream is then passed onto the transport sink, which then writes out to the communications connection. The server side reads the requests from the communications connection and passes the request stream to the server channel sink chain. The server formatter sink deserializes the request into a message and passes the message to the remoting infrastructure to be processed.

When you're deciding which .NET-supplied channels to use, you must choose between performance and portability. The TcpChannel has better performance and is based on the .NET Framework's TCP socket communications layer. The TcpChannel also provides for the capability to encode the messages as binary and SOAP, an XML standard. The HttpChannel uses the HTTP protocol as a transport and provides SOAP encoding. Although the HttpChannel isn't as efficient, it's compatible with other platforms.

Building a Host and Client for TCP Connections

In this section, we are going to build two console applications. The first is the command-line host program that services requests. The second, which also runs from the command line, is the client that sends data to the host and expects a returned result. In the exercise following this lesson, you'll build a third program—a Windows Form that calls on the services of the host and displays the result.

This remoting application accepts an area's length value and width value from the client, calculates the square footage, and returns the result. Although this calculation is trivial, you could replace it with one of enormous complexity that requires a high-powered computer or proprietary algorithms.

 Tip

> When designing a class that other applications will use remotely, you need to take into account how the class will be used (copied or by reference) and what the class interface will have. If it's a referenced class, it should be well encapsulated to minimize the amount of traffic needed to work with the class. If it will be copied, it should be small to minimize the transfer size.

Hosting Applications for Remote Objects

One way to host remote objects is to create a hosting application. Hosting applications set up which channels they listen to for incoming requests from client applications. A hosting application can create one or more channels to which it responds. It's also the hosting application's responsibility to indicate which objects are hosted and whether they are well known or client activated.

Creating a Host Application

Creating a simple host application is as easy as creating a console application that registers a channel and service. The console application then sits and waits indefinitely before letting the .NET remoting features take over.

Here's how to put the hosting application together:

1. Create an empty solution called Remoting.
2. Add a Visual Basic .NET console project called `vbServiceHost`.
3. Rename the default filename to vbServiceHost.vb.
4. In your VisualBasic .NET project references area, add a reference to `System.Runtime.Remoting`.
5. In vbServiceHost.vb, substitute the contents of Listing 17.2.

LISTING 17.2   vbServiceHost.vb—Sample Remote Object Hosting Application

```
Imports System
Imports System.Runtime.Remoting
Imports System.Runtime.Remoting.Channels
imports System.Runtime.Remoting.Channels.Tcp

Namespace RemotingExample
```

LISTING 17.2   continued

```
Public Class Example

Public Shared Function Main() As Integer
  Dim chan As TcpChannel
  chan = New TcpChannel(8085)
  ChannelServices.RegisterChannel(chan)
  RemotingConfiguration.RegisterWellKnownServiceType _
  (GetType(vbServiceObject.RemotingExample.Calculate), "Calculate", _
  WellKnownObjectMode.SingleCall)
  System.Console.WriteLine _
    ("Service: Calculate service processing on port 8085")
  System.Console.WriteLine("Hit <enter> to exit...")
  System.Console.ReadLine()
  Return 0
End Function

End Class

End Namespace
```

ANALYSIS   The Main() subroutine is the entry point for the console application. As soon as it starts, it registers a TCP channel on port 8085. It then registers a well-known service of type vbServiceObject.RemotingExample.Calculate. (In case you're wondering, that service object doesn't exist yet. That's the next step.)

After setting itself up, the host waits to process requests until someone presses Enter to terminate the program. We'll revisit the host after assembling the workhorse object and the client component that belong in our remoting solution.

Creating the Service Object

The service object is the "smarts" in the remoting scenario; it performs the calculation. Follow these steps in your Remoting solution to set up this object:

1. Add a VisualBasic .NET class library project called vbServiceObject.

2. Rename the default filename to vbServiceObject.vb.

3. In the project references area for this project, add a reference to System.Runtime.Remoting.

4. In vbServiceObject.vb, substitute the contents of Listing 17.3.

LISTING 17.3 vbServiceObject.vb—Service Object for a Hosting Application

```vb
Imports System
Imports System.Runtime.Remoting
Imports System.Runtime.Remoting.Channels
Imports System.Runtime.Remoting.Channels.Tcp

Namespace RemotingExample

  Public Class Calculate
    Inherits MarshalByRefObject

    Public Sub Calculate()
      Console.WriteLine("Calculate service activated")
    End Sub

    Public Function Square(ByVal valueOne As Integer, _
      ByVal valueTwo As Integer) As Integer
      Console.WriteLine("ServiceObject.Calculate : {0} * {1}", _
      valueOne, valueTwo, (valueOne * valueTwo))
      Return (valueOne * valueTwo)
    End Function

  End Class

End Namespace
```

ANALYSIS The Calculate() subroutine writes a status message to the console. The real work is handled by the Square() function, which accepts two integers, writes a status message about them to the console, and returns the result of multiplying the first value by the second.

We now have a calculation object but nothing to initiate the process. That requires the client, which we'll build in the next step.

Building a Client to Use the Remote Object

Building a client application that uses remote objects isn't unlike building any other application. In fact, you add a reference to the remote object DLL file as though you were going to use it directly. The difference occurs when the object is actually created. Rather than use the New keyword, which would create a new object using the referenced DLL object within your application, you use the Activator.GetObject() method.

Follow these steps in your remoting solution to set up this client:

1. Add a VisualBasic .NET console project called vbClient.

2. Rename the default filename to vbClient.vb.

3. In your vbClient project references, add a reference to
   System.Runtime.Remoting.

4. In vbClient.vb, substitute the contents of Listing 17.4.

LISTING 17.4   vbClient.vb—Command-Line Client Remoting Project

```
Imports System
Imports System.Runtime.Remoting
Imports System.Runtime.Remoting.Channels
Imports System.Runtime.Remoting.Channels.Tcp
Imports vbServiceObject.RemotingExample

Public Class vbClient

  Public Shared Sub Main()
    Dim args As Array
    args = System.Environment.GetCommandLineArgs()
    Dim valueOne, valueTwo As Integer
    If args.Length = 3 Then
      valueOne = args.GetValue(1)
      valueTwo = args.GetValue(2)
    End If

    Dim chan As TcpChannel
    chan = New TcpChannel()
    ChannelServices.RegisterChannel(chan)

    Dim calc As Calculate
    Try
      calc = CType(Activator.GetObject(GetType(Calculate), _
      "tcp://localhost:8085/Calculate"), Calculate)
    Catch ex As Exception
      Console.WriteLine("Error message: " & ex.Message)
    End Try
    If calc Is Nothing Then
      System.Console.WriteLine("Could not locate server")
    Else
      If args.Length < 3 Then
        System.Console.WriteLine _
        ("Usage: vbClient valueOne valueTwo")
        System.Console.WriteLine("    e.g., vbClient 4 5")
      Else
        Try
```

17

LISTING 17.4   continued

```
            Console.WriteLine("Calculation result: " & _
               calc.Square(valueOne, valueTwo))
        Catch ex As Exception
            System.Console.WriteLine("Error: " & ex.Message)
        End Try
      End If
    End If

    End Sub

End Class
```

ANALYSIS   The Main() subroutine starts by collecting the arguments passed from the command line and storing them in the array called args. Here's a sample command line for using this client application:

```
vbClient 5 6
```

Because the first element of the array (index of 0) will be the executable name (vbClient), we bypass it and start collecting the second and third elements. To do so, we use the GetValue() method and assign it the index value. Notice that we try to collect the command-line values only if there are three of them. This way, we can avoid an error.

The client uses the Activator.GetObject() method to create a proxy for the remote object. The parameters it passes include the URL for the well-known object. Notice that we do some rudimentary error handling here when using GetObject(). If the host service hasn't been started, the method throws an exception.

Assuming that the correct values are in place, the client calls the following remote method while writing the output to the console:

```
calc.Square(valueOne, valueTwo)
```

The remoting project is just about ready to build and test. Be sure that you've added a reference to vbServiceObject.dll in the vbClient and vbServiceHost projects. Figure 17.2 shows how the References sections should look in Solution Explorer.

Build your solution by choosing Build Solution from the Build menu. Alternatively, you can build each project separately. After you fix any errors, it's time to test the remoting project. Here's the sequence:

1. Open a command window and change directories to the location of vbServiceHost.exe.

2. Run vbServiceHost.exe. The host initializes and waits for requests. Figure 17.3 shows a sample command window.

FIGURE 17.2

Project references for vbClient *and* vbServiceHost.

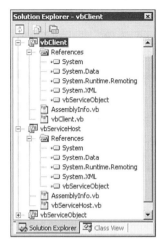

FIGURE 17.3

The host application, vbServiceHost, *running in a command window.*

3. Open a second command window and change directories to the location of vbClient.exe.

4. Execute vbClient.exe and pass two integers as parameters, such as 5 and 6. Figure 17.4 shows a sample command window for the client, including the output of the calculation result.

FIGURE 17.4

The client application, vbClient, *executed in a command window.*

5. Return to vbServiceHost in its command window. Notice that it has reported the activity as shown in Figure 17.5.

FIGURE 17.5

The activity of the client application is shown in the host, vbServiceHost.

17

> **Tip** To avoid a build error, you need to stop `vbServiceHost` before recompiling your solution.

Our testing has taken place on one computer. However, because you're using TCP, you can change the URLs and make calls to other network addresses. You can see the potential of harnessing machines in multiple locations to handle complicated and resource-intensive computing tasks.

Summary

Today you learned how to create and use remote objects with the .NET remoting framework. You used this powerful feature to write distributed applications, and the .NET Framework encapsulates the functionality to make this task easy. You also learned that there are multiple ways to host remote objects for client use. Today's lesson also discussed configuring the host and the different options to make remote objects usable.

Remote objects are sure to be part of any distributed application, and designing your objects correctly will allow them to work efficiently with minimal bandwidth usage.

Q&A

Q Can a host provide access to classes within more than one DLL?

A Yes. A host can host many different objects on one or more channels. The objects can reside in one or more DLL files and be in multiple namespaces.

Q When would I use a remote object instead of a Web Service?

A Although Web Services provide some communication between an application and an object on another machine and are useful when one-way communication is needed, remoting allows interaction between the objects in both directions. Use remote objects whenever flexibility is required within the interface between the client and server and two-way communication is a requirement. In fact, if a remote object defines events, the client application can handle the events when they are triggered. This allows a server to notify the client when an action occurs.

Workshop

The Workshop provides quiz questions and an exercise to help solidify your understanding of remote objects and provide you with experience in using what you've learned. Answers are provided in Appendix A, "Answers to Quizzes."

Quiz

1. What are the two types of remote object activation?

2. What's the difference between copied and referenced remote objects?

3. What's the base class for a referenced remote object?

4. What are the two .NET-provided channels for remote objects?

Exercise

Create a Windows Form as a substitute for the command-line client. Make the form accept two integers, call the remote service (vbHostService), and display the resulting value in the form.

17

DAY 18

Designing a Project Management Application

Every application development project begins with a concept that's translated into a design which is then implemented, tested, and deployed. All the lessons in this book have focused on teaching you how to think and work in an object-oriented manner. Today's lesson and the following lessons will put the concepts that you have learned up to this point into practice. You will develop a project management application for a fictitious client named XYZCompany.

It's imperative that any application development project begins with a complete design that includes both business requirements and technical design. Today's lesson isn't geared to teach you how to do project management as much as it is to teach you how to design an application using object-oriented programming techniques. If you're looking for help with project management, several books on the market cover that subject. However, today's lesson covers some project management skills required to build a design. Today you will accomplish the following:

- Compile a list of business requirements.
- Identify the components of the project.
- Identify object classes and their relationships.
- Build a set of UML diagrams for the project design.

Meeting with the Client

Before you can design an application, you have to know what the application is supposed to do. My favorite saying is, "How can you get there if you don't know where you're going?" In application development, you can't build the application unless you know what it's supposed to do.

Every application has a target client, whether it's you personally, another individual, a company, or the general software buying market. The client, whoever it is, is trying to fill a need with the application. Identifying that need and understanding the problem are key to a good design.

To understand the client's problem, you generally have some sort of meeting. If the software is for personal use, you will sit down by yourself. If it's for another individual or company, you will most likely have several meetings with the clients to understand their problem. If the software is for a retail product, you will typically meet with a product manager who gathers requirements based on customer input and market research. In any case, a meeting occurs.

Working in a Domain

In the process of meeting with the client for the project, your objective is to outline the problem that the client wants to solve. This conceptual outline of the problem doesn't necessarily represent the result; it's merely a representation of the real world. This type of diagram is generally created as a domain model diagram.

 Note
> Because a detailed discussion of Unified Modeling Language (UML) is outside the scope of this book, refer to *Sams Teach Yourself UML in 24 Hours*, Second Edition, by Joseph Schmuller (ISBN: 0-672-32238-2) if you want more information.

A domain model using UML notation is created with a set of class diagrams that have no operations defined. It should generally show the domain objects or conceptual classes, class associations, and attributes of the conceptual classes.

When you meet with XYZCompany's representatives to talk about the problem they want to solve, they describe the need to have a project management system that can keep track of their resources, projects, individual items within the project and to which resource they are assigned, and the status of each item within a project. They also want to keep track of products managed by the product manager and the projects within the products managed by the project managers. At a high level, you now have a basic understanding of what the client wants, so you diagram a domain model as shown in Figure 18.1.

Figure 18.1

Domain model diagram of XYZCompany problem to be solved.

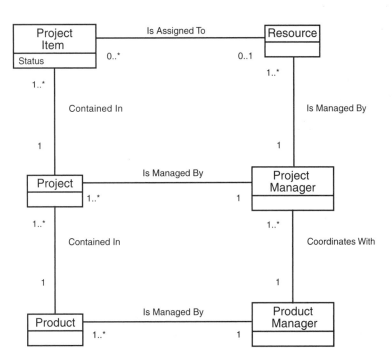

This domain model doesn't necessarily describe the software class architecture but instead describes the visualization of tasks, products, and people as they are in the real world. It provides a road map to help design the software later.

You identify conceptual real-world classes within a domain model by listening to what the client's requirements are and identifying the nouns. For example, the client's requirements list *project*, *resources*, *project items*, and so on. All these terms become conceptual classes in the domain model.

You identify relationships between the conceptual classes by using the verbs used by the client to describe the requirements. For example, a project manager *manages* a project. Therefore, the project manager class has a management relationship with a project.

The final step in the domain model is to indicate any conceptual class states indicated by the client. In this case, the client wants to track the status of each item within the project. Therefore, the status becomes a state within the project item conceptual class.

Decomposing the Domain Model

NEW TERM Some software solutions can be complex and difficult to conceptualize as one large unit. By breaking the domain model into smaller units, you can focus on a smaller portion of the problem at a time. In object-oriented analysis, decomposition occurs by dealing with separate entities within the domain. Therefore, the task of *decomposing* a domain model is to identify the different concepts in the problem domain and document the results.

For example, in the real-world domain shown in Figure 18.1, the conceptual classes Project Manager, Resource, and Project are related in that a project manager manages a project and resources, which are ultimately assigned to a project. Figure 18.2 shows a partial domain model of the project.

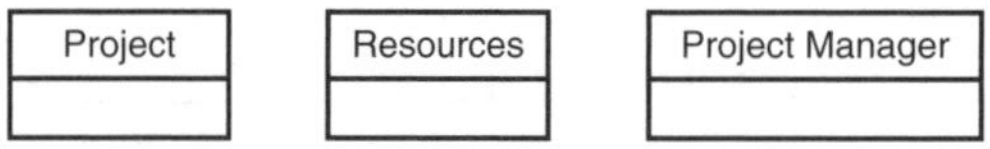

FIGURE 18.2

Decomposed portion of the domain model diagram.

Project		Resources		Project Manager

For the purposes of this project, decomposing the domain model isn't necessary because it's relatively simple and easy to manage as defined.

Designing with the Requirements

Now that you have the general requirements and a domain model for the project, it's time to turn the requirements into a design. How far you take the design is up to you and how detailed you want to be. UML provides several different diagrams you can use in designing an application. For some complex applications, you might use all the different diagrams to some extent in your application design.

For the XYZCompany project, you will create only a subset of the types of diagrams UML defines because the project isn't very complex. The class diagram is one of the most fundamental of the diagrams for a technical design. You shouldn't design an object-oriented application without it.

Creating an Interaction Design

The interaction diagram is a valuable tool in object-oriented design projects. Many developers don't use it often enough. This diagram shows how objects interact with each other by using messages in a time line that shows the objects' life span as they are used by other objects.

By spending some time on the interactive diagrams during the design process, you will gain a better understanding of how the objects need to interact with each other. Without the diagram, you may have some vague idea of how they should interact, but it won't be defined and small issues that would normally be apparent will inevitably slip through the design process undetected.

The XYZCompany project initially has limited interaction between the objects. Later phases of the project will be enhanced to include other features and thus interactions. For the initial phase, the client requires the application to keep track of products, which encompasses multiple projects with their own project items. The project items are assigned to resources that can report the project items' status as they make progress completing the items.

The first interaction diagram (see Figure 18.3) describes the interaction between the objects when a new project is created within a product. Keep in mind that you may need to revise your diagrams as the project progresses and you get a deeper understanding of the complexities and requirements.

18

FIGURE 18.3

Interactive diagram for adding a new project.

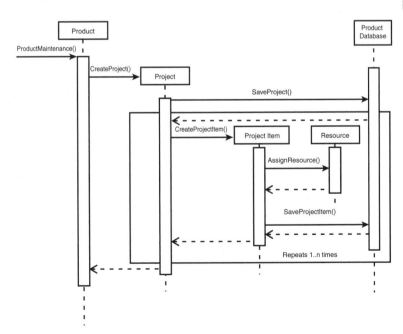

The diagram shows that when a new project is created, it's saved to the product database. Then new project items are created for the project, assigned to a resource, and then saved to the product database. A project can have more than one project item, so this process can continue as often as necessary until the user is finished adding project items.

The other interaction diagram in this design shows the interaction that occurs when a resource marks the status of a project item. The resource updates the project item status with the new status, which is then saved in the product database (see Figure 18.4).

FIGURE 18.4

Interaction diagram for updating the status of a project item.

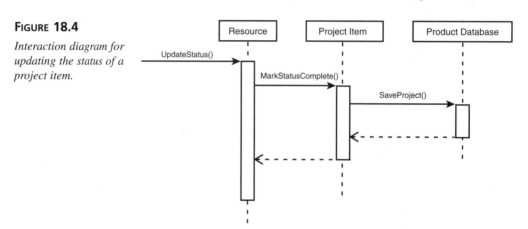

Creating Software Classes from Conceptual Classes

Creating a class diagram from the conceptual classes you created earlier isn't necessarily a one-to-one transfer of class entities. Many applications aren't actually created exactly as their real-world classes would lead you to believe. However, in cases in which the application is somewhat simple and the real-world entities are well defined, it makes sense that the software classes generally follow the lines of the conceptual classes.

The first step in creating a UML class diagram from the conceptual class diagram is to identify the classes that you will create for the application. This high-level class diagram doesn't indicate members or methods; it shows the classes and their associations with each other (see Figure 18.5).

Notice that the relationships are similar to the ones shown in the conceptual class design. The aggregations are shown for the `Product`, `Project`, and `ProjectItems` classes so that their relationship is obvious.

FIGURE 18.5

High-level UML class diagram with relationships.

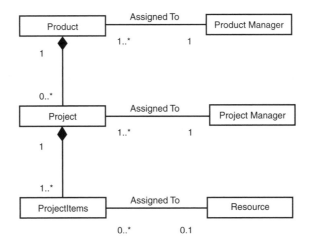

> **Note**
>
> No classes represent the user interface in this project because good design starts with the underlying class architecture. After the architecture is designed, a user interface is designed to encompass the underlying classes. The two designs are created separately, and the UI design will contain references only to the underlying classes. This design makes sense because it mirrors how an object-oriented application should be developed. Therefore, the UI design will be created in the next lesson.

18

When you know what the high-level classes are and their relationships with each other, the next step in the design is to identify the properties that each class should have. For example, the Product class should have a unique ID, name, description, and assigned manager's ID. Going through each class identified in the high-level diagram, the class state information for each class is defined as shown in Figure 18.6.

UML Notation Symbols

Unified Modeling Language defines three visibility levels for attributes and operations in classes. These levels are represented on diagrams with the following symbols:

- \- represents private
- \# represents protected
- \+ represents public

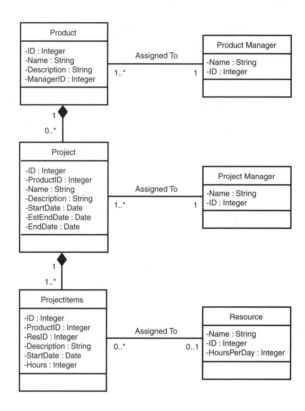

As you can see in Figure 18.6, all the classes have state information defined. The
`Product`, `Project`, and `ProjectItems` classes have information that allows them to be
tied together by their unique ID values. They also have references to the manager or
resource ID to which they are assigned.

As you look at Figure 18.6, notice that Product Manager, Project Manager, and Resource
are all somewhat related in that they share common state information and all have assign-
ments. The great benefit from creating a proper design is that you spot these issues
before you write any code. At this point, it makes sense to create a new abstract class
that the Product Manager, Project Manager, and Resource classes will inherit. The new
class should include all the common state information currently being replicated. You
include this information by declaring a new `Employee` class and changing the diagram to
the one shown in Figure 18.7.

Another member, `Position`, is added to the `Employee` class to indicate the position held
by the employee; this member identifies the employee's role. That role is defined within
each class derived from the `Employee` class.

FIGURE 18.7

Updated class diagram with the new abstract `Employee` class.

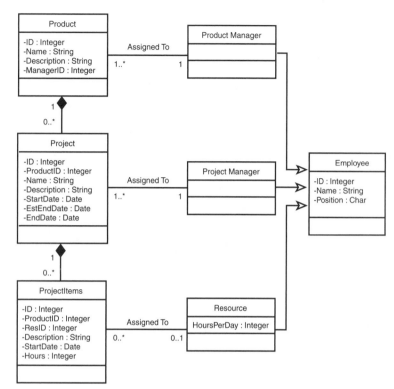

The final step in building the class diagram is to define all methods and properties for each class. Each class has `New()` and `Dispose()` methods for creation and cleanup. Each class also provides properties for each member within the class. Finally, each class provides `Save()`, `Read()`, and `Delete()` methods for saving, reading, and deleting the class object from the data source. Figure 18.8 shows the resulting UML class diagram.

When you look at the class diagram in Figure 18.8, notice a common feature that all major classes have: They all have a unique identity and can read, write, and delete themselves from a data source. This is a good opportunity for defining an interface that each class can implement and for providing a generic interface for dealing with each class. The interface, `IDBIdentity`, should declare the `ID()`, `Name()`, `Description()`, `Save()`, `Delete()`, and `Read()` properties and methods. Although not all classes have members to support the `Description()` property, those classes can implement it by returning an empty string. Figure 18.9 shows the final class diagram, which is the final diagram in the design.

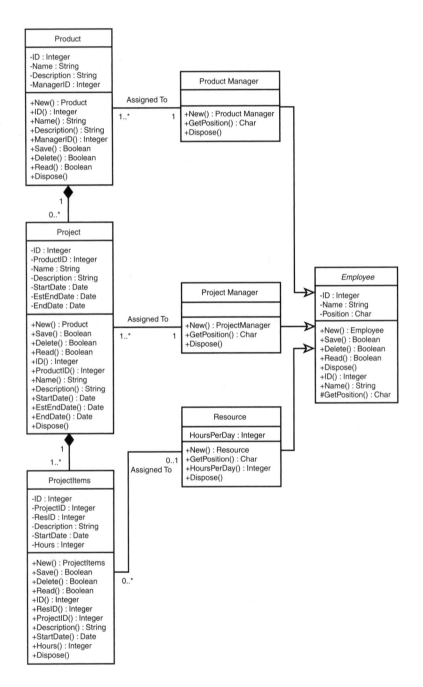

FIGURE 18.8

UML class diagram with all methods and properties shown for each class.

FIGURE **18.9**

Final UML class diagram with IDBIdentity *interface.*

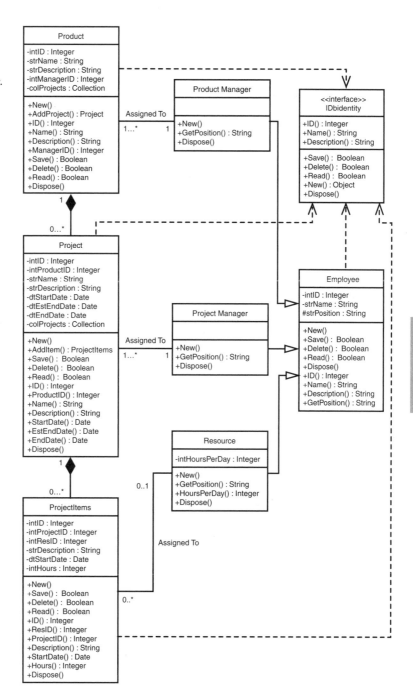

18

Summary

Today you went through an object-oriented design process for a fictitious client's application. You learned that you gather requirements, take that information to a conceptual diagram, and then produce the UML diagrams from that. You ended the day with your final class diagram for the application. While going through the design process, you learned that problems that arise and design opportunities are easily integrated at this stage of the application development process.

The final three lessons in this book deal with creating and enhancing the application designed in this lesson. You will continue to use this design and enhance it throughout the coming lessons.

Q&A

Q What if I like to do other types of design diagrams? Can I use them for object-oriented programming?

A UML is just one form of diagramming used for object-oriented design. Although many others are used, UML is an industry standard for most object-oriented programming.

Q Can user interface design and functional design intermingle?

A You can design an application any way you want to unless you work for a company that requires you to design a particular way. The important point is that you identify the different aspects of the application which should be the same regardless of the design methods. However, user interface design shouldn't dictate the underlying functionality; the functionality should dictate the user interface. That's why I keep the design separate; this approach also provides a nice separation that enables me to easily make changes to the appearance without affecting the underlying functionality.

Workshop

The Workshop provides quiz questions and an exercise to help solidify your understanding of today's lesson. Answers are provided in Appendix A, "Answers to Quizzes."

Quiz

1. Before you design an application, what's your first step?
2. Do conceptual classes reflect actual classes?

3. Name some elements and characteristics that UML class diagrams reveal about the classes within the application.

Exercise

XYZCompany has come back to you and asked that the system be able to keep track of project teams. The company wants to know what resources are assigned to a team. The team also has a team leader who reports directly to the project manager. Draw the matching diagrams needed to reflect the new client request. However, make the diagrams separate and just reference objects from today's design.

18

DAY 19

Creating the Project Management Application

After creating the object-oriented design, you'll want to turn that design into code. Yesterday you worked with the client to create a UML design that reflects the way the client does business. The object-oriented design process maps the elements of the business into classes, derived classes, and interfaces.

Today you will create the Visual Basic .NET code that implements that design. After you lay out a class design, turning that design into code is usually very simple. That's the beauty of UML diagrams. Just take the diagram that represents a class or interface, create it in Visual Basic .NET, and then add the properties, methods, and events as shown in the diagram.

In today's lesson, you will accomplish the following:

- Create a class module in Visual Studio .NET.
- Code an interface.
- Code classes.

Creating a Class Module

To map the UML object-oriented design to Visual Basic .NET code, you start by creating a class module. This process is similar to creating class modules in Visual Basic 6.0. The big difference is the syntax, which you learned on Day 4, "Making New Objects by Expanding Existing Objects."

After a class module is built as part of a solution, you can use it anywhere in that solution. You also can build a class module into a standalone assembly that you can use as a part of other Visual Studio .NET solutions.

 Tip

> You might have noticed that the terms *solution* and *project* seem to be used interchangeably. In fact, every project in Visual Studio .NET is part of a solution. But a solution can have more than one project in it, similar to project groups in Visual Basic 6.0. Because a new project needs a new solution, however, the terms mean almost the same thing.

Let's get started with our class module. In Visual Studio .NET, start a new Visual Basic Class Library project (from the File menu, choose New, Project, Visual Basic Projects, and then Class Library). Name the project ProjectManager and click OK.

At this point, Visual Studio .NET will generate a solution consisting of one project with three parts: some built-in standard references, an AssemblyInfo.VB component, and a class module named Class1.vb.

In Solution Explorer, rename the default class module file (Class1.vb) to PM.vb. Also, erase the default `class1` definition code so that you're starting with a clean slate. You're now ready to code the interface.

Creating the Interface

In the class design from yesterday, you learned that the designed classes share a set of common properties and methods. The properties have to do with identification and the methods with reading, writing, and deleting themselves from whatever data storage you choose. As a result, you designed an interface, `IDBIdentity`, that has the standard set of properties and methods. Because all the classes you will create use that interface, start with that definition.

When you create an interface, you merely define the names of its properties, events, and methods. No code other than that is found in the interface. The code that the properties and methods use will be defined in the class definitions. Any parameters for methods or events also have to be defined. The one limitation of interfaces is that they have to be exactly matched in the class definitions.

Properties are defined with their data types. Functions are also defined with a data type for the return value, and parameters are defined with their types.

Tip

> A nice Visual Studio .NET feature enables you to type only what is necessary, and Visual Studio .NET will fill in the rest. For example, if you type
>
> ```
> public interface IDBIdentity
> ```
>
> Visual Studio .NET will capitalize the first two words and add the End Interface syntax two lines below, leaving the cursor on the line between. You don't need to indent the other lines or type the parentheses. The IDE takes care of all that.

Listing 19.1 shows the code for the IDBIdentity interface. Enter it in the code window for PM.vb.

LISTING 19.1   Defining the IDBIdentity Interface

```
Public Interface IDBIdentity
    ReadOnly Property ID() As Integer
    Property Name() As String
    Property Description() As String
    Function Save() As Boolean
    Function Delete() As Boolean
    Function Read() As Boolean
    Sub Dispose()
End Interface
```

19

Creating Classes

Classes are created in class modules. If you want, you can create a different class module for each class, but you also can create all the classes you need within one module. If the classes are interlinked with each other in their code, putting them in one class module would be best. If the classes are independent of each other and will be used separately depending on the solution, it would be best to put each class, or a small set of classes, in separate modules.

Code maintenance is another reason to keep classes together, whereas readability may dictate separating classes. If you have no other compelling reason to keep classes together, you can choose any method you like.

For this project, because the classes are interlinked and used together, they all will be placed in the PM.vb class module.

You can divide the classes in this project into three parts:

- The Employee class, which is an abstract class
- The derived classes of the Employee class: ProductManager, ProjectManager, and Resource
- The other classes: Product, Project, and ProjectItems

Employee Class

NEW TERM   The Employee class is an *abstract* class, meaning that it won't be used to create any objects in any programs that use this class library. Instead, other classes, sometimes called *derived* classes, will inherit from the Employee class, making the job of creating them that much easier.

To create an abstract class in Visual Basic .NET, use the MustInherit keyword in the class definition, between the scope (in this case, Public) and the word Class.

Interface Code

Because the Employee class will use the IDBIdentity interface, the first code line in the class definition indicates that the class implements this interface. To create the definition, you use the Implements keyword. After you type it, the IDE will offer up any types defined within your class, as well as any in the class libraries specified in your project's References section. Typing **i**, **d**, **b**, **i**, and then pressing Tab will select the IDBIdentity class.

After you enter that line, a squiggly underline appears under IDBIdentity. This squiggly underline indicates a syntax problem that Visual Studio .NET has detected. If you position the mouse pointer over the word, a ToolTip will appear explaining what the problem is (see Figure 19.1).

FIGURE **19.1**

The PM.vb code window showing a squiggly line under IDBIdentity.

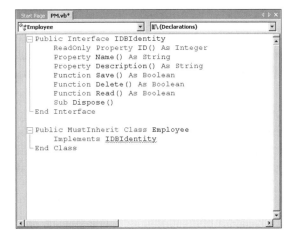

Unfortunately, that tip is just one of several things that are wrong at this point. Because the interface involves three properties and four methods, the interface implementation really has seven problems. To see all the problems, you open the Task List window, which usually appears at the bottom of the IDE. To see it, choose Show Tasks and then All from the View menu. At the top of the Task List window, you see that seven tasks in the list all start with "ProjectManager.Employee" must be implemented (see Figure 19.2).

FIGURE **19.2**

Task List window from ProjectManager *project.*

Whenever you use an interface in a class, the class must define all the element members of that interface. This means that all properties, functions, and subs have to be defined in the class definition. This is the downside of using interfaces because Visual Studio .NET doesn't automatically insert the necessary code to implement them.

Type in the property, function, or sub exactly as it was defined in the interface, but then add the key phrase Implements at the end of the defining line, followed by the interface name, a dot, and the appropriate property or method from the interface. The IDE will make this procedure relatively painless.

Because properties and functions must do something in class code, add some standard code to make it work. The actual code developed for the classes will be entered later. When you enter the standard code for the property Gets and functions, make sure that they return a value of the data type specified in the interface.

To that end, some private members should be defined in the class to store the values passed in and out via the property code. For the Employee class, create two private variables, intID and strName. They will store the property values from ID() and Name().

Employee Class–Specific Code

Along with all the code for the interface, you also need a new property and function, strPosition and GetPosition(). You must manipulate the strPosition property at the derived class level, so it needs to be accessible by those classes. To do that, you must define the property as Protected. The function will be public so that other code in a solution can read the position. Add a protected declaration for strPosition, and in the function GetPosition(), return that variable. This is a variation on properties. Rather than allow others to read or modify through a property, you force them to use a method to read it.

> **Tip**
>
> The Visual Studio .NET IDE comes to your aid again. After you type in a property definition, the IDE automatically adds the Get and Set structures, leaving you with only the important code to write. In the case of a Get, add a line to return a value, and in Set, assign the Value parameter to the appropriate member.

All this code for the class definition of Employee is shown in Listing 19.2. Notice that a read-only property has only a Get function, no Set sub. Also, notice that because the Employee class has no internal member to store the Description property, Get returns an empty string and Set does nothing.

LISTING 19.2   Starting Code for the Employee Class

```
Public MustInherit Class Employee
    Implements IDBIdentity

    Dim intID As Integer
    Dim strName As String
    Protected strPosition As String
```

LISTING 19.2   continued

```
Public ReadOnly Property ID() As Integer Implements IDBIdentity.ID
    Get
        Return intID
    End Get
End Property

Public Property Name() As String Implements IDBIdentity.Name
    Get
        Return strName
    End Get
    Set(ByVal Value As String)
        strName = Value
    End Set
End Property

Public Property Description() As String Implements IDBIdentity.Description
    Get
        Return ""
    End Get
    Set(ByVal Value As String)

    End Set
End Property

Public Function Save() As Boolean Implements IDBIdentity.Save
    Return True
End Function

Public Function Delete() As Boolean Implements IDBIdentity.Delete
    Return True
End Function

Public Function Read() As Boolean Implements IDBIdentity.Read
    Return True
End Function

Public Sub Dispose() Implements IDBIdentity.Dispose

End Sub

Protected Function GetPosition() As String
    Return strPosition
End Function
End Class
```

19

Employee Class Constructor

At this point, the class doesn't have code in it to do much. That's okay because there's no storage device yet for the class. The Save() method is intended to save the information from an instance of the Employee class to some storage device. The Delete() method will remove the information from the storage, and the Read() method will retrieve that information. On Day 21, you'll design that storage device.

You need to add the class constructor at this time. In Visual Basic 6.0, some of the tasks of a constructor were handled by the Initialize event, but now Visual Basic .NET uses a New() method when an object is created. The advantage of New() is that it can accept parameters when the object is created. The really great advantage of New() is that it can be overloaded, allowing multiple manners of instantiating a class.

In the Employee class, the only information that is modifiable is the Name property. There are member variables for the ID and position of an employee, but users can't change them. Instead, those members are set when an instance of the class is created in the constructor.

Because the position isn't defined in the Employee class definition but will be handled in the derived classes of the Employee class, the only properties that concern us are ID and Name. The ID must be set at the time an Employee object is created but may be unknown if the object represents a new hire. This scenario sets up three possible ways of creating the object:

- No ID yet
- ID known, but name will be set later
- ID and name known right away

To handle these three possibilities, create three different versions of the New() method:

- One with no parameters
- One with just one parameter, for the ID
- One with two parameters, for both the ID and the name

If no parameters are used, the intID member will be set to −1. This way, when you want to save that employee, either the Save() method will figure the ID to use, or the storage engine will determine the value and pass it to the Save() method.

If one parameter is used, it will be used for the intID member. It is assumed that the Name() property will be used to set the name.

If two parameters are used when this object is created, the first parameter will be for the intID member, and the second parameter will be used for the strName member. The name can still be changed later during the lifetime of this object.

Listing 19.3 shows the code for the Employee class constructors.

LISTING 19.3 Employee Class Constructors

```
Public Sub New()
    intID = -1
End Sub

Public Sub New(ByVal intNewID As Integer)
    intID = intNewID
End Sub

Public Sub New(ByVal intNewID As Integer, ByVal strNewName As String)
    intID = intNewID
    strName = strNewName
End Sub
```

When the class is instantiated, the system automatically determines which constructor to use. This choice depends on the number and data types of the parameters. This type of overloading is available throughout Visual Basic .NET, but this is the only place where the keyword Overloads doesn't have to be used.

Derived Classes

The Employee class was designed as an abstract class, meaning that no objects can be created directly from that class. Instead, derived classes that inherit from the abstract class are created, and then those classes are used to instantiate objects. In this design, three classes inherit from the Employee class: ProductManager, ProjectManager, and Resource.

Class View Window

The best way to see how this process works is to use the Class View window while you enter the new classes. (Choose Class View from the View menu, or click the Class View toolbar button to see this window.) The Class View window appears with the Solution Explorer, usually in the upper-right frame of the IDE. These windows are tabbed at the bottom, so you can use the tabs to switch between the Solution Explorer and Class View.

After you open the Class View window, expand the ProjectManager namespace, which is indicated by braces. You will see both the Employee class and IDBIdentity interface.

19

Expand the `Employee` class, and a folder called Bases and Interfaces will appear, along with all the methods and properties of the `Employee` class (see Figure 19.3).

FIGURE 19.3

Class View window showing the Employee *class expanded.*

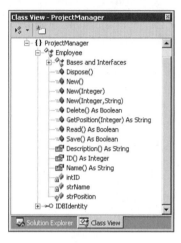

After you view the properties and methods of the `Employee` class, collapse the lines until you see only the elements that make up the `ProjectManager` namespace—`Employee` and `IDBIdentity`.

Derived Classes

Creating the derived classes is easy, and similar to creating any class. Simply type the `ProductManager` class definition line first, and you will see the following in the code window:

```
Public Class ProductManager

End Class
```

The cursor will be positioned on the blank line. In the Class View window, you can see that the namespace has a new class, the one you just created. No expand icon appears next to the name because the class definition doesn't include any members yet. Now type the following in the blank line:

```
Inherits Employee
```

Notice the expand icon next to the `ProductManager` class name in the Class View window. Expanding the class shows that all definitions of `Employee` have been inherited by the `ProductManager` class and appear to be a part of the `ProductManager` class definition. The only difference is that no code other than the `Inherits` line appears in the module.

Do the same for the `ProjectManager` and `Resource` classes so that the result looks like Listing 19.4.

LISTING 19.4   Derived Classes of `Employee`

```
Public Class ProductManager
    Inherits Employee
End Class

Public Class ProjectManager
    Inherits Employee
End Class

Public Class Resource
    Inherits Employee
End Class
```

Derived Class Constructors

The constructors written for the `Employee` class are fine as far they go, but one extra member in that class wasn't processed at the base class level. That member is `strPosition`, which stores the position of an employee. That member wasn't set at the base class level because the derived classes are responsible for setting that value.

This means that all constructors for the `Employee` class must be overridden in the derived classes. You can easily set them up this way by writing the `New()` methods in each class. Rather than rewrite the entire constructors, you can use the base class constructors through the use of the `MyBase` keyword.

You can use `MyBase` in derived classes to refer to members of the base class, such as calling methods of the base class. This way, you can add to the behavior of a base class method by overriding the method in the derived class and calling the base class method. This must be done as the first command of the derived class's method.

Because the base class has three constructors, the derived classes will also have three constructors. The parameter values passed into the creation of the derived class objects will be passed into the base class's `New()` methods.

Listing 19.5 shows the code for the `ProductManager` class, while the `ProjectManager` class is almost the same except for the change in value for `strPosition`.

19

LISTING 19.5   `ProductManager` Class Constructors

```
Public Sub New()
    MyBase.New()
    strPosition = "Product Manager"
End Sub
Public Sub New(ByVal intNewID As Integer)
    MyBase.New(intNewID)
    strPosition = "Product Manager"
End Sub
Public Sub New(ByVal intNewID As Integer, ByVal strNewName As String)
    MyBase.New(intNewID, strNewName)
    strPosition = "Product Manager"
End Sub
```

The `Resource` class is handled a little differently. Because the position of a resource can be almost anything else, the constructors for the `Resource` class have an extra required parameter to specify the job for the employee being instantiated. Listing 19.6 shows the code for the constructors for the `Resource` class.

LISTING 19.6   `Resource` Class Constructors

```
Public Sub New(ByVal strJob As String)
    MyBase.New()
    strPosition = strJob
End Sub
Public Sub New(ByVal strJob As String, ByVal intNewID As Integer)
    MyBase.New(intNewID)
    strPosition = strJob
End Sub
Public Sub New(ByVal strJob As String, ByVal intNewID As Integer, _
            ByVal strNewName As String)
    MyBase.New(intNewID, strNewName)
    strPosition = strJob
End Sub
```

You need to make one last change for the `Resource` class. A private member sets the number of hours per day that the resource devotes to project items, and you need to create property procedures for reading and storing that value. Add the code in Listing 19.7 to the beginning of the `Resource` class, right after the inherits line.

LISTING 19.7   Handling Hours Per Day in the `Resource` Class

```
Dim intHoursPerDay As Integer
Public Property HoursPerDay() As Integer
```

LISTING 19.7   continued

```
        Get
            Return intHoursPerDay
        End Get
        Set(ByVal Value As Integer)
            intHoursPerDay = Value
        End Set
    End Property
```

The Rest of the Classes

The rest of the classes—Product, Project, and ProjectItems—are similar to the Employee class because they all use the IDBIdentity interface. They vary because they aren't abstract classes and because each has its own set of other private members, properties, and methods. The other difference is that they all use the Description member and property from the interface.

Listing 19.8 shows the initial code for the Product class. The other two class definitions are identical, except for the class name.

LISTING 19.8   Product Class Code

```
Public Class Product
    Implements IDBIdentity

    Dim intID As Integer
    Dim strName As String
    Dim strDescription As String

    Public ReadOnly Property ID() As Integer Implements IDBIdentity.ID
        Get
            Return intID
        End Get
    End Property

    Public Property Name() As String Implements IDBIdentity.Name
        Get
            Return strName
        End Get
        Set(ByVal Value As String)
            strName = Value
        End Set
    End Property

    Public Property Description() As String Implements IDBIdentity.Description
        Get
```

19

LISTING 19.8   continued

```
        End Get
        Set(ByVal Value As String)
            strDescription = Value
        End Set
    End Property
    Public Function Save() As Boolean Implements IDBIdentity.Save
        Return True
    End Function
    Public Function Delete() As Boolean Implements IDBIdentity.Delete
        Return True
    End Function
    Public Function Read() As Boolean Implements IDBIdentity.Read
        Return True
    End Function
    Public Sub Dispose() Implements IDBIdentity.Dispose

    End Sub
End Class
```

Product **Class**

The Product class has three constructors, as the Employee class does, so that you can
instantiate a product with no parameters, just the ID parameter, or both the ID and name
parameters. The code is identical to the Employee class constructor code (refer to Listing
19.3) because the same parameter and member names are used, taking advantage of the
concept of polymorphism.

The only additions to the Product class are an intManagerID private member and a
matching ManagerID public property (see Listing 19.9).

LISTING 19.9   Handling Manager IDs in the Product Class

```
Dim intManagerID As Integer

Public Property ManagerID() As Integer
    Get
        Return intManagerID
    End Get
    Set(ByVal Value As Integer)
        intManagerID = Value
    End Set
End Property
```

Project **Class**

The basics of the Project class are identical to the Product class, but because a project is part of a product, the constructors will include a parameter for the ProductID. This class also includes five private members for a project: intManagerID, intProductID, dtStartDate, dtEndDate, and dtEstEndDate. It also has public properties for the last four items.

Listing 19.10 shows the extra code for these members and properties.

LISTING 19.10   Handling Extra Properties in the Project Class

```
Dim intProductID As Integer
Dim intManagerID As Integer
Dim dtStartDate As Date
Dim dtEndDate As Date
Dim dtEstEndDate As Date

Public Property ManagerID() As Integer
    Get
        Return intManagerID
    End Get
    Set(ByVal Value As Integer)
        intManagerID = Value
    End Set
End Property

Public Property StartDate() As Date
    Get
        Return dtStartDate
    End Get
    Set(ByVal Value As Date)
        dtStartDate = Value
    End Set
End Property

Public Property EndDate() As Date
    Get
        Return dtEndDate
    End Get
    Set(ByVal Value As Date)
        dtEndDate = Value
    End Set
End Property

Public Property EstEndDate() As Date
    Get
        Return dtEstEndDate
    End Get
```

19

LISTING 19.10   continued

```
    Set(ByVal Value As Date)
        dtEstEndDate = Value
    End Set
End Property
```

ANALYSIS   intProductID doesn't have a matching property because that value is set in the
constructors by an extra parameter, intProduct, that's required by the New()
methods, as shown in Listing 19.11.

LISTING 19.11   Code to Add to the Project Class for the Constructors

```
Public Sub New(ByVal intProduct As Integer)
    intID = -1
    intProductID = intProduct
End Sub

Public Sub New(ByVal intProduct As Integer, ByVal intNewID As Integer)
    intID = intNewID
    intProductID = intProduct
End Sub

Public Sub New(ByVal intProduct As Integer, ByVal intNewID As Integer, _
               ByVal strNewName As String)
    intID = intNewID
    intProductID = intProduct
    strName = strNewName
End Sub
```

ProjectItems Class

The ProjectItems class is similar to the other two classes, except that the strName
member and Name property don't do anything. Like with the Project class, a project item
is created with a reference to the project it's for, so the project ID is passed into the constructors as a parameter.

The ProjectItems class also has members for the project ID (intProjectID), the
resource ID (intResID), the start date (dtStartDate), and the number of hours spent on
an item (intHours). It also includes properties for accessing the last three values.

Listing 19.12 shows the special code for this class.

LISTING 19.12   Extra Code to Add to the `ProjectItems` Class

```
Dim intProjectID As Integer
Dim intResID As Integer
Dim dtStartDate As Date
Dim intHours As Integer

Public Property ResID() As Integer
    Get
        Return intResID
    End Get
    Set(ByVal Value As Integer)
        intResID = Value
    End Set
End Property

Public Property StartDate() As Date
    Get
        Return dtStartDate
    End Get
    Set(ByVal Value As Date)
        dtStartDate = Value
    End Set
End Property

Public Property Hours() As Integer
    Get
        Return intHours
    End Get
    Set(ByVal Value As Integer)
        intHours = Value
    End Set
End Property

Public Sub New(ByVal intProject As Integer)
    intID = -1
    intProjectID = intProject
End Sub

Public Sub New(ByVal intProject As Integer, ByVal intNewID As Integer)
    intID = intNewID
    intProjectID = intProject
End Sub
```

ANALYSIS   The `ProjectItems` class has only two constructors because you don't need to pass a name as a parameter. As we stated before, this class doesn't use the `Name` property.

19

Final Code in the Product Class

The Project class requires an extra ID because it isn't created from outside the class library. Instead, extra methods are included in the Product class for instantiating an object from this class. This way, a project that isn't a part of some product can't be created.

For the Product class, three new methods need to be added, all with the same name. The three methods all have the same name because of the three constructors for the Project class. The difference between using your own overloaded methods and overloading the New() method is that you have to use the keyword Overloads in the definition of the methods.

You also need to create a collection within the class definition so that an instance of the Product class can be used to reference the projects within it. Add the following line to the Product class to define the collection object:

```
Dim colProjects As New Collection
```

Now add the code in Listing 19.13 to create the overloaded methods for adding a Project object. Note that these methods are placed in the Product class definition.

LISTING 19.13   Code to Add to the Product Class with the AddProject Methods

```
Public Overloads Function AddProject() As Project
    Dim intCount As Integer

    intCount = colProjects.Count + 1
    colProjects.Add(New Project(intID), intCount.ToString)
    Return colProjects.Item(intCount.ToString)
End Function

Public Overloads Function AddProject(ByVal intProjectID As Integer) As Project
    Dim intCount As Integer

    intCount = colProjects.Count + 1
    colProjects.Add(New Project(intID, intProjectID), _
                    intCount.ToString)
    Return colProjects.Item(intCount.ToString)
End Function

Public Overloads Function AddProject(ByVal intProjectID As Integer, _
        ByVal strName As String) As Project
    Dim intCount As Integer

    intCount = colProjects.Count + 1
    colProjects.Add(New Project(intID, intProjectID, strName), _
```

LISTING 19.13   continued

```
        intCount.ToString)
    Return colProjects.Item(intCount.ToString)
End Function
```

> **ANALYSIS** Notice that the AddProject() methods are functions that return the Project object created. This way, the program using these classes can manipulate the Project objects separately from the Product object. In some designs, the Project class definition itself might be private, and the Product class's collection member would be public, so other programs would have to use the Product objects to refer to the Project objects.

Summary

Today you created Visual Basic .NET classes based on the class design of yesterday's process. You learned how to code interfaces, classes, and derived classes. You also learned about the implementation of interfaces and the required code that must be placed in a class definition so that you can use the interface. You learned about coding constructors, overloading them, and creating overloaded methods of your own. Finally, you learned about using collections within a class definition and some of the methods and properties associated with them.

Tomorrow you'll design and code a Windows Form interface for interacting with these classes. That way, your application's users can supply data to be used in the classes. You'll also use the code for instantiating objects from your classes.

19

Q&A

Q What if I want to create another set of classes with the same names but with different behavior but still able to use both sets of classes in the same solution?

A You can do so easily by using namespaces. Each set of classes would be in its own namespace. Then, when you use the classes, you can specify which class you want by prefixing the namespace before the class name, as in ProjectManager.Employee and Company.Employee.

Q This lesson contained a lot of code to copy from one class definition to another. Can I make this code transfer easier?

A Yes. You can use the toolbox. When you copy some text into the Clipboard, you can paste into the General section of the toolbox. Then place the cursor in the code

window where you want the code, and go to the toolbox and just double-click the code segment. You can also drag and drop the code entry from the toolbox to the code window. You can even give the entry in the toolbox a meaningful name. These entries will also persist into your next session with Visual Studio .NET.

Workshop

The Workshop provides quiz questions and an exercise to help solidify your understanding of today's lesson. Answers are provided in Appendix A, "Answers to Quizzes."

Quiz

1. What's the keyword for using an interface in a class definition?

2. What's the keyword for using a base class when defining a derived class?

3. What's the keyword for using the same method name multiple times in a class definition?

4. Why would you use a method name more than once in a class definition?

Exercise

In today's lesson, you learned how to use one class to instantiate objects from another class. You made changes to the Product class so that a Product object contains Project objects. Now do the same for the ProjectItems objects by making the appropriate additions to the Project class. Remember that the ProjectItems class has only two constructors.

DAY 20

Adding Features to the Application

Yesterday you wrote the classes for the Project Manager application in Visual Basic .NET. This code implemented the class design of Day 18. What's missing is a user interface to actually start using the project manager classes.

Today you will create the visual interface that users will see when working with the classes you designed. You will use Windows Forms to create the visual interface. You'll use inheritance so that you can create a standard form for data entry. Furthermore, you could just as easily create Web Forms for the interface. The classes you designed yesterday have no code for any particular type of user interface.

In today's lesson, you will accomplish the following:

- Design a visual interface.
- Create visual classes.
- Create Windows Forms in Visual Basic .NET.
- Write code to instantiate objects.

Designing a Visual Class

NEW TERM   When you designed the classes yesterday, you used a technique of application
building that separates form from function. What you created in yesterday's lesson is called the middle layer of a three-layer component. This layering is referred to as an *n-tier design*, and this project has three tiers. The first layer is presentation, and the third layer is data storage.

Today you'll create the visual, or presentation, tier. The first step in creating a presentation tier is to know how the data-entry people at XYZCompany interact with the data. Then you need to come up with a design for the application that matches their method of data input and output.

After doing the research, you decide that a standard data-entry form would be the best way for the XYZCompany to enter, edit, and retrieve the data. Four types of data are input: employees, products, projects, and project items. Therefore, you will create four forms. Only one form is used for employees because the position entered will determine the type to be used for that employee.

After analyzing the forms' requirements, you realize that these simple forms require just a few types of controls: labels, text boxes, command buttons, radio buttons, groups, and date/time pickers.

The text boxes will allow users to enter the data, a label will signal what data goes into a text box, and the command buttons will be used to take actions. Radio buttons will give users a fixed set of choices within a group. Date/time pickers will be used for date-type entry. The actions for the command buttons are creating a data item, saving the data, reading some data, and deleting data. The forms will also contain buttons to start other forms.

The forms appear to be nearly identical. Each form will have at least four buttons and a set of two labels and two text boxes for the ID and name. This "sameness" among objects in the object-oriented programming world usually indicates a class.

Forms are objects, instances of the Form class from the System.Windows.Forms namespace. When you create a form, you are really creating a derived class of that Form class, and when the application runs, it's creating an instance of your derived class. Because it's a class, you can create a derived form class and then use that class to create other forms.

For this project, you will create a Form class, which incorporates the main functionality of the forms. Then you'll use that class to create the four forms for the project.

Creating a Visual Class

Creating visual classes is different from coding classes because you use a drawing surface to create the class. The "visual" classes, however, are the same as the coded classes because Visual Basic .NET creates the code for you. This approach varies from the approach used in Visual Basic 6.0, where the visual aspects of forms and controls were set behind the scenes. In Visual Basic .NET, you create a form as in earlier versions of Visual Basic, but the result is code that you can read and modify.

When you're using inheritance, it's best to create a separate solution for the class. Then you can reference it in another solution where it will be used. Another way to use inheritance would be through the code itself.

For this project, you will use the method of creating separate solutions, building them, and then using them in later projects. In yesterday's lesson, you created a set of classes called `ProjectManager`. For the `Form` base class, you will create a new project called `PMFormClass`.

Laying Out the Form

To lay out your first form, start a new project in Visual Studio .NET, selecting Windows application as the starting template for the form base class. This way, you have a standard form to work with, and it's used to create a `Form` class. Call the project `PMFormClass`.

After you open the project, rename the form to `frmPM.vb` for this project. Notice that the References section in the Solution Explorer window has more namespaces than the class project that you created yesterday. The new namespaces are `System.Drawing` and `System.Windows.Forms`. Figure 20.1 shows the Solution Explorer with these references. These namespaces are needed for placing standard controls on the design surface.

FIGURE 20.1

The Solution Explorer window showing the references in the project.

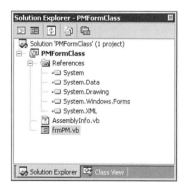

20

First, set any properties that you want the standard form to have. The only properties to change for this form are Text, which provides the form's caption on the title bar, and Name, which creates the class name for the form. Change the Text property to "Project Manager" to make sure that any future forms you create from this form will have an appropriate default title. Change the Name property to frmPM.

 Tip

In Visual Basic 6.0, the title in the title bar was the Caption property. In Visual Basic .NET, the Caption property has been changed to the Text property to give different controls uniform behavior.

What's standard about all the forms are two sets of data-entry controls and four buttons. The data controls consist of a descriptive label and a text box. The standard buttons are for creating, saving, retrieving, and deleting the information displayed in the form.

 Caution

There's no code for actually working with data storage. That topic will be covered in tomorrow's lesson. Nevertheless, the buttons will take the appropriate actions as soon as the storage mechanism and code are in place.

Now it's simply a matter of getting the different controls onto the form. Go to the toolbox (usually located on the left side of the IDE) and select Label. Then draw the label or just click the design surface. Repeat the process to place the second label below the first. Then place two text boxes to the right of the labels.

Next, do the same for four buttons, placing them along the bottom of the form.

After you add the controls, set the properties as shown in Table 20.1. Three buttons have their Enabled properties set to False to prevent the user from selecting one of them until after the Create button is selected. Code to enable the buttons will be written later today in the discussion on derived classes.

TABLE 20.1 Control Property Settings

Control Name	Property	Value
Label1	(Name)	lblID
	Text	ID:
	AutoSize	True
	TextAlign	TopRight

TABLE 20.1 continued

Control Name	Property	Value
Label2	(Name)	lblName
	Text	Name:
	AutoSize	True
	TextAlign	TopRight
Textbox1	(Name)	txtID
	Text	Make blank
Textbox2	(Name)	txtName
	Text	Make blank
Button1	(Name)	btnCreate
	Text	Create
Button2	(Name)	btnRead
	Text	Read
	Enabled	False
Button3	(Name)	btnSave
	Text	Save
	Enabled	False
Button4	(Name)	btnDelete
	Text	Delete
	Enabled	False

After you set these properties, arrange the controls similar to Figure 20.2.

FIGURE 20.2

The frmPM *form with controls.*

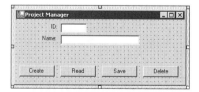

Notice that the buttons are arranged along the bottom of the form. Placing the button controls on the bottom or right of a form is one way to build forms. When you use this form to build the other forms, more controls may be needed in the space below the txtName control and above the buttons. When you use the Form class, you might resize the form to accommodate more controls, and then you would have to move the buttons.

20

Instead, you can set a new property, Anchor, that makes sure a control maintains the appropriate position in its container. In the past, controls were always anchored to the top and left of the container. This position is still the default, but by changing the Anchor property to a different set of container sides, you enable the control to move as the container is resized. If you anchor a control to all sides, it will be resized as the form is resized.

To make sure that the buttons stay on the bottom of the form, no matter how the form is resized, change the Anchor property for all the buttons to Bottom, Right. You use a graphic tool in the Property window, where you click a bar representing the sides to anchor. Clear the top and left bars, and set the bottom and right bars.

Viewing the Generated Code

As we stated earlier, Visual Basic .NET actually turns the design into code, and you can see this code by opening the module's code window (double-click somewhere on the form being designed). Another way is to click the View Code button on the Solution Explorer window with the desired module selected.

Here, you can see that you've created a class named frmPM and that this class is inherited from the System.Windows.Forms.Form class. The Windows Form designer generated the rest of the code. When you expand that section, you see the generated code. This code has a class constructor for the form that calls the InitializeComponent() method. The designer-generated code declares all controls as Friend, and the InitializeComponent() method sets the properties of these controls.

Friend means that the control can be referenced by code elsewhere in the project but implies that the control is also Private. This means that derived classes can't reference the controls within any methods. To fix this problem, you will modify the generated code, adding the word Protected before Friend in each control declaration. Protected means that although the controls are still excluded from being referenced outside the class project, derived classes can reference them. Making controls Protected is important for later today when you create forms that inherit from this class.

Note

There's a comment recommending that the InitializeComponent() method not be modified in the code editor. If you want to add your own code to do something when an instance of the class is created, you add that code in the New() method, after the call to the generated method. That way, you can modify the form in the designer later without worrying about what would happen to the custom code you wrote.

Although the buttons with all the different forms have similar behavior, that code depends on the classes used by a form, so there's no point in writing the code in this Form class. Having examined the code window, you can save and close this module.

Now that this class is completed, you have to compile the project so that the class can be inherited. If it was built in the normal fashion, you would have an executable. Such a file is useful for testing, but because you would never "execute" this program, you'll want the form compiled into a dynamic link library file (.DLL). To do that, change the Output type property of the project by following these steps:

1. Right-click the project name and select Properties from the context menu.

2. In the Common Properties/General section is the Output Type drop-down list. Select Class Library from this list. Automatically, Visual Studio .NET will change the Startup object to (None), as shown in Figure 20.3.

FIGURE 20.3

The PMFormClass *Property Pages window, showing an Output Type of Class Library.*

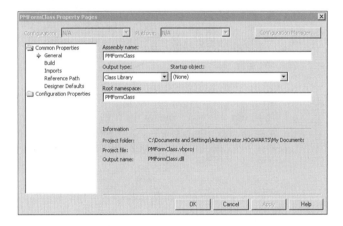

3. Click OK.

4. Complete the compile process by choosing Build Solution from the Build menu.

20

Creating the Forms

Now that you've created two class libraries for your application, start a new project to use those classes. As you did with the Form class, select Windows Application as your starting point. Name the project PMApp. This project starts with a blank form called form1.vb in the same way that the project you used to build the Form base class started.

This form is based on the standard Form class from the System.Windows.Forms namespace. To create a form based on an already-created form, follow these steps:

1. Right-click the project name in the Solution Explorer and select Add and then Add Inherited Form from the context menu.

2. The Add Item dialog box appears with the Inherited Form icon already selected. Type the name of the form you're creating (in this example, **frmEmployee.vb** for the employee form) and then click Open.

3. In the Inheritance Picker dialog box, click Browse and navigate to the PMFormClass.DLL file that you built in the previous section. The dialog box changes to show the classes in that file (see Figure 20.4). Specify the component from the file you want to use as the base class and click OK.

FIGURE 20.4

The Inheritance Picker dialog box.

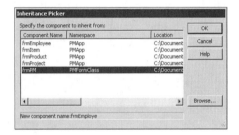

Note	If you get a screen showing the frmEmployee.vb form in design mode with an error message, along with the Task List window showing the errors to fix, open the frmEmployee.vb code window and change the Inherits line to read:

```
Inherits PMFormClass.frmPM
```

This change will eliminate the error and the messages in the Task List window.

After you add this form to the project, notice that two new namespaces are added to the References section of your project: Microsoft.VisualBasic and PMFormClass. The latter is the class you created earlier. The layout of the form will look exactly like the Form class designed earlier, but dropping arrow icons will be added to each control within the form. These icons indicate that the controls are inherited and can't be deleted from this form.

Laying Out the Employee Form

To complete the employee form, you need to add controls to handle the entry of the employee's position and possibly his or her hours. Furthermore, the employee form will have an extra button to launch the product form. Because two of the positions are fixed, and the hours depend on the employee's having a non-managerial position, a group control with three radio buttons will do the trick.

This group control is similar to the frame control in Visual Basic 6, and radio buttons are what used to be called option buttons. So, put a group under the `txtName` control to include three radio buttons, two text boxes, and a label. Then don't forget to add a button to open the product form. Finally, change the title of the form (the `Text` property) so that it shows the type of form you're using—`Employee`.

The result should look something like Figure 20.5. Change the controls' name properties to names such as `rdoProdMgr` and `txtHours`, as shown in Table 20.2. Also, change the text properties so that the controls look like Figure 20.5.

TABLE 20.2   Control Names for the Employee Form

Control Type	Control Name	Control Text
GroupBox	`grpPosition`	`Position`
RadioButton	`rdoProdMgr`	`Product Manager`
RadioButton	`rdoProjMgr`	`Project Manager`
RadioButton	`rdoResource`	`Other`
TextBox	`txtResource`	Make blank
Label	`lblHours`	`Hours Per Day:`
TextBox	`txtHours`	Make blank
Button	`btnProduct`	`Products`

FIGURE 20.5

The `frmEmployee` *form with data-entry controls.*

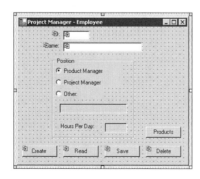

20

Notice that the text boxes in the group, `txtResource` and `txtHours`, are grayed out. This is to prevent a user from entering data unless he or she enables the Other radio button. Setting the `Enabled` property to `False` disables the text boxes and setting the `BackColor` property to `Inactive Border` makes them appear disabled to users.

You're nearly ready to test the appearance of the form at runtime by starting the project while in design mode. Before you test it, though, you need to complete these two steps:

1. Delete the Form1.vb form that Visual Basic .NET added to your project automatically when you created a Windows application. To do so, right-click the module in the Solution Explorer window and choose Delete from the context menu.

2. Right-click the project name, select Properties from the context menu, and then change the Startup Object to be frmEmployee.

Now click the Start button on the toolbar. When you're satisfied with the way the form looks and works, close it or click the Stop Debugging button.

Viewing the Employee Form's Code

Now you can enter code for the employee form's events. This example will have very simple code. The txtResource and txtHours controls are wired to the rdoResource radio button's Checked property through an event. In the click event for btnCreate, an employee object will be created, but which type of employee is used depends on the position entered. The other buttons will act on the methods of an instantiated object.

First, you need a member variable referring to the current employee object. But, until the position is filled in, you don't know which derived class to use. To handle this situation, create a member as the standard Object type and then later specify which class. Because this form will launch the product form, you also need a variable to hold that form. Add the following lines to the beginning of the class definition, after the Inherits line:

```
Dim oEmp As Object
Dim oProdForm As frmProduct
```

At some point, you'll have to use the classes created in yesterday's lesson. To do that, you must have a reference to that class library in this project. Set up this reference by right-clicking the References section in the Solution Explorer and choosing Add Reference. In the Add Reference dialog box, select the Projects tab, then the Browse button, and locate the compiled DLL file for the ProjectManager class library. The dialog box should look similar to Figure 20.6. Then click OK.

The first code to enter is for the rdoResource control's CheckChanged event. Double-click the control, and Visual Basic .NET will take you to the code window and automatically put in the code for handling that event. Type the lines from Listing 20.1 into this method.

FIGURE 20.6

The Add Reference dialog box.

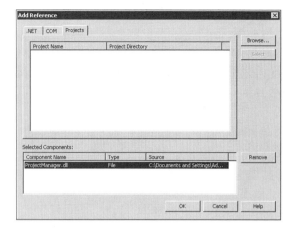

LISTING 20.1 The `rdoResource`'s `CheckChanged` Event

```
Me.lblHours.Enabled = Me.rdoResource.Checked
Me.txtHours.Enabled = Me.rdoResource.Checked
Me.txtResource.Enabled = Me.rdoResource.Checked
If Me.txtResource.Enabled = True Then
    Me.txtResource.BackColor = System.Drawing.SystemColors.Window
    Me.txtHours.BackColor = System.Drawing.SystemColors.Window
Else
    Me.txtResource.BackColor = System.Drawing.SystemColors.InactiveBorder
    Me.txtHours.BackColor = System.Drawing.SystemColors.InactiveBorder
End If
```

ANALYSIS This code uses the `SystemColors` namespace colors instead of actual colors from the `Color` namespace. This means that if a user changes the desktop scheme or colors in any way, your application will also change to match the user's choices. This is good design for today's computer world in which users change colors on their desktops and versions of Windows use different schemes altogether.

Now you're ready to enter the code for the Create button. Double-click that button, and in the method automatically created, add the code in Listing 20.2.

LISTING 20.2 The Create Button's Click Event

```
Private Sub btnCreate_Click(ByVal sender As System.Object, _
        ByVal e As System.EventArgs) Handles btnCreate.Click
    Dim intIdent As Short, strPerson As String
    intIdent = CInt(Val(Me.txtID.Text))
    strPerson = Trim(Me.txtName.Text)
```

20

LISTING 20.2 continued

```
      ' outer check is for position
      ' inner checks are for whether id, name
      ' or both are present
      If Me.rdoProdMgr.Checked = True Then
          If intIdent <= 0 Then
              oEmp = New ProjectManager.ProductManager()
          ElseIf strPerson.Length = 0 Then
              oEmp = New ProjectManager.ProductManager(intIdent)
          Else
              oEmp = New ProjectManager.ProductManager(intIdent, _
                  strPerson)
          End If
      ElseIf Me.rdoProjMgr.Checked = True Then
          If intIdent <= 0 Then
              oEmp = New ProjectManager.ProjectManager()
          ElseIf strPerson.Length = 0 Then
              oEmp = New ProjectManager.ProjectManager(intIdent)
          Else
              oEmp = New ProjectManager.ProjectManager(intIdent, _
                  strPerson)
          End If
      Else
          ' Make sure that a position is
          ' filled in for other
          Dim strRes As String
          strRes = Trim(Me.txtResource.Text)
          If strRes.Length = 0 Then
              Dim strMessage As String
              strMessage = "Position title " & _
                  "must be filled in to " & _
                  "create employee."
              MsgBox(strMessage)
              ' to cut down on tabs
              Exit Sub
          End If

          If intIdent <= 0 Then
              oEmp = New ProjectManager.Resource(strRes)
          ElseIf strPerson.Length = 0 Then
              oEmp = New ProjectManager.Resource(strRes, intIdent)
          Else
              oEmp = New ProjectManager.Resource(strRes, intIdent, _
                  strPerson)
          End If
      End If
      Me.btnCreate.Enabled = False
      Me.btnRead.Enabled = True
      Me.btnSave.Enabled = True
      Me.btnDelete.Enabled = True
  End Sub
```

ANALYSIS This code is lengthy because two factors are involved in creating an employee object:

- The first is which type of employee and therefore which class should be used.
- The second factor is which constructor of the class to use. Recall from yesterday that almost every class has three different constructors. Why? A user might know both the employee's ID and name before the class is created, or just the ID, or neither. This approach creates a lot of flexibility when you're creating an object. Does the data source generate IDs? Should the data-entry people create them? The different constructors allow different scenarios to be used when adding other code.

Also, one last bit of code at the end disables the Create button and enables the other three buttons. This way, users will be forced to deal with the employee object created before creating another. Code to reverse this is found in the procedures for saving and deleting the employee object.

The code for the three other buttons is simple by comparison. The Read button code will run the Read method of the Employee class and then fill in values from the retrieved employee object. The Save button code will store the form's values into the properties of the employee object and then run the Save method. The Delete button will run the Delete method and set the object to Nothing. Because all these actions depend on an object that is created from the Create button, the code will check first for the existence of the object. The Save and Delete activities will also clear the controls on the form and reset the buttons so that only Create can be selected. Listing 20.3 shows all three event codes.

LISTING 20.3 The Click Events for the Read, Save, and Delete Buttons

```
Private Sub btnRead_Click(ByVal sender As System.Object, _
        ByVal e As System.EventArgs) Handles btnRead.Click
    If Not oEmp Is Nothing Then
        oEmp.Read()
        Me.txtName.Text = oEmp.Name
        If oEmp.ToString = "ProjectManager.Resource" Then
            Me.txtHours.Text = oEmp.HoursPerDay
            Me.rdoResource.Checked = True
            Me.txtResource.Text = oEmp.GetPosition(oEmp.ID)
        ElseIf oEmp.ToString = "ProjectManager.ProductManager" Then
            Me.rdoProdMgr.Checked = True
        ElseIf oEmp.ToString = "ProjectManager.ProjectManager" Then
            Me.rdoProjMgr.Checked = True
        End If
    End If
End Sub
```

20

LISTING 20.3   continued

```
Private Sub btnSave_Click(ByVal sender As System.Object, _
            ByVal e As System.EventArgs) Handles btnSave.Click
    If Not oEmp Is Nothing Then
        oEmp.Name = Me.txtName.Text
        If Me.rdoResource.Checked = True Then
            oEmp.HoursPerDay = CInt(Val(Me.txtHours.Text))
        End If
        oEmp.Save()
        Me.txtID.Text = ""
        Me.txtName.Text = ""
        Me.txtResource.Text = ""
        Me.txtHours.Text = ""
        Me.rdoProdMgr.Checked = True
        Me.btnCreate.Enabled = True
        Me.btnRead.Enabled = False
        Me.btnSave.Enabled = False
        Me.btnDelete.Enabled = False
    End If
End Sub

Private Sub btnDelete_Click(ByVal sender As System.Object, _
            ByVal e As System.EventArgs) Handles btnDelete.Click
    If Not oEmp Is Nothing Then
        oEmp.Delete()
        oEmp = Nothing
        Me.txtID.Text = ""
        Me.txtName.Text = ""
        Me.txtResource.Text = ""
        Me.txtHours.Text = ""
        Me.rdoProdMgr.Checked = True
        Me.btnCreate.Enabled = True
        Me.btnRead.Enabled = False
        Me.btnSave.Enabled = False
        Me.btnDelete.Enabled = False
    End If
End Sub
```

ANALYSIS   In the code for the Read button, the ToString method is used with the object to return the name of the class. The ToString method is a part of the standard Object type in Visual Basic .NET, and in the case of reference type classes will return the name of the class.

The final piece of code for this form is the click event code for the btnProduct control. This button will create and show a form by instantiating it and running the Show() method. This is a big change from Visual Basic 6. In the earlier product, forms could be referenced by name any time in a project, and Visual Basic took care of the instantiation behind the scenes. In Visual Basic .NET, your code has to do that work.

This code uses the oProdForm member created earlier in this section. Until the frmProduct form is created, these code lines will be shown as errors:

```
OprodForm + New frmProduct ()
OproducForm.Show ()
```

If you want to avoid these errors, leave off this code until you create the next form.

Laying Out the Product Form

The next step is to add another inherited form for products, using the frmPM base class as you did for the employee form. This time the form is much simpler because you need only two extra pieces of data: a description and the Product Manager ID. Because a description is free form, one property, MultiLine, needs to be set to True for that text box. Then you can increase the text box's height and width. The result should look something like Figure 20.7.

FIGURE 20.7

The frmProduct *form with data-entry controls.*

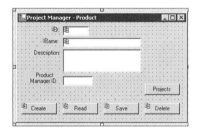

Viewing the Product Form's Code

The product form's code is actually simpler than the code for the employee form. Just as you did in the first form, add the following two code lines at the beginning of the Form class definition to create two member variables—one for the product object and one for the project form. (As we mentioned earlier, it might be a good idea to add the second line after you create the project form.)

```
Dim oProd As ProjectManager.Product
Dim oProjForm As frmProject
```

In this form, there's no question which class is being used, so there's no extra code when creating the object for determining that factor. The Create button code simply checks for the entry of an ID, name, or both, and then uses the appropriate constructor.

The other three buttons run the matching methods of the Product class, copying data one way or the other. Listing 20.4 shows the code for all four buttons.

20

LISTING 20.4   frmProduct.vb: The Click Events of the Create, Read, Save, and Delete Buttons

```vb
Private Sub btnCreate_Click(ByVal sender As System.Object, _
            ByVal e As System.EventArgs) Handles btnCreate.Click
    Dim intIdent As Integer
    Dim strProduct As String

    intIdent = CInt(Val(Me.txtID.Text))
    strProduct = Trim(Me.txtName.Text)

    If intIdent <= 0 Then
        oProd = New ProjectManager.Product()
    ElseIf strProduct.Length = 0 Then
        oProd = New ProjectManager.Product(intIdent)
    Else
        oProd = New ProjectManager.Product(intIdent, strProduct)
    End If
    Me.btnCreate.Enabled = False
    Me.btnRead.Enabled = True
    Me.btnSave.Enabled = True
    Me.btnDelete.Enabled = True
End Sub

Private Sub btnRead_Click(ByVal sender As System.Object, _
            ByVal e As System.EventArgs) Handles btnRead.Click
    If Not oProd Is Nothing Then
        oProd.Read()
        Me.txtName.Text = oProd.Name
        Me.txtDescription.Text = oProd.Description
        Me.txtMgrID.Text = oProd.ManagerID
    End If
End Sub

Private Sub btnSave_Click(ByVal sender As System.Object, _
            ByVal e As System.EventArgs) Handles btnSave.Click
    If Not oProd Is Nothing Then
        oProd.Name = Me.txtName.Text
        oProd.Description = Me.txtDescription.Text
        oProd.ManagerID = CInt(Val(Me.txtMgrID.Text))
        oProd.Save()
        Me.txtID.Text = ""
        Me.txtName.Text = ""
        Me.txtDescription.Text = ""
        Me.txtMgrID.Text = ""
        Me.btnCreate.Enabled = True
        Me.btnRead.Enabled = False
        Me.btnSave.Enabled = False
        Me.btnDelete.Enabled = False
    End If
End Sub
```

LISTING 20.4   continued

```
Private Sub btnDelete_Click(ByVal sender As System.Object, _
        ByVal e As System.EventArgs) Handles btnDelete.Click
    If Not oProd Is Nothing Then
        oProd.Delete()
        oProd = Nothing
        Me.txtID.Text = ""
        Me.txtName.Text = ""
        Me.txtDescription.Text = ""
        Me.txtMgrID.Text = ""
        Me.btnCreate.Enabled = True
        Me.btnRead.Enabled = False
        Me.btnSave.Enabled = False
        Me.btnDelete.Enabled = False
    End If
End Sub
```

The code for the button that launches the project form is a bit different because projects are tied to products, and in this sample, you must have a valid product before you create projects for that product. Another way the code varies is that the method for creating projects is a part of the Product class. To handle these two issues, the code in Listing 20.5 first checks to see whether a valid product object exists. This check requires two If statements because the entire condition is checked at runtime. The first check, whether a Product object exists, must be true before the second check, for a valid ID, is made. Then the Product object is passed as an argument to the frmProject constructor. Because this code uses a form and constructor that you have not yet written, add this code and comment it out, if you don't like the temporary syntax errors. After you create the frmProject form, uncomment the code.

LISTING 20.5   The Project Button's Click Event

```
Private Sub btnProject_Click(ByVal sender As System.Object, _
        ByVal e As System.EventArgs) Handles btnProject.Click
    If Not oProd Is Nothing Then
        If oProd.ID > 0 Then
            oProjForm = New frmProject(oProd)
            oProjForm.Show()
        End If
    End If
End Sub
```

20

Laying Out the Project Form

To create the project form, start by adding an inherited form and choose the PMFormClass as this form's base class.

This form has a description and a manager ID, just like the product form, but it also has a number of other data items, as well as one piece of data that comes from the product form. The extra data are the start, estimated end, and end dates for the project. The extra item is the product ID.

Because the product ID can't be modified, use a label control and set the BorderStyle property to Fixed3D to give it a nice look.

For the date values, use the date/time picker control from the toolbox. This control allows users to enter dates by typing, or they can use the drop-down arrow to select dates from a mini-calendar. Set the Format property for each control to Short and change the Value property to 1/1/2002, as a default date. When the form runs, the dates will end up with the current date through code.

Your form should look something like Figure 20.8.

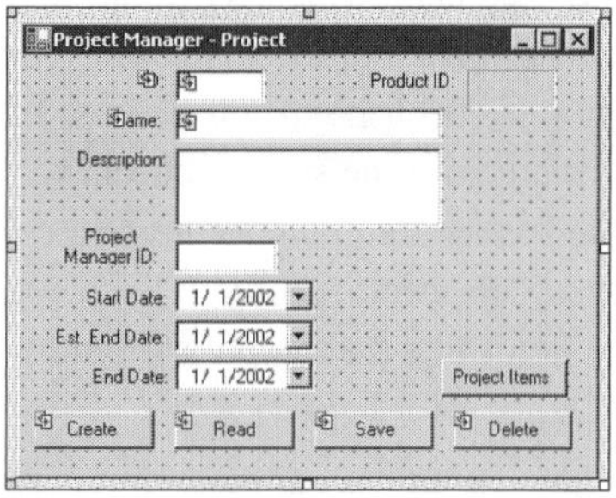

FIGURE 20.8

The frmProject *form with data-entry controls.*

Viewing the Project Form's Code

The first difference with the project form's code is that besides member variables for a project object and the project items form, you also need a variable for the product object that represents the container for the projects created here. You therefore need three declaration lines at the beginning of the form class definitions:

```
Dim oProj As ProjectManager.Project
Dim oProd As ProjectManager.Product
Dim oItemForm As frmItem
```

The next difference is something that's done right inside the generated code. You need to get a reference to the product object used on the product form at the time this form is created. To do that, you create a constructor that accepts an object as a parameter.

Open the section of code called `Windows Form Designer Generated Code` and add the code in Listing 20.6 near the beginning of that section, perhaps right after the default constructor (the `New()` method).

LISTING 20.6 The `New()` Method for the Project Form

```
Public Sub New(ByVal oProduct As ProjectManager.Product)
    MyBase.New()

    'This call is required by the Windows Form Designer.
    InitializeComponent()

    'Add any initialization after the InitializeComponent() call
    oProd = oProduct
    Me.lblProduct.Text = oProd.ID
    Me.dtpStart.Value = Today
    Me.dtpEstEnd.Value = Today
    Me.dtpEnd.Value = Today
End Sub
```

ANALYSIS The first difference in Listing 20.6 is the argument to the `New()` method. Remember from yesterday that you can overload the `New()` method simply by adding different sets of parameters to the extra methods. The parameter here is a variable that represents the product object being passed in as part of instantiating the form.

Later in the same method, the parameter value is passed to the member variable declared at the beginning of the class. This way, the reference to the product object persists throughout the life of the form. Then the `ID` property is used to populate the product ID label, and the current date is stored as the value for all the date/time picker controls. The `Today()` function retrieves the system's current date.

When a project object is created, rather than use the normal constructors, you use a method of the `Product` class. Yesterday, you created the set of overloaded `AddProject` methods so that a project could be added to a collection within the product itself. The `AddProject` methods are functions that return a reference to the new project object that's created. This is effectively the same behavior as using the `New` keyword when creating an object.

This change actually simplifies the Create button event code considerably. Other than that, all the code for the click events for the buttons is similar to the `Product` form class. Listing 20.7 shows all this code.

20

LISTING 20.7   frmProject.vb: The Click Events of the Create, Read, Save, Delete, and Project Items Buttons

```vb
Private Sub btnCreate_Click(ByVal sender As System.Object, _
        ByVal e As System.EventArgs) Handles btnCreate.Click
    Dim intIdent As Integer
    Dim strProject As String

    intIdent = CInt(Val(Me.txtID.Text))
    strProject = Trim(Me.txtName.Text)

    If intIdent <= 0 Then
        oProj = oProd.AddProject()
    ElseIf strProject.Length = 0 Then
        oProj = oProd.AddProject(intIdent)
    Else
        oProj = oProd.AddProject(intIdent, strProject)
    End If
    Me.btnCreate.Enabled = False
    Me.btnRead.Enabled = True
    Me.btnSave.Enabled = True
    Me.btnDelete.Enabled = True
End Sub

Private Sub btnRead_Click(ByVal sender As System.Object, _
        ByVal e As System.EventArgs) Handles btnRead.Click
    If Not oProj Is Nothing Then
        oProj.Read()
        Me.txtName.Text = oProj.Name
        Me.txtDescription.Text = oProj.Description
        Me.txtMgrID.Text = oProj.ManagerID
        Me.dtpStart.Value = oProj.StartDate
        Me.dtpEstEnd.Value = oProj.EstEndDate
        Me.dtpEnd.Value = oProj.EndDate
    End If
End Sub

Private Sub btnSave_Click(ByVal sender As System.Object, _
        ByVal e As System.EventArgs) Handles btnSave.Click
    If Not oProj Is Nothing Then
        oProj.Name = Me.txtName.Text
        oProj.Description = Me.txtDescription.Text
        oProj.ManagerID = CInt(Val(Me.txtMgrID.Text))
        oProj.StartDate = Me.dtpStart.Value
        oProj.EstEndDate = Me.dtpEstEnd.Value
        oProj.EndDate = Me.dtpEnd.Value
        oProj.Save()
        Me.txtID.Text = ""
        Me.txtName.Text = ""
        Me.txtDescription.Text = ""
```

LISTING 20.7   continued

```
            Me.txtMgrID.Text = ""
            Me.dtpStart.Value = Today
            Me.dtpEstEnd.Value = Today
            Me.dtpEnd.Value = Today
            Me.btnCreate.Enabled = True
            Me.btnRead.Enabled = False
            Me.btnSave.Enabled = False
            Me.btnDelete.Enabled = False
        End If
    End Sub

    Private Sub btnDelete_Click(ByVal sender As System.Object, _
                ByVal e As System.EventArgs) Handles btnDelete.Click
        If Not oProj Is Nothing Then
            oProj.Delete()
            oProj = Nothing
            Me.txtID.Text = ""
            Me.txtName.Text = ""
            Me.txtDescription.Text = ""
            Me.txtMgrID.Text = ""
            Me.dtpStart.Value = Today
            Me.dtpEstEnd.Value = Today
            Me.dtpEnd.Value = Today
            Me.btnCreate.Enabled = True
            Me.btnRead.Enabled = False
            Me.btnSave.Enabled = False
            Me.btnDelete.Enabled = False
        End If
    End Sub

    Private Sub btnItem_Click(ByVal sender As System.Object, _
                ByVal e As System.EventArgs) Handles btnItem.Click
        If Not oProj Is Nothing Then
            If oProj.ID > 0 Then
                oItemForm = New frmItem(oProj)
                oItemForm.Show()
            End If
        End If
    End Sub
```

20

Laying Out the Project Items Form

To lay out the last form, for project items, once again start by adding an inherited form.
Then locate the PMFormClass.dll file so that you can use that file's class as the base
class. Call the module frmItem.vb.

The problem with this form is that project items have no name. Because the form base class you designed has a label and a text box for the name and you can't delete inherited controls, you must change the `Visible` property of the two controls. If you set that property to `False`, users won't see the controls, and you can move them out of the way. When you're in Visual Studio .NET's design mode, those controls will be visible.

The project items form needs a description and resource ID, like the last two, and a start date and hours entry. This form doesn't require a button to start another form. When you're finished laying out your form, it should look like the one in Figure 20.9.

FIGURE 20.9

The `frmItem` *form with data-entry controls.*

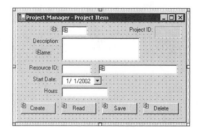

Remember that even though the name label and text box are shown here, at runtime they will be made invisible. If you want to be sure about that, set the `Visible` property to `False` in the `New()` method created in the next section.

Viewing the Project Items Form's Code

The code for the project items form is very much the same as the code for the project form. You need to create two member variables to hold references to the project item instance and to the project object used when this form was opened:

```
Dim oItem As ProjectManager.ProjectItems
Dim oProj As ProjectManager.Project
```

This code belongs at the beginning of the class definition. Then create a constructor that accepts the project object as a parameter, passes that value to the member created above, and initializes a couple of the controls. Listing 20.8 shows this code. Here, you also can set `Visible` to `False` for the `lblName` and `txtName` controls.

LISTING 20.8   The New() Method for the Project Items Form

```
Public Sub New(ByVal oProject As ProjectManager.Project)
    MyBase.New()

    'This call is required by the Windows Form Designer.
    InitializeComponent()
```

LISTING 20.8   continued

```
       'Add any initialization after the InitializeComponent() call
       oProj = oProject
       Me.lblProject.Text = oProj.ID
       Me.dtpStart.Value = Today
       Me.txtHours.Text = 0
  End Sub
```

You'll create the rest of the code for this form in the exercise.

Summary

Today you learned how to add features to the `ProjectManager` class. The main feature that had been missing was an interface for the system users. Today you created that interface by first creating a standard `Form` class that you used as a base class to construct your forms. This class had the standard look that you wanted for all the forms. You learned how to add an inherited form to a project and add code to a form.

Although most of the code you wrote today was fairly simple, you learned how to add constructors to a form so that you could pass in a parameter, and you discovered how to display a form using code in Visual Basic .NET.

Tomorrow you'll extend the `ProjectManager` class library by adding the capability to store the data on disk as XML.

Q&A

Q What if I want to run all the forms from a common source, such as a menu?

A Menus are available in Visual Basic .NET. You'll find them much easier to use than in previous versions. First, you can add menus to any form. Second, you can find menus in the toolbox, just like any other control. Finally, you can create menu items just by typing in the menu control that is placed at the top of the form.

Q When I added controls to an inherited form, I noticed that the tab order was wrong because the form tabbed to the added controls after the inherited buttons at the bottom of the form. How can I fix this problem?

A You can handle this problem in two ways. The hard way is to change each control's `TabIndex` property. The easy way is to choose Tab Order from the View menu. In the resulting screen, the current tab index is shown in a little box in the upper left of each control. Click the controls in the tab order you want, and the numbers will change appropriately. When you're finished, choose Tab Order from the View menu again.

20

Workshop

The Workshop provides quiz questions and an exercise to help solidify your understanding of today's lesson and provide you with experience in using what you've learned. Answers are provided in Appendix A, "Answers to Quizzes."

Quiz

1. What property of a form represents the title in the title bar?
2. What property affects a control's size and location within a form when the form is resized?
3. What keyword is used to create an object?

Exercise

In this lesson, you learned how to design forms so that users can interface with the classes and methods you wrote yesterday. You created four forms, all inherited from one form base class. You added code to accomplish certain objectives of data entry in these forms. You put in code to correspond to buttons on all the forms except for the last one. Now complete the code for the four inherited buttons in the frmItem form.

DAY 21

Enhancing the Application's Features

Yesterday you created an application to use the classes designed on Day 19, "Creating the Project Management Application." The classes and forms you created include methods and code to save, read, and delete the data. The problem with that code is that you don't have any place to store the data so that it can be saved, read, or deleted. As of now, you don't have any code to take care of that functionality.

Today you will extend the Project Manager application's feature set by adding a mechanism for storing the data in files on disk. You will save and retrieve the data through the use of XML document files. As a result, today's lesson will also serve as a brief introduction to the world of XML. If you already know XML, skip to the section "Coding the Class Module."

In today's lesson, you will accomplish the following:

- Understand the need for storage.
- Learn about eXtensible Markup Language (XML).

- Code the XML Document Object Model (XML-DOM).
- Write routines to save, read, and delete data.

Persisting Data

NEW TERM Data gathered during the execution of a program is practically no good unless you have some way to persist that data. *Persisting data* means that after the data is created in one session of an application, it will be available at a later date.

Most development today centers around databases that store data in files on disk. These databases are usually handled by database management systems (DBMSs), programs that ensure that the data is stored properly, falls within specified constraints, and even keeps the wrong people from gaining access to the data. Some of the more popular database products are Microsoft SQL Server, Oracle, DB2, and Sybase.

Because the Project Manager application should persist the data entered, it would be nice to use a database management system to store, retrieve, and protect the data. To do that, you need to have the software for that system and then learn how to process that system's data.

Most DBMS software requires more learning. That is, to use the database system, you have to learn another computer language or another object model that you tap into from Visual Basic .NET. That's just one aspect of programming around data.

Furthermore, you need to have the DBMS software to implement for this lesson. Rather than use some proprietary and perhaps even costly database system for today's activity, you will use XML document files to store the data for this project.

Introducing XML

XML, or eXtensible Markup Language, is a way to store data in an easy-to-read, easy-to-process, simple-to-transfer format. XML was designed by the same group that set the standard for Hypertext Markup Language (HTML), the standard used for Web browsers. That group is the World Wide Web Consortium, often referred to as the W3C.

HTML was designed for the purpose of marking up documents for browser presentation. It uses a series of tags that set off parts of text within a document so that the browser will know how to present the information and in some cases how to format the text. HTML is limited in that no description of the text is required. HTML explains how to present the data, but not what it is. For example, the following is a simple and standard HTML document:

```
<html>
<head>
<title>Sample HTML</title>
</head>
<body>
<h1>An HTML Example</h1>
<p>Meriweather Hughes</p>
</body>
</html>
```

As you can see, the <p> tag contains some text, which could be someone's name, a company name, or anything else, but nothing in the HTML itself explains what that data means.

XML was developed to address this lack within HTML. XML wasn't designed to be a replacement for HTML, but to serve as a complement to it. HTML handles the presentation of information within the browser, and XML handles the explanation of the data. The following example is a well-formed XML document:

```
<?xml version="1.0"?>
<Customers>
<Customer>
<Name>Meriweather Hughes</Name>
</Customer>
</Customers>
```

Here, you have no question about what the data is. The tags used within the document explain exactly what information is stored there. You can tell that the actual string of characters is a customer's name. You also could guess, correctly, that the document can easily store more than one customer.

Well-Formed XML Rules

NEW TERM The example in the preceding section is referred to as *well-formed* XML. This means that the example followed certain rules that made it a "proper" XML document. Unlike HTML, XML doesn't have a predefined set of tags to use in the data. Instead, you can think of XML as simply a set of rules to follow when you create your own XML data:

- A prolog should be used at the start of a well-formed XML document. The prolog is not required but it helps since it is the document declaration. This declaration announces what the document is and what version of XML is being used. It looks exactly like this:

  ```
  <?xml version="1.0" ?>
  ```

  Currently, there's only one version of XML. Even so, the version number still must be specified.

21

- The tags in an XML document are called *elements*. Just as in HTML, the elements can contain attributes within the starting tags. Every starting tag must have an ending tag. The only exception is that you can use an empty tag in place of starting and ending tags that have no content. This means that you can use `<Customer/>` in place of `<Customer></Customer>`.

- A document can have only one root element. This element's starting tag is at the top, or beginning, of the document, and its ending tag is at the bottom, or end. This way, everything else in the XML data is contained within the root element.

- The element tags must be properly nested. This means an ending tag for an inner element must come before the ending tag for the outer element. An example of illegal nesting follows:

```
<Outer>
<Inner>This cannot be processed.
</Outer>
</Inner>
```

- XML is case sensitive. This means that the ending tag element names must match the starting tag element names precisely.

There is more for you to learn about XML, but this information will be enough for you to create well-formed XML documents to store data from the application.

Supporting Technologies

NEW TERM   One of the most significant aspects of XML is its extensibility. Besides the rules for XML, the W3C has developed documents (called *recommendations*) for all kinds of technology to make XML more useful. Another tool called Document Type Definitions (DTD) describes exactly how an XML document should look. This way, a processor can validate the XML document making sure that all data that should be there is there, that it has the right number of elements, that it is in the correct order, and so on.

After a while, many XML users were dissatisfied with the limitations of DTDs, and another technology called XML Schemas was developed to describe the contents of XML documents. XML Schemas have the advantage of actually being XML as well and, therefore, are just as extensible as XML itself.

NEW TERM   Using DTDs or XML Schemas makes your XML data *valid*. This label means more than *well-formed*. This means that if someone examined your XML data, compared that data to the schema describing it, and found it to be a match, the document is said to be valid.

Many companies in the Internet business, including Microsoft, accepted XML almost overnight. In fact, the entire .NET technology is based on XML, as well as other standards that have emerged in the last few years. Although the code you've written is all Visual Basic .NET, not XML, other files generated by Visual Studio .NET are XML, which helps describe the solutions, projects, assemblies, and other things around your code.

Understanding XML is important in understanding much of what goes into a Visual Basic .NET application. You should invest quite a bit of effort into learning more about XML as you create more and more Visual Basic .NET projects.

Understanding the Document Object Model and XPath

Two technologies developed to augment the use of XML are important for using XML documents to store persistent data: the XML Document Object Model (XML-DOM, or just DOM) and XPath queries. By using these technologies, you can save the data from the Project Manager application and then retrieve it later.

DOM

NEW TERM DOM is another standard developed by the W3C for the purpose of turning XML data into a binary object within memory. After the XML data is cached in the computer's memory as a DOM, it can be searched, queried, modified, and then finally written back into its original text form. When the data is loaded into memory, it's sometimes referred to as a *tree*.

Because XML-DOM is a standard, any computer software company can design a component or program that reads XML data from a source, such as a file, and process that data into the binary representation in memory.

Processing causes elements within the XML to become nodes within the DOM. Not only do the elements become nodes, but so also does the text that can be an element's content. By turning the document into a collection of nodes, DOM enables programs to traverse the nodes, searching, extracting, and modifying the data and elements found within the XML data.

Because DOM is an object model, a program can use properties and methods to perform the searches, reading, and changing of the data. This enables you to easily write programs to manipulate the data. Because the DOM is in memory, a program can access the XML data a virtually unlimited number of times. When the object is released from memory, the data is no longer accessible. Usually, before releasing, you write the DOM back to an XML file, which puts the memory representation back into its textual format.

21

The .NET Framework provides a namespace for working with XML documents, called, appropriately enough, System.XML.

Querying the DOM

To locate a particular node within the DOM, the W3C developed another standard for querying the tree. This query language is called XPath, short for XML Path. XPath refers to the fact that the query language looks a lot like the paths used to fully qualify file-names. Nevertheless, XPath queries are rarely like the pathnames of files.

NEW TERM To start with, to locate the DOM's root, you just use / for an XPath query. Then, if you're looking for a particular element in the tree, you use an XPath query such as /Customers/Customer/Name/FirstName. This is referred to as an *absolute* path. It starts at the root of the document, indicated by the beginning slash, and then searches for the Customers element, which is the root element; then the Customer element one level below the root; then the Name element one level below Customer; and finally the FirstName element one level below Name. If you just want to find the FirstName element regardless of its exact position in the tree, you use //FirstName.

NEW TERM Performing a search of this type changes the *context node*, the location that is your base for the next operation. This means that XPath queries can be relative to the context node. This way, if you first did a query for /Customers/Customer/Name, you would start another search by using just FirstName. Because the query doesn't start with a slash, XPath assumes that you're starting at the context node and looks for an element called FirstName one level below that node.

After locating that node, you can run the query ../LastName to move to the LastName element, which is at the same depth as the FirstName node. The .. indicates the parent node of the context node. Another query could be ../../Address to locate the node that holds the customer's address information.

NEW TERM Besides querying on the basis of node locations, you also can query on the con-tents of a text node by using *predicates* as a part of the query. The preceding examples just used the "node-set" portion of an XPath query. The predicate is enclosed in square brackets immediately after the node-set. This sample query uses a predicate to search for a node with specific content:

//LastName[Smith]

NEW TERM You can think of XPath query searches in the same way that you might look for something. That is, after you find what you're looking for, you stop looking. In XPath, this is referred to as a *single node*. However, you also can use XPath to return a node list that contains all nodes matching the query. This node list can then be processed one node at a time.

The DOM Object Model

After you load XML data into a DOM tree, your program has access to many methods and properties. Some built-in methods perform the same tasks as XPath queries, but do so more clearly because of the methods' names. For example, you learned that .. refers to the parent node of the context node. The Microsoft implementation of the DOM object model has a .ParentNode property that can do the same thing. The difference is that using the property doesn't cause the context node to change, but the XPath query does change the context.

This discussion of XML, XPath, and the DOM object model has served as an introduction to the rich set of special characters, functions, and capabilities of these technologies. There is much more to learn, but you've learned enough to use these technologies in the Project Manager application.

Coding the Class Module

On Day 19, you created classes to handle the activities associated with the employee, product, project, and project item classes. Furthermore, all these classes implemented the IDBIdentity interface, which defined Save(), Read(), and Delete() methods. You didn't create any code, however, to implement these methods. Today, you will write that code.

In the following sections, you'll write the code for the Employee class and one derived class of the Employee class. The other three classes have standard code because they don't have the derived classes. All these methods are written as functions so that the class code can return a Boolean value indicating success or failure. Because these classes don't have any interface with the user, they don't display messages when a failure occurs. The new code will be added to the PM.vb class module from Day 19. In this section, the code is going into the Employee class.

The Save() Method

At the start of the Save() method, you will declare several variables. One will point to an XMLDocument object, a bunch will be XMLNodes, and there are a few others. To avoid having to type the full qualifier for the class types that you're using, you can type the following Imports commands at the beginning of the PM.vb class module:

```
Imports System
Imports System.XML
```

Then, at the beginning of the Save() method, declare the needed variables with the following code:

21

```
Dim oXml As New XmlDocument()
Dim oRoot As XmlNode
Dim oEmp As XmlNode
Dim oSubNode As XmlNode
Dim oElem As XmlElement
Dim oIDNodes As XmlNodeList
Dim oIDNode As XmlNode
Dim intIDContent As Integer
Dim boolNewEmp As Boolean
Dim boolSuccess As Boolean
```

ANALYSIS The first variable, oXml, is not only declared at this point, but also instantiated by use of the New keyword before the class type.

The first check in the Save() method is that the Name property of the Employee class must have a value. Storing an entry without that information makes no sense. The first check in the Save() method then checks for a value by checking the length property of the private member variable.

If the strName member is empty, the program sets a Boolean variable, boolSuccess, to False without having to access the XML data file. The boolSuccess variable is used as the return value of the Save() method. The following code fragment checks for an empty strName:

```
If strName.Length = 0 Then
    boolSuccess = False
```

If a name is there, you will load the XML data file that contains the employee data. For this sample application, use a file at the root of drive C. We chose that location so that this code would work on almost any computer.

The XML file is called Employees.xml, and because this might be the first time the program is run, the file might not be there. As a result, the code tries to load the XML file in a Try...Catch block. Catch is set up to trap for FileNotFoundException, and if it traps such an exception, the program will start the XML document with a string. The object variable for the document is used here. The method for loading an XML data file into the DOM is Load, and the method for using a string to create the DOM is LoadXml. The code fragment looks like this:

```
Else
    Try
        oXml.Load("C:\Employees.xml")
    Catch ex As IO.FileNotFoundException
        oXml.LoadXml("<?xml version='1.0'?><Employees></Employees>")
    End Try
```

Else is the second part of the test to see whether strName is empty.

As you can see, the document starts with the minimum required text. The XML declaration is followed by an empty set of element tags. This element, Employees, serves as the root element for the entire document.

To work with the DOM, you need a reference to the root node of the loaded document. You add a reference by assigning the result of the document's DocumentElement property to a variable:

```
oRoot = oXml.DocumentElement
```

Here, things get a bit complicated. Before you can save an employee to the file, you have to determine whether this is a new entry or an old entry that has been modified. Furthermore, it's possible that if it is a new entry, the program has to assign the employee's ID property if the user hasn't supplied it.

This next section of code checks to see whether the intID member variable is less than 1, which indicates that the program has to assign the value. If so, the program needs to search through the DOM, locating the highest ID value, and then increment that value by 1 and assign it to intID. If the intID is a positive value, the program just checks for the existence of that value in the document. Because the actual saving is not done in this section, you have to store the result of this check in a Boolean variable indicating whether the employee entry is new or an edit. Here is the code:

```
If intID < 1 Then
    intIDContent = 0
    oIDNodes = oRoot.SelectNodes("//ID")
    For Each oIDNode In oIDNodes
        If intIDContent < CInt(oIDNode.InnerText) Then
            intIDContent = CInt(oIDNode.InnerText)
        End If
    Next
    intID = intIDContent + 1
    boolNewEmp = True
Else
    oIDNode = oRoot.SelectSingleNode("//Employee[ID='" & _
      intID.ToString & "']")
    If oIDNode Is Nothing Then
        boolNewEmp = True
    Else
        boolNewEmp = False
    End If
End If
```

The first check is for an intID less than 1, which means that the program has to generate the ID. The first step is to initialize a variable to zero. Then the program creates a nodeset of all the ID nodes in the document. This is accomplished through the SelectNodes method of the document element using the XPath query //ID. This method returns a set

21

of all ID nodes from anywhere in the document, regardless of their relative position to the root element.

Then the code checks each individual node's value against the initialized variable by fetching the node's InnerText property. If the node's value is higher, the variable is set to the node's value. When this process is complete, the intID member is set to the variable plus 1, and another variable is set to true to indicate that this is a new entry.

If intID is positive, the SelectSingleNode method of the document element searches the DOM document. This method is an extension to the W3C specification. As long as you're using the Microsoft implementation of that specification, the function will work. Because you're using Microsoft's .NET Framework, there's no chance that this search will fail.

This time, the XPath query searches for the first Employee node with an ID element matching the ID you're searching for. If no node matches, the result is an undefined object. If an object exists, the new entry Boolean variable is set to False.

At this point, you're ready to record the employee data to the file. If it's a new employee, new nodes need to be added to the DOM. If it's an existing entry, it has to be replaced. The first check is of the Boolean variable that stores whether this is a new entry. If it is, new elements must be created and filled with the data from the class members. The first step is to use the factory method of the document to create the element, add it to the appropriate node, and then add the text.

The employee data includes the employee's ID, name, and position. But you must consider one other factor. Because the Employee class is a base class, the code written here is used with instances of the derived classes of the Employee class. One of those derived classes, Resource, has one other piece of data to be saved: hours per day.

NEW TERM   The best way to handle a variable situation such as this is to use a *hook*. A hook is a place in a program that can be coded differently, at a later time or in a different place, so that the originating code doesn't have to be modified at all. This code needs a hook because the extra data item has to be added to the document after the other items and before the document is saved to the disk. In the Employee class, the hook will have no code but will allow any derived class to fill in code where needed.

The first hook will be a subroutine, WriteExtra, for adding or changing elements in the document. This subroutine will have two parameters:

- A reference to the node where the elements are attached
- A Boolean expression indicating whether the element should be added or modified

The code for this procedure is as follows:

```
Protected Overridable Sub WriteExtra(ByVal oNode As XmlNode, _
          ByVal boolNew As Boolean)
   'In this class, it does nothing
End Sub
```

This code is placed anywhere within the `Employee` class definition, but not within the `Save()` method. The subroutine is marked as `Overridable` so that derived classes can modify it. Because it's also marked as `Protected`, it can't be called from outside the instances of the derived classes.

Adding elements with text involves four lines of code that are the same for each element. A good technique in this situation is to create a subroutine to handle those same code lines and just define parameters to handle the variables of the process.

This code will be so generic that it can be used by all the classes in this project, not just the `Employee` class. To make procedures like this available globally, follow these steps:

1. Add a new module to the project and name it Utility.vb.

2. Before the file's `Module` declaration, add the two `Imports` commands that support the `System` and `Xml` namespaces.

3. Add the next two sets of code to that file.

The steps for creating an element with text are to create the element node, create the text node, append the element to the appropriate parent node, and append the text node to the new element node. To do so, use the `PlaceElements` subroutine in Listing 21.1.

LISTING 21.1 Utility.vb: The `PlaceElement` Subroutine

```
Public Sub PlaceElement(ByVal oNode As XmlNode, _
        ByVal strElement As String, ByVal strText As String)
    Dim oElement As XmlElement
    Dim oContent As XmlText
    Dim oDoc As XmlDocument
    Dim oNewNode As XmlNode

    oDoc = oNode.OwnerDocument
    oElement = oDoc.CreateElement(strElement)
    oContent = oDoc.CreateTextNode(strText)

    oNewNode = oNode.AppendChild(oElement)
    oNewNode.AppendChild(oContent)
End Sub
```

21

ANALYSIS   Three parameters are defined for this procedure: the parent node for the new element, the name of the element, and the text for that element. After the routine starts, a reference to the DOM document is obtained through the `OwnerDocument` property. Then the factory methods to create an element and a text node are used. The `AppendChild` method adds the element itself, which returns a reference to the node just added, and then the text node is added to the new element.

A different procedure is needed for modifying the text of an existing node. This procedure takes arguments of the node where the modification is to be made and the new text. Listing 21.2 shows the code for this subroutine.

LISTING 21.2   utility.vb: The `ReplaceElement` Subroutine

```
Public Sub ReplaceElement(ByVal oNode As XmlNode, ByVal strText As String)
    Dim oContent As XmlText
    Dim oDoc As XmlDocument

    oDoc = oNode.OwnerDocument
    oContent = oDoc.CreateTextNode(strText)

    oNode.ReplaceChild(oContent, oNode.FirstChild)
End Sub
```

Make sure that this code is in the Utility.vb module along with `PlaceElement`.

Now that the new procedures are in place, you can return to the `Save()` method code for the finishing touches. First, check to see whether this is a new entry. If so, create a new `Employee` node and then add the `ID`, `Name`, and `Position` nodes by using `PlaceElement`. Then call the `WriteExtra` subroutine.

If this entry is a replacement, locate the `Name` node within the pre-existing node, modify it by using `ReplaceElement`, and then call `WriteExtra`. The `Name` node is the only thing that can be modified in this design.

After the writing is finished, save the XML document to the Employees.xml file. This method overwrites the file if it already exists. Then set the `boolSuccess` variable to `True`, and you're done with the `Save()` method. Here's the last code fragment, which wraps up the code that you started at the beginning of this section:

```
If boolNewEmp Then

    oElem = oXml.CreateElement("Employee")
    oEmp = oRoot.AppendChild(oElem)
```

```
        PlaceElement(oEmp, "ID", intID.ToString)
        PlaceElement(oEmp, "Name", strName)
        PlaceElement(oEmp, "Position", strPosition)
        WriteExtra(oEmp, True)
    Else
        oSubNode = oIDNode.SelectSingleNode("Name")
        ReplaceElement(oSubNode, strName)
        WriteExtra(oIDNode, False)
    End If

    oXml.Save("C:\Employees.xml")

    boolSuccess = True
End If

Return boolSuccess
```

The `Read()` Method

The `Read()` method is much simpler but has one thing in common with the `Save()`
method. You must create a hook so that the hours per day value can be read from the
`Resource` derived class.

The `Read()` method starts with variable declarations and then checks for a valid `intID`
value. If the ID is not valid, you won't find it in the XML file. Then the file is opened,
and if an ID is not found, a `False` return is set up, indicating read failure.

The code fragment for the beginning of the `Read()` method is as follows:

```
Dim oXml As New XmlDocument()
Dim oName As XmlNode
Dim oPosition As XmlNode
Dim boolSuccess As Boolean

If intID < 1 Then
    ' cannot read an Employee
    ' without an id
    boolSuccess = False
Else
    Try
        oXml.Load("C:\Employees.xml")
        boolSuccess = True
    Catch ex As IO.FileNotFoundException
        boolSuccess = False
    End Try
End If
```

21

ANALYSIS Rather than encapsulate the rest of the method within `Else...End If`, you can
use the `boolSuccess` variable value to see whether the method should execute
the next portion of code. If it is `True`, a search is done using an XPath query. If nothing

is found, `boolSuccess` is set to `False`; otherwise, the text node contents are passed to the properties of the `Employee` class. Because the `Resource` derived class has to read the hours per day in addition to the standard employee properties, the `ReadExtra` subroutine is called. There is no code in this class, but there will be in the `Resource` class. The code for `ReadExtra` is as follows and should be placed anywhere in the `Employee` class, but not in the `Read()` method:

```
Protected Overridable Sub ReadExtra(ByVal oNode As XmlNode)
    'In this class, it does nothing
End Sub
```

The only parameter you need is for the parent node of the node to be read. The rest of the `Read()` method's code follows:

```
If boolSuccess Then
    oName = oXml.SelectSingleNode("//Employee[ID='" & _
      intID.ToString & "']/Name")
    If oName Is Nothing Then
        boolSuccess = False
    Else
        strName = oName.InnerText
        oPosition = oName.SelectSingleNode("../Position")
        strPosition = oPosition.InnerText
        ReadExtra(oName.ParentNode)
    End If
End If

Return boolSuccess
```

ANALYSIS   Notice that because the search produces a reference to the `Name` node, that node is used as the context node for the rest of the needed data. The XPath query used to locate the `Position` node is `../Position`, which goes to the parent node of `Name` and then to the child node called `Position`. When `ReadExtra` is called, the `ParentNode` property of the `Name` node is passed to the subroutine.

The `Delete()` Method

By this time, you should be getting the hang of writing these methods and realize how similar all this code is to the first routine you wrote. The `Delete()` method uses the same techniques as the `Read()` method, except that after the node is located, the `RemoveChild` method deletes the data entry. The only real difference is that this method doesn't need a hook. Listing 21.3 shows the code for the `Delete()` method.

LISTING 21.3   The Employee Class `Delete()` Method

```
Public Function Delete() As Boolean Implements IDBIdentity.Delete
    Dim oXml As New XmlDocument()
    Dim oEmp As XmlNode
    Dim boolSuccess As Boolean

    If intID < 1 Then
        ' cannot delete an Employee
        ' without an id
        boolSuccess = False
    Else
        Try
            oXml.Load("C:\Employees.xml")
            boolSuccess = True
        Catch ex As IO.FileNotFoundException
            boolSuccess = False
        End Try
    End If

    If boolSuccess Then
        oEmp = oXml.SelectSingleNode("//Employee[ID='" & _
          intID.ToString & "']")
        If oEmp Is Nothing Then
            boolSuccess = False
        Else
            oEmp.ParentNode.RemoveChild(oEmp)
        End If
    End If

    If boolSuccess Then
        oXml.Save("C:\Employees.xml")
    End If
    Return boolSuccess
End Function
```

The Resource Class

In the `Save()` and `Read()` methods of the `Employee` class, you called the `WriteExtra` and `ReadExtra` subroutines. You also created these subroutines in `Employee` but with no code. The procedures were set as `Overridable`, so that in a derived class, they could be overridden.

The `Resource` class is such a derived class. Resources have an extra property, `HoursPerDay` and the supporting member variable, `intHoursPerDay`. Therefore, the XML file should have an `HoursPerDay` element to store that value. No rule in XML says

21

that every set of an element must have the exact same child elements. In fact, it's because of the extensibility and flexibility of the standard that XML has gained such wide acceptance.

Resources are employees as well, and there is no reason why they shouldn't be stored in the same file as the other employees, product managers, and project managers. Now is the time to add the code to the `Resource` class to handle the extra data item. Listing 21.4 has the code that is to be added.

LISTING 21.4   The `WriteExtra` and `ReadExtra` Subroutines for the `Resource` Class

```
Protected Overrides Sub WriteExtra(ByVal oNode As System.Xml.XmlNode, _
                            ByVal boolNew As Boolean)
    If boolNew Then
        PlaceElement(oNode, "HoursPerDay", intHoursPerDay.ToString)
    Else
        Dim oHours As XmlNode
        Dim oPosition As XmlNode

        oHours = oNode.SelectSingleNode("HoursPerDay")
        ReplaceElement(oHours, intHoursPerDay.ToString)
        oPosition = oNode.SelectSingleNode("Position")
        ReplaceElement(oPosition, strPosition)
    End If
End Sub

Protected Overrides Sub ReadExtra(ByVal oNode As System.Xml.XmlNode)
    Dim oHours As XmlNode
    oHours = oNode.SelectSingleNode("HoursPerDay")
    intHoursPerDay = CInt(oHours.InnerText)
End Sub
```

In the section for changing existing elements, you see that because the position of `Resource` is editable, the position is modified, as well as the hours per day.

Seeing the Data

After these changes are made, you can rebuild the project and then run the PMApp program created on Day 20. After you enter some data for employees, an XML file will exist with the employee information you entered.

One feature of Visual Studio .NET is that you can load any file into the design environment. Visual Studio .NET will adjust its presentation according to the file type loaded.

When you load an XML document, the Visual Studio .NET interface processes the data just like Internet Explorer, using color coding and indentation to make the XML data readable, just like in Figure 21.1. It also puts a pair of buttons labeled XML and Data at the bottom of the screen. When you click the Data button, Visual Studio .NET takes the XML data and presents it in an editable grid, as though it were tabular data from a database (see Figure 21.2).

FIGURE 21.1

Employees.XML document in Visual Studio .NET.

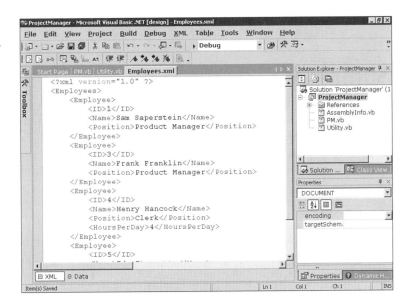

FIGURE 21.2

Employees.XML document in Data view in Visual Studio .NET.

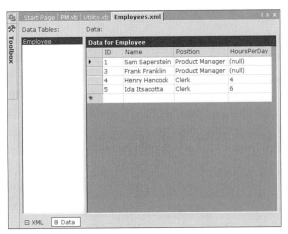

21

The `Product`, `Project`, and `ProjectItems` Classes

Because nothing is really different about the `Product`, `Project`, and `ProjectItems` classes and their `Save()`, `Read()`, and `Delete()` methods, you can find the code for these classes in XtraXml.txt, one of the downloadable files for this book. Instructions in the file point out which listings should be inserted into which classes. PM.txt contains all the completed code for the entire PM.vb class module.

Summary

Today you wrapped up your project by extending it with data persistence. Along the way, you learned a little bit about XML and some of the supporting technologies that have helped establish XML as the future in computing. We hope that you'll continue to learn more about this exciting technology, especially because it's a basic building block of Microsoft's .NET initiative.

Today you also learned how to code methods in the classes to take care of some of this application's data storage needs. Storing data is almost always a necessity in programs.

Finally, today's lesson wrapped up the Project Manager application as well as the past three weeks of learning about object-oriented programming using the new Visual Basic .NET.

Q&A

Q How do I code a derived class method so that it augments the code of the base class method?

A You use the `MyBase` keyword, which acts as a variable pointing to the base class of the derived class. Then, by specifying the base class's method name, you execute the code of the base class method, as well as any extra code in the derived class method. This technique is good even when there's no code in the base class method because someone may add code to the base class method in the future and you'll want to make sure that you inherit that code.

Q If I use XML, can I somehow create an index on the data for faster access?

A Yes and no. You can't create a *permanent* index on the XML document; however, you can speed up access to elements in the DOM by creating an attribute for those elements that can be specified as an ID type. To do so, you use a DTD for the XML document. Then you use the very fast `GetElementByID` method of the document element.

Workshop

The Workshop provides quiz questions and an exercise to help solidify your understanding of today's lesson. Answers are provided in Appendix A, "Answers to Quizzes."

Quiz

1. What technology is used to query the XML-DOM in memory?
2. What object and method are used to build an element node?
3. What keyword is used on an inherited method when the derived class modifies it?
4. What extended XML function is used to return just one node?

Exercise

Table 21.1 contains XPath queries for searching through an XML document. For this exercise, construct the XML document node-set that these queries use. In each case, the context node is listed. *Previous* indicates the results of the last search. Except where specified in the queries, element contents can be anything you want. The XML document that you create should cause all the XPath queries to be successful.

TABLE 21.1 XPath Queries of an XML Document

Context Node	XPath Query
Root	`/Products/Product[ID="4"]`
Previous	`Projects/Project[StartDate="20020312"]`
Previous	`Items/Item/Description`
Root	`/Products/Product/Name`
Root	`//Item/Hours`
Root	`//Project[Name="Manufacturing"]`
Previous	`../../Description`
Previous	`../Projects`
Root	`//Item[ID="10002"]`
Previous	`Description`
Previous	`../../../ID`

21

WEEK 3

In Review

Congratulations on making it through 21 days of intense learning about object-oriented programming and Visual Basic .NET! In this final week, you had a chance to put all the information together. You learned how to handle events, messages, and notifications. Recall the Directory Monitor project from Day 15? In that lesson, you created an application that displays an updated list of files and monitors changes to the list with the `FileSystemWatcher` class. The following day, you learned about error handling and how to cope gracefully with situations that don't go as expected. You can see the advantages of providing meaningful error messages by trapping exactly what went wrong. You'll probably find many uses for remoting, as you discovered it in Day 17. The ability to call objects from anywhere that you can make a TCP connection opens up a whole new world in distributed computing.

An example of how far you've come is clear from Day 18. You can now read and make sense of an object-oriented project's diagram. In fact, you can design a project that you can hand off to others to implement, just as an architect creates blueprints and leaves the actual building to tradespeople. To that end, the architect became the builder in the final three chapters. First, you wrote the base classes and created the objects; then you designed the user interface. Finally, you wrapped up the whole project by creating the code that stores all the data on the disk drive in XML format.

Working through these 21 lessons has been quite an adventure into OOP, with a few side trips along the way to master the tools and technologies. At this point, you know enough

15

16

17

18

19

20

21

about OOP that you can learn even more. Or, as Aristotle put it, "For the things we have to learn before we can do them, we learn by doing them."

APPENDIX A

Answers to Quizzes

Day 1, "Object-Oriented Programming 101: Making the Task Application"

Quiz

1. It shows class relationships to other classes, member data, and methods and properties.
2. Serialization.
3. Class inheritance or derivation.
4. A property.
5. `Dispose()`.

Exercise

Change the `SmartMsg` class to receive a filename on the `New()` method, as follows:

```
Class SmartMsg
   Inherits SimpleMsg

   Private strFileName As String

   Public Sub New(ByVal FileName As String)
      'Always good to call MyBase's New()
      MyBase.New()

      Me.strFileName = FileName

      Read()
   End Sub
   ...
```

Change the `Write()` method to create a new file using the `FileName` member instead of the `"msg.bin"` string:

```
Public Function Write() As Boolean
...
   Try
      'Allocate and create a new file and serialize object
      MsgFile = (New File(FileName)).Open(FileMode.Create)
...
```

Change the `Read()` method the same as the `Write()` method to use the `FileName` member:

```
   Public Function Write() As Boolean
      ...
      Try
         'Allocate and create a new file and serialize object
         MsgFile = File.Open(strFileName, FileMode.Create)
      ...
```

Add a new member variable, `Msg2`, to the `MsgReader` class and allocate it as follows:

```
Class MsgReader
   Inherits System.Windows.Forms.Form

   Private Msg As SmartMsg
   Private Msg2 As SmartMsg

   Public Sub New(ByRef Msg As SmartMsg)
      MyBase.New()

      MsgReader = Me
      Me.Msg = Msg

      Msg2 = New SmartMsg("msg2.bin")
```

```
        'This call is required by the Win Form Designer.
        InitializeComponent()

        'TODO: Add any initialization after the InitializeComponent() call
        TextBox.Text = Msg.MsgText()
        TextBox2.Text = Msg2.MsgText()
    End Sub
...
```

Call the `Dispose()` method on the new `Msg2` object in the `Dispose()` subroutine of the `MsgReader` class:

```
    Protected Overloads Overrides Sub Dispose(ByVal disposing As Boolean)
        If Disposing Then
            If Not (components Is Nothing) Then
                components.Dispose()
            End If
        End If
        MyBase.Dispose(disposing)

        'Dispose messages
        Msg.Dispose()
        Msg2.Dispose()
    End Sub
```

Declare, create, and initialize a new text box control for the Windows Form and resize the first TextBox to make room for the new one:

```
'Control variables
Private WithEvents TextBox As TextBox
Private WithEvents TextBox2 As TextBox
Private WithEvents btnCancel As Button
Private WithEvents btnOK As Button

Dim WithEvents MsgReader As Form

'NOTE: The following procedure is required by the Windows Form Designer
'It can be modified using the Windows Form Designer.
'Do not modify it using the code editor.
Private Sub InitializeComponent()
    components = New System.ComponentModel.Container()

    Me.btnOK = New System.Windows.Forms.Button()
    Me.TextBox = New System.Windows.Forms.TextBox()
    Me.btnCancel = New System.Windows.Forms.Button()
    Me.TextBox2 = New System.Windows.Forms.TextBox()
    Me.SuspendLayout()
    '
    'TextBox
    '
    Me.TextBox.AcceptsReturn = True
```

```
    Me.TextBox.Multiline = True
    Me.TextBox.Name = "TextBox"
    Me.TextBox.ScrollBars = System.Windows.Forms.ScrollBars.Vertical
    Me.TextBox.Size = New System.Drawing.Size(288, 110)
    Me.TextBox.TabIndex = 0
    Me.TextBox.Text = ""
    '
    'TextBox2
    '
    Me.TextBox2.AcceptsReturn = True
    Me.TextBox2.Location = New System.Drawing.Point(0, 112)
    Me.TextBox2.Multiline = True
    Me.TextBox2.Name = "TextBox2"
    Me.TextBox2.ScrollBars = System.Windows.Forms.ScrollBars.Vertical
    Me.TextBox2.Size = New System.Drawing.Size(288, 110)
    Me.TextBox2.TabIndex = 1
    Me.TextBox2.Text = ""
    '
    'btnOK
    '
    Me.btnOK.Location = New System.Drawing.Point(128, 232)
    Me.btnOK.Name = "btnOK"
    Me.btnOK.TabIndex = 2
    Me.btnOK.Text = "OK"
    '
    'btnCancel
    '
    Me.btnCancel.Location = New System.Drawing.Point(208, 232)
    Me.btnCancel.Name = "btnCancel"
    Me.btnCancel.TabIndex = 3
    Me.btnCancel.Text = "Cancel"
    '
    'MsgReader
    '
    Me.AutoScaleBaseSize = New System.Drawing.Size(5, 13)
    Me.ClientSize = New System.Drawing.Size(288, 261)
    Me.Controls.AddRange(New System.Windows.Forms.Control() _
        {Me.TextBox, Me.TextBox2, Me.btnOK, Me.btnCancel})
    Me.Name = "MsgReader"
    Me.Text = "Task"
    Me.ResumeLayout(False)
End Sub
```

Assign the text from the new TextBox control into the new SmartMsg object when the user clicks OK:

```
Protected Sub btnOK_Click(ByVal sender As Object, _
    ByVal e As System.EventArgs) Handles btnOK.Click
    ' Save the simple message
```

```
    Msg.MsgText = TextBox.Text()
    Msg2.MsgText = TextBox2.Text()

    Close()
End Sub
```

Change the allocation of the `SmartMsg` object in the `main()` subroutine to include the filename:

```
Sub main()
  System.Windows.Forms.Application.Run(New MsgReader(New SmartMsg("msg.bin")))
End Sub

End Sub
```

Day 2, "Learning to Speak OOP"

Quiz

1. An entity with state, a defined boundary, behavior, and characteristics.

2. A class is a blueprint or template from which objects are created. It describes the member data, methods, and functionality of an object.

3. `Finalize()`.

4. Events.

Exercise

Create a new class interface named `IMyInterface1`:

```
Interface IMyInterface1
End Interface
```

Create a new class named `MyClass2`:

```
Class MyClass2
End Class
```

Create a new class named `MyClass1` that inherits `MyClass2` and implements `IMyInterface1`:

```
Class MyClass1
     Inherits MyClass2
     Implements IMyInterface1

End Class
```

Day 3, "Enclosing Features and Data in Objects"

Quiz

1. `Private`. In some cases, `Protected`, for use in derived classes.

2. To provide "black box" objects that take care of the implementation details and provide users with a simple interface.

3. All methods declared as `Public` within the class definition. Any member data declared as `Public` is also part of the interface; however, declaring data this way isn't recommended.

Exercise

The subroutine definition is shown in Listing A.1 and is added to the `Books` class.

LISTING A.1   Books.vb: `FillList()` Method Definition

```
Public Sub FillList(ByRef List As ListView)
    'Display a wait cursor since this process can take a while
    Cursor.Current = Cursors.WaitCursor()

    'Query the book list and fill the listview
    Me.Query()
    While Me.Fetch()
        List.Items.Add(Me.Title()).SubItems.AddRange(New System.String() _
            {Me.Author(), Me.Price()})
    End While

    'Change the cursor back to the default
    Cursor.Current = Cursors.Default()
End Sub
```

Day 4, "Making New Objects by Extending Existing Objects"

Quiz

1. `Inherits`.

2. `Public` and `Protected`. The derived class can also see `Friend` and `Shared` members and methods. Only `Private` members and methods are hidden from the derived class.

3. MustInherit.

4. Overridable and Overrides.

Exercise

Listing A.2 shows the code for the WithdrawForm class definition. It's similar to the DepositForm class, except that it has a different control and text.

LISTING A.2 WithdrawForm.vb: WithdrawForm Class Derived from TransactionForm

```
Public Class WithdrawForm
    Inherits TransactionForm

    Public Sub New()
        MyBase.New()

        'This call is required by the Windows Form Designer.
        InitializeComponent()

        'Add any initialization after the InitializeComponent() call

    End Sub

    'Form overrides dispose to clean up the component list.
    Protected Overloads Overrides Sub Dispose(ByVal disposing As Boolean)
        If disposing Then
            If Not (components Is Nothing) Then
                components.Dispose()
            End If
        End If
        MyBase.Dispose(disposing)
    End Sub

    '
    'Additional Controls
    '
    Protected WithEvents PayToField As System.Windows.Forms.TextBox
    Protected WithEvents PayToText As System.Windows.Forms.Label

    Protected Overrides Sub InitializeComponent()
        MyBase.InitializeComponent()

        Me.PayToField = New System.Windows.Forms.TextBox()
        Me.PayToText = New System.Windows.Forms.Label()

        '
        'PayToField
        '
        Me.PayToField.Location = New System.Drawing.Point(80, 62)
```

LISTING A.2 continued

```
        Me.PayToField.Size = New System.Drawing.Size(176, 20)
        Me.PayToField.TabIndex = 4
        '
        'PayToText
        '
        Me.PayToText.Location = New System.Drawing.Point(10, 64)
        Me.PayToText.Name = "PayToText"
        Me.PayToText.Size = New System.Drawing.Size(70, 16)
        Me.PayToText.TabIndex = 5
        Me.PayToText.Text = "Pay To:"


        '
        'Re-order the memo field and text
        '
        Me.MemoField.TabIndex = 6
        Me.MemoText.TabIndex = 7

        MyBase.InitializeComponent()
        Me.Text = "Withdraw Form"


        '
        'Re-add controls to form
        '
        Me.Controls.Clear()
        Me.Controls.AddRange(New System.Windows.Forms.Control() _
                {Me.DateText, Me.DateField, Me.PayToText, Me.PayToField, _
                 Me.MemoText, Me.MemoField, Me.AmountText, Me.AmountField})
    End Sub
End Class
```

Day 5, "Giving Objects Polymorphic Behavior"

Quiz

1. Because every implementation of the interface can be unique, the same interface can have different behavior.

2. No. Because the method must be overridden and the original has no implementation, it is polymorphic the first time it is implemented in a derived class.

3. Yes. If you declare your method without the Overridable keyword, it can never be overridden by a derived class and therefore will always have the same functionality.

4. No. If the overridden subroutine performs the same implementation as the subroutine it overrides, it isn't polymorphic. Just because a subroutine is re-implemented, doesn't make it polymorphic. It must have different behavior.

Exercise

Add the `Read()` and `ReadData()` method declarations to the `TransactionForm` class as shown in Listing A.3.

LISTING A.3   TransactionForm.vb: The `Read()` and `ReadData()` Methods

```
Public MustInherit Class TransactionForm
    Inherits System.Windows.Forms.Form

    Public Overridable Function Read(ByVal FileName As String) As Boolean
        'declare a file and serialize class
        Dim TranFile As Stream
        Dim BinSerialize As BinaryFormatter

        'Set the return value to True
        Read = True

        'Use Try/Catch to handle any errors
        Try
            'Allocate and open the file and de-serialize objects
            TranFile = File.Open(FileName, FileMode.Open)
            BinSerialize = New BinaryFormatter()

            'Serialize the MsgText() property which is a String object
            AmountField.Text = CType(BinSerialize.Deserialize(TranFile), String)
            MemoField.Text = CType(BinSerialize.Deserialize(TranFile), String)
            DateField.Text = CType(BinSerialize.Deserialize(TranFile), String)

            'Call ReadData() to read derived class's data
            ReadData(BinSerialize, TranFile)
        Catch
            'Indicate an error occurred
            Read = False
        End Try

        TranFile.Close()
    End Function

    'Declare Abstract method to read derived class's data
    Protected MustOverride Sub ReadData(ByRef BinSerialize As BinaryFormatter,_
                            ByRef TranFile As Stream)

    ...

End Class
```

Now provide the implementation of the ReadData() method to the DepositForm and WithdrawForm, as shown in Listing A.4.

LISTING A.4   DepositForm.vb and WithdrawForm.vb: Implementing ReadData() in the DepositForm and WithdrawForm Classes

```
Public Class DepositForm
    Inherits TransactionForm
    Implements IPrint

    Protected Overrides Sub ReadData(ByRef BinSerialize As BinaryFormatter,_
                            ByRef TranFile As Stream)
        DepositToField.Text = CType(BinSerialize.Deserialize(TranFile), String)
    End Sub

    ...

End Class

Public Class WithdrawForm
    Inherits TransactionForm
    Implements IPrint

    Protected Overrides Sub ReadData(ByRef BinSerialize As BinaryFormatter, _
                            ByRef TranFile As Stream)
        PayToField.Text = CType(BinSerialize.Deserialize(TranFile), String)
    End Sub

    ...

End Class
```

Day 6, "Building Complex Objects by Combining Objects"

Quiz

1. Association, aggregation, and composition

2. Association

3. Composition or aggregation as a reference

Exercise

Add a private member data item, CkBook, to the WithdrawForm and DepositForm classes. On the constructor, New(), receive a reference to a CheckBook object and store the reference in the CkBook member, as shown in Listing A.5.

A

LISTING A.5 WithdrawForm.vb: Using an Aggregate Association with the CkBook Class

```
Public Class WithdrawForm
    Inherits TransactionForm
    Implements IPrint

    Private CkBook As CheckBookReg

    Public Sub New(ByRef CkBook As CheckBookReg)
        MyBase.New()

        Me.CkBook = CkBook

        'This call is required by the Windows Form Designer.
        InitializeComponent()
    End Sub

    ...

End Class

Public Class DepositForm
    Inherits TransactionForm
    Implements IPrint

    Private CkBook As CheckBookReg

    Public Sub New(ByRef CkBook As CheckBookReg)
        MyBase.New()

        Me.CkBook = CkBook

        'This call is required by the Windows Form Designer.
        InitializeComponent()
    End Sub

    ...

End Class
```

Day 7, "Getting to Know the Visual Basic .NET Programming Environment"

Quiz

1. A solution is a collection of one or more projects and related files in Visual Studio .NET.

2. Yes.

3. The common language runtime (CLR) manages all memory.

4. In your current project, go to Solution Explorer and select the project name (for example, MyApp). From the Project Menu, choose Add Existing Item. In the Add Existing Item dialog box, navigate to the file that you want to link. Click the down arrow next to the Open button and select Link File. The small arrow on the file's icon indicates that it's linked rather than physically included in the project.

5. This was a bit of a trick question because you are asked *how* you find out. The answer is to open the online help index, look for the phrase *hidden files*, and open the topic. The help topic shows the use of the Show All Files button.

Exercise

Figure A.1 shows how the form should look after it is designed. The key to this exercise is to double-click Button1 to create an event handler for a click event. Inside the handler, enter the following code:

```
Label1.Text = TextBox1.Text
```

As always, if you need information on how to carry out a task in Visual Basic .NET, check first with the online help.

FIGURE A.1

The sample form.

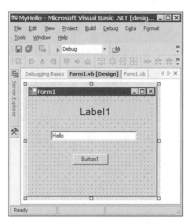

Day 8, "Working with Visual Basic .NET Data Types"

A

Quiz

1. System.ValueType

2. 0

3. public

Exercise

The following code shows the declaration of the MyNewStruct structure. This example is just one possible implementation; other implementation possibilities can accomplish the same task.

```
Structure MyNewStruct
    Public nValue As Integer
    Public strString As String
    Public aryArray() As Integer

    Public Sub InitializeArray(ByRef ary As Array)
        Dim i As Integer
        ReDim aryArray(ary.GetUpperBound(0))

        For i = ary.GetLowerBound(0) To ary.GetUpperBound(0)
            aryArray(i) = ary(i)
        Next
    End Sub
End Structure
```

Day 9, "Organizing Classes into Groups"

Quiz

1. System and Microsoft

2. Yes

3. Organization of classes and structures and name conflict avoidance

Exercise

The following code shows one possible solution to the exercise. It declares classes in each of four namespaces, which create three levels of namespaces under the root namespace:

```
Namespace MyRoot
    Public Class MyOwnClass
    End Class
End Namespace

Namespace MyRoot.Level1
    Public Class MyOwnClass
    End Class

    Namespace Level2
        Public Class MyOwnClass
        End Class
    End Namespace
End Namespace

Namespace MyRoot.Level1.Level2.Level3
    Public Class MyOwnClass
    End Class
End Namespace
```

Day 10, "Creating a User Interface"

Quiz

1. System.Windows.Forms.Form

2. System.Web.UI.Page

3. .ASPX and .ASPX.VB

4. No. Windows Forms can also be MDI containers and have no data-entry related use.

Exercise

Add the boldfaced statement in Listing A.6 to the Submit button event handler to save the entered name value in the Session state.

LISTING A.6   Storing the Text Value of edtName to a Session Variable in Webform1.aspx.vb

```
Private Sub btnSubmit_Click _
    (ByVal sender As System.Object, ByVal e As System.EventArgs) _
    Handles btnSubmit.Click
  Session.Item("Name") = edtName.Text()
  Response.Redirect("webform2.aspx")
End Sub
```

Create a new Web Form called `WebForm2` and add a Label control to the page. Next, insert the boldface code into the `Page_Load` subroutine, as shown in Listing A.7.

LISTING A.7 Assigning the Value of the Session Variable to the Label Control in Webform2.aspx.vb

```
Private Sub Page_Load _
  (ByVal sender As System.Object, ByVal e As System.EventArgs) Handles _
    MyBase.Load
  'Put user code to initialize the page here
  Label1.Text = "Welcome " + Session.Item("Name")
End Sub
```

Day 11, "Creating and Using Components"

Quiz

1. Perform late binding to external types defined in other assemblies.

2. Structures, classes, types, and enumerations.

3. Yes. By adding the component to the toolbox for the designer, you can use the component at design time.

4. `Assembly`.

Exercise

The code in Listing A.8 shows one way of completing this exercise. Notice that most of the activity is in the button objects' `Click` events. The first button calls the component while the second button ends the program. Closing the form stops the beep.

LISTING A.8 Form1.vb: Using a Button Object to Invoke the `DemoComp` Component

```
Public Class Form1
    Inherits System.Windows.Forms.Form

#Region " Windows Form Designer generated code "

    Public Sub New()
        MyBase.New()
        InitializeComponent()
    End Sub

    Protected Overloads Overrides Sub Dispose _
    (ByVal disposing As Boolean)
```

LISTING A.8 continued

```
            If disposing Then
                If Not (components Is Nothing) Then
                    components.Dispose()
                End If
            End If
            MyBase.Dispose(disposing)
        End Sub
        Friend WithEvents Button1 As System.Windows.Forms.Button
        Friend WithEvents Button2 As System.Windows.Forms.Button

        Private components As System.ComponentModel.IContainer
        <System.Diagnostics.DebuggerStepThrough()> _
    Private Sub InitializeComponent()
            Me.Button1 = New System.Windows.Forms.Button()
            Me.Button2 = New System.Windows.Forms.Button()
            Me.SuspendLayout()
            Me.Button1.Location = New System.Drawing.Point(72, 32)
            Me.Button1.Name = "Button1"
            Me.Button1.TabIndex = 0
            Me.Button1.Text = "Start Beep"
            Me.Button2.Location = New System.Drawing.Point(72, 80)
            Me.Button2.Name = "Button2"
            Me.Button2.TabIndex = 1
            Me.Button2.Text = "Exit"
            Me.AutoScaleBaseSize = New System.Drawing.Size(5, 13)
            Me.ClientSize = New System.Drawing.Size(232, 181)
            Me.Controls.AddRange _
    (New System.Windows.Forms.Control() {Me.Button2, Me.Button1})
            Me.Name = "Form1"
            Me.Text = "Form1"
            Me.ResumeLayout(False)
        End Sub

#End Region
    Private Sub Button1_Click(ByVal sender As System.Object, _
    ByVal e As System.EventArgs) Handles Button1.Click
        Dim objComponent As New MyComponents.DemoComp()
        objComponent.Timer1.Start()
    End Sub

    Private Sub Button2_Click(ByVal sender As System.Object, _
    ByVal e As System.EventArgs) Handles Button2.Click
        End
    End Sub
End Class
```

Day 12, "Building Web Applications"

A

Quiz

1. As a Web Reference.

2. ASP.NET running on the Web server with the help of the compiled Visual Basic .NET code.

3. Yes.

4. The service is located within the referenced host. For example, on your machine, it's referenced as localhost.myservice.

Exercise

Add the boldfaced code to the Service1 service class:

```
Imports System.Web.Services

<WebService(Namespace:="http://rich-dell/webservices/")> Public Class Service1
    Inherits System.Web.Services.WebService

+  " Web Services Designer Generated Code "

    <WebMethod()> Public Function DateTime() As String
       DateTime = Date.Now.ToString("M/dd/yyyy hh:mm:ss")
     End Function

    <WebMethod()> Public Function CurrentDate() As String
       CurrentDate = Date.Today.ToString("M/dd/yyy")
    End Function

    <WebMethod()> Public Function CurrentTime() As String
       CurrentTime = Date.Now.ToString("hh:mm:ss")
    End Function

End Class
```

Day 13, "Deploying Visual Basic .NET Projects"

Quiz

1. A manifest

2. Using a Windows Installer created with Visual Studio .NET

Exercise

Using the MyFormApp solution, add a Setup Project called MyFormSetup, as shown in Figure A.2. Using the Properties page for the MyFormSetup project, ensure that you are including the primary output of MyFormApp (refer to Figure 13.9 for guidance).

FIGURE A.2

Adding a setup project to the MyFormApp *solution.*

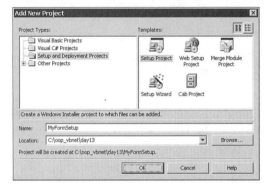

Check the Configuration Manager to ensure that MyFormSetup is included in the build process (refer to Figure 13.7 for an example). Then build the project and check the output, as shown in Figure A.3.

FIGURE A.3

The Output window shows the build progress of MyFormSetup.

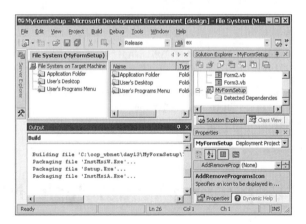

Day 14, "Working with Object Interfaces"

Quiz

1. Interface.

2. Implements.

3. No. A class has to implement all methods, properties, and events within an implemented interface.

4. As many interfaces as necessary; there is no limit.

5. Structures can implement interfaces.

Exercise

First, declare the new `IError` interface as shown in the following code segment:

```
Public Interface IError
   Sub DisplayError( ByVal sMsg As String )
End Interface
```

Then declare a class, `MyClass`, that implements the `IError` interface by displaying the message as shown in the following code segment:

```
Public Class MyOwnClass
   Implements IError

   Sub DisplayError( ByVal sMsg As String ) Implements IError.DisplayError
      MsgBox(sMsg)
   End Sub

End Class
```

Day 15, "Handling Events, Messages, and Notifications"

Quiz

1. Event.

2. To provide a template for the handler of an event. The handler for an event must have the same parameters as the delegate with which the event was declared.

3. Handles.

4. No. Because an event is raised and the code that raised the event isn't waiting for a return value, using a function to handle an event serves no purpose; therefore, the compiler won't allow it.

Exercise

First, declare the class with the events and delegates as shown in the following code segment:

```
Public Class MyEvents
   Public Delegate Sub Event1Delegate(ByVal nValue As Integer)
   Public Delegate Sub Event2Delegate _
   (ByVal sValue As String, ByVal sender As Object)
   Public Event Event1 As Event1Delegate
   Public Event Event2 As Event2Delegate

   Public Sub PerformProcess()
      'Perform Step
      RaiseEvent Event1(50)

      'Perform Final Step
      RaiseEvent Event2("Done", Me)
   End Sub
End Class
```

Then, declare a class to use the MyEvents class and create subroutines that handle the events in the MyEvents class, as shown in the following code segment:

```
Public Class MyUser
   Private WithEvents Events As MyEvents

   Public Sub New()
      Events = New MyEvents()
   End Sub

   Private Sub Event1Handler(ByVal nValue As Integer) Handles Events.Event1
      MsgBox(nValue.ToString())
   End Sub

   Private Sub Event2Handler _
   (ByVal sValue As String, ByVal sender As Object) Handles Events.Event2
      MsgBox(sValue)
   End Sub

   Public Sub UseObject()
      Events.PerformProcess()
   End Sub
End Class
```

Day 16, "Gracefully Capturing Errors"

Quiz

1. Try...Catch...Finally.

2. Throw.

3. It's executed whenever the Try block exits or after any exception is handled.

Exercise

The following class definition provides the three constructors and the property to gain access to the `Object`:

```
Public Class ExerciseException
   Inherits Exception

   Private m_Source As Object

   Public Sub New()
      MyBase.New()
   End Sub

   Public Sub New(ByVal sMsg As String)
      MyBase.New(sMsg)
   End Sub

   Public Sub New(ByVal sMsg As String, ByVal source As Object)
      MyBase.New(sMsg)

      m_Source = source
   End Sub

   Public ReadOnly Property SourceObject() As Object
   Get
      SourceObject = m_Source
   End Get
   End Property
End Class
```

Day 17, "Developing and Using Remote Objects"

Quiz

1. Well-known (server-side) and client-activated.

2. A copied object is copied into the local application's domain. The referenced object is used within the local application's domain through a proxy, and the real object exists on the server.

3. `MarshalByRefObject`.

4. `TcpChannel` and `HttpChannel`.

Exercise

To complete this exercise, follow these steps:

1. In your Remoting solution, add a Windows application and call it `vbWinFormClient`.

2. Rename the default form file to vbWinformClient.vb.

3. Design a graphical interface with two text boxes, two buttons, and the required labels, as shown in Figure A.4.

FIGURE A.4

Graphical user interface for the Windows Form client application that uses vbServiceHost.

4. Use the code shown in Listing A.9 to assemble the values accepted from the user. Call the remote object in the click event of the Calculate button.

LISTING A.9 vbWinFormClient.vb—Windows Form to Call and Display Values Calculated by the Remote Object

```vbnet
Imports System.Runtime.Remoting
Imports System.Runtime.Remoting.Channels
Imports System.Runtime.Remoting.Channels.Tcp
Imports vbServiceObject.RemotingExample

Public Class Form1
  Inherits System.Windows.Forms.Form
' Windows Form Designer generated code omitted

  Private Sub btnCalculate_Click _
  (ByVal sender As System.Object, ByVal e As System.EventArgs) _
  Handles btnCalculate.Click
    btnCalculate.Enabled = False
    Dim chan As TcpChannel
    chan = New TcpChannel()
    Try
      ChannelServices.RegisterChannel(chan)
    Catch ex As Exception
      MsgBox(ex.Message)
    End Try
    Dim calc As Calculate
    calc = CType(Activator.GetObject(GetType(Calculate), _
```

LISTING A.9 continued

```
      "tcp://localhost:8085/Calculate"), Calculate)

    If calc Is Nothing Then
      MsgBox("Could not find Server...")
    Else
      Try
        Me.lblSquare.Text = calc.Square _
        (Me.txtLength.Text, Me.txtWidth.Text)
      Catch ex As Exception
        MsgBox("Error message: " & ex.Message)
      End Try
    End If

  End Sub

  Private Sub btnExit_Click _
  (ByVal sender As System.Object, ByVal e As System.EventArgs) _
  Handles btnExit.Click
    End
  End Sub
End Class
```

Day 18, "Designing a Project Management Application"

Quiz

1. Gather requirements from the client.

2. No. They are conceptual real-world classes. However, they can have corresponding application classes.

3. Relationships, aggregation, members, properties, methods, derivations, and interfaces implemented.

Exercise

The first step is to create an additional conceptual class diagram as shown in Figure A.5.

Figure A.5

Conceptual class dia-gram for adding the team and team leader to the project for XYZCompany.

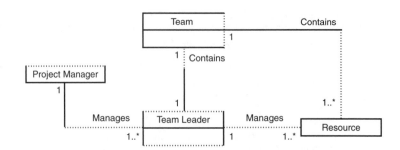

The diagram in Figure A.5 shows the relationship between the project manager and team leader. The team itself contains a single team leader and one or more resources managed by the team leader.

Drawing the UML class diagram for the necessary classes requires only a single new class, `Team`, which contains the manager's ID and the team leader's ID. This information ties the class back to its project manager and its team leader. The team leader doesn't need its own class because it's the same as the existing `Resource` class.

Also, a `TeamID` member is added to the `Resource` class to identify the team to which it's a member. The resulting class diagram is shown in Figure A.6.

Figure A.6

The UML Class dia-gram for the `Team` *Class includes the IDs of the manager and the team leader.*

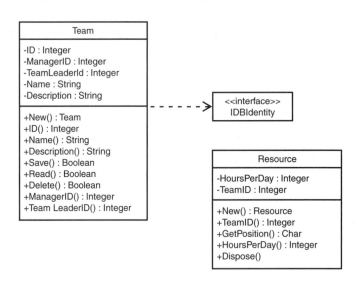

Day 19, "Creating the Project Management Application"

A

Quiz

1. Implements

2. Inherits

3. Overloads

4. When you have different sets of parameters, whether in number or data type

Exercise

First, define a collection member for the Project class definition:

```
Dim colItems As New Collection
```

Then add the code in Listing A.10 to the Project class definition for creating project item objects, storing them in the collection, and returning the item to the calling procedure.

LISTING A.10 Code for the Project Class for the AddItem Methods

```
Public Overloads Function AddItem() As ProjectItems
    Dim intCount As Integer

    intCount = colItems.Count + 1
    colItems.Add(New ProjectItems(intID), intCount.ToString)
    Return colItems.Item(intCount.ToString)
End Function

Public Overloads Function AddItem(ByVal intItemID As Integer) As ProjectItems
    Dim intCount As Integer

    intCount = colItems.Count + 1
    colItems.Add(New ProjectItems(intID, intItemID), intCount.ToString)
    Return colItems.Item(intCount.ToString)

End Function
```

Day 20 "Adding Features to the Application"

Quiz

1. Text

2. Anchor

3. New

Exercise

Listing A.11 shows the code for the Create, Read, Save, and Delete buttons' click events in the frmItem form.

LISTING A.11   The Click Events for the Create, Read, Save, and Delete Buttons

```
Private Sub btnCreate_Click(ByVal sender As System.Object, _
        ByVal e As System.EventArgs) Handles btnCreate.Click
    Dim intIdent As Integer

    If intIdent <= 0 Then
        oItem = oProj.AddItem()
    Else
        oItem = oProj.AddItem(intIdent)
    End If
    Me.btnCreate.Enabled = False
    Me.btnRead.Enabled = True
    Me.btnSave.Enabled = True
    Me.btnDelete.Enabled = True
End Sub

Private Sub btnRead_Click(ByVal sender As System.Object, _
        ByVal e As System.EventArgs) Handles btnRead.Click
    If Not oItem Is Nothing Then
        oItem.Read()
        Me.txtDescription.Text = oItem.Description
        Me.txtResID.Text = oItem.ResID
        Me.dtpStart.Value = oItem.StartDate
        Me.txtHours.Text = oItem.Hours
    End If
End Sub

Private Sub btnSave_Click(ByVal sender As System.Object, _
        ByVal e As System.EventArgs) Handles btnSave.Click
    If Not oItem Is Nothing Then
        oItem.Description = Me.txtDescription.Text
        oItem.ResID = CInt(Val(Me.txtResID.Text))
        oItem.StartDate = Me.dtpStart.Value
```

LISTING A.11 continued

```
              oItem.Hours = CInt(Val(Me.txtHours.Text))
              oItem.Save()
              Me.txtID.Text = ""
              Me.txtDescription.Text = ""
              Me.txtResID.Text = ""
              Me.dtpStart.Value = Today
              Me.txtHours.Text = ""
              Me.btnCreate.Enabled = True
              Me.btnRead.Enabled = False
              Me.btnSave.Enabled = False
              Me.btnDelete.Enabled = False
          End If
      End Sub

      Private Sub btnDelete_Click(ByVal sender As System.Object, _
              ByVal e As System.EventArgs) Handles btnDelete.Click
          If Not oItem Is Nothing Then
              oItem.Delete()
              oItem = Nothing
              Me.txtID.Text = ""
              Me.txtDescription.Text = ""
              Me.txtResID.Text = ""
              Me.dtpStart.Value = Today
              Me.txtHours.Text = ""
              Me.btnCreate.Enabled = True
              Me.btnRead.Enabled = False
              Me.btnSave.Enabled = False
              Me.btnDelete.Enabled = False
          End If
      End Sub
```

Day 21 "Enhancing the Application's Features"

Quiz

1. XPath

2. `DOMDocument.CreateElement`

3. `Overrides`

4. `SelectSingleNode`

Exercise

The following XML document would satisfy all the XPath queries specified:

```
<Products>
  <Product>
    <ID>4</ID>
    <Name>Spyglass</Name>
    <Description>Magnifying glass for detectives</Description>
    <Projects>
      <Project>
        <ID>101</ID>
        <Name>Market Research</Name>
        <StartDate>20020130</StartDate>
        <Items>
          <Item>
            <ID>10001</ID>
            <Description>Search for professionals</Description>
            <Hours>40</Hours>
          </Item>
          <Item>
            <ID>10002</ID>
            <Description>Survey mailing</Description>
            <Hours>15</Hours>
          </Item>
        </Items>
      </Project>
      <Project>
        <ID>106</ID>
        <Name>Manufacturing</Name>
        <StartDate>20020312</StartDate>
        <Items>
          <Item>
            <ID>10011</ID>
            <Description>Prototype creation</Description>
            <Hours>80</Hours>
          </Item>
          <Item>
            <ID>10012</ID>
            <Description>Assembly line orders</Description>
            <Hours>45</Hours>
          </Item>
        </Items>
      </Project>
    </Projects>
  </Product>
</Products>
```

Index

S